WORL WAR II
WAR CRIMES & ESPIONAGE

Karen Farrington

ABBEYDALE PRESS

This paperback edition published in 2003 by
Abbeydale Press
An imprint of Bookmart Ltd
Registered Number 2372865
Blaby Road, Wigston,
Leicestershire, LE18 4SE
United Kingdom

3 5 7 9 10 8 6 4

ISBN 1-86147-114-9

Originally published by Bookmart Ltd as part of
Witness to World War II.

PICTURE CREDITS

The publisher would like to thank the following organisations for supplying
photographs for use in this book.
Every effort has been made to contact the copyright holders for the pictures.
In some cases they have been untraceable, for which we offer our apologies.

US Library of Congress; US National Archives; BFI; J Baker Collection;
British Airways; Imperial War Museum; Australian High Commission,
London; Musee d'Histoire Contemporaine; Bundesarchiv; The Scout
Association; The Morning Star via The Marx Memorial Library, London;
Oxfam; Novosti; National Archives of Singapore; US Army; Daimler Benz;
RCA; London Transport Museum; Boeing Corp; National Museum of
Labour History; The Truman Library. ; Polish Underground Movement;
Manx Museum; Red Cross Archives; Robert Hunt Library; Far East War
Collection/Vic Brown; Kyodo News Services; Public Records Office of Hong
Kong; Hulton Deutsch; Norsk Hydro; The Public Archives of Canada;
Associated Press; State of Israel Government Press Office; Embassy of The
Federal Republic of Germany; Nato Photo; UN Photo; EEC London;
National Film Archive; Tanjug.

THE AUTHOR

Karen Farrington is a writer and former Fleet Street journalist who has
specialised in the study of conflict throughout the 20th Century. In
compiling Witness to World War II she has personally interviewed scores of
veterans from around the world, obtaining a unique insight into the war
through the eyes of the men on the front line. Among her previous books is
'Fated Destiny', an historical pot pourri of the curious, shocking and
mysterious which includes accounts of some of the greatest military
blunders in recent history. Karen Farrington is married with three children
and lives in Exmoor, Devon.

Printed in Singapore

CONTENTS

WWII WAR CRIMES AND ESPIONAGE

War can bring out reserves of heroism, loyalty and chivalry in some individuals; but in others it brings out the very worst aspects of their personalities – leading them to behaviour which they subsequently wish to hide, or to disown. And there is also a secret, hidden side to all warfare, because of the need for effective intelligence, and the requirement to mislead the enemy. As Winston Churchill explained to his World War II ally (and later Cold War enemy), Joseph Stalin: 'In wartime, truth is so precious that she should always be attended by a bodyguard of lies.'

WWll WAR CRIMES & ESPIONAGE shows how this 'bodyguard of lies' affected the fighting at sea, on land or in the air. The course of events was heavily, and often decisively, influenced by a secret war of intelligence gathering, of 'black propaganda', of spies and double agents. Crucial decisions were taken on the basis of good or faulty intelligence. Some institutions, such as the British code-breaking establishment at Bletchlcy, were more valuable than tank divisions, while some spies, like the Soviet agent in Japan, Richard Sorge, were responsible for winning important battles.

The other menace that brooded under the surface of the fighting at the front lines was the horror of a war in which atrocities and genocide became part of policy, and in which the treatment of civilians and military prisoners could be shockingly far removed from agreed standards. Some of this was known at the time; some was suspected; but much was hidden until revealed later – and has cast a shadow over the world and the very concept of humanity ever since.

Secret War

SPY ACTIVITY

The risky business of spying has excited and intrigued people for generations. It has been the source of novels, films and gossip for years. Those armchair experts who rely on Ian Fleming and Graham Greene – themselves ex-intelligence men – for their information drink in every detail of espionage and how it works. Those in the know generally keep quiet.

During World War II, spying was more thrilling than any book and more daring than any movie. Spies were motivated by nationalism, ideology, a fierce sense of right and wrong, love, lust or simply cash. Those who were caught in action paid with their lives – or abruptly switched loyalties. Luckier spies who survived rarely saw their names in lights.

The groundwork carried out by agents during the war was of almost inestimable value to the governments for which they worked.

In Britain, spies were controlled by the Special Operations Executive. In America, the Office of Strategic Services was set up in June 1942.

Yet not all the authorities were quick to realise the value of what was being presented to them.

■ CICERO ■

The information passed on by Cicero, the spy they didn't believe, is a classic case of a missed opportunity by the Germans.

Cicero was in fact an Albanian by the name of Elyesa Bazna. He worked at the British embassy in Ankara, Turkey first as a servant then as a valet. It seems that the ambassador, Sir Hughe Knatchbull-Hugessen, was very lackadaisical in matters of security.

Even the untrained eye of the valet appreciated that the chances to rifle through top secret papers were too frequent to miss. Bazna decided to make some extra cash by selling the secrets that he found lying around his master's bedroom to the Germans.

Bazna set about his task of photographing papers during evenings when Knatchbull-Hugessen was elsewhere. His booty included a list of Allied agents working in Turkey, confidential minutes of many top level conferences, details of diplomatic code and even the plans for the forthcoming invasion of Europe, codenamed 'Operation Overlord'.

To the delight of the German spymasters in the region who named him 'Cicero', the information just kept coming. So valuable was the link that documents from the ambassador's boudoir were sent straight to Joachim von Ribbentrop in Berlin for assessment at the highest level.

Strangely enough, von Ribbentrop dismissed 'Cicero' out of hand as a hoaxer. He could not believe that a mere servant would have access to such highly classified information.

Moreover, he decided Cicero's claims to be anti-British after his father had been shot by an Englishman were dubious. For one thing, Bazna spoke excellent English; for another, he kept changing his story, and neither fact did much to enhance his credibility with the Germans. Von Ribbentrop suspected he had been planted by the British themselves. Franz von Papen, the German ambassador to Turkey, was instructed to

Documents went straight to von Ribbentrop for assessment at the highest level

disregard the information received through this channel.

Little did Hitler's Foreign Minister realise the woeful lack of security at the British embassy.

Germany's spymasters were outraged at von Ribbentrop's attitude, and continued to find the cash to finance Cicero, despite opposition from Berlin. Cicero apparently operated between October 1943 and March 1944. Then, the British were tipped off about his covert activities and began their own investigations. It took them a long time to plug the leak because it came from the ambassador's residence, rather than from the embassy as had long been suspected.

Cicero was forewarned of the risk by Germany and fled with £300,000 in counterfeit British notes. The fake payment by the Germans resulted in Bazna languishing for some time in a Turkish prison after he had tried to use them. In 1962, now living in

Opposite: Franz von Papen was Hitler's ambassador to Turkey when Cicero's secrets began to filter through.
Below: Radio transmitters like those carried by spies Joseph Waldberg and Karl Meier when they entered Britain posing as refugees: they were arrested.

Above: The original offices in central London which housed Special Operations Executive, the heartbeat of Britain's espionage activities.

Germany and working as a night watchman, Bazna wrote a book called 'I was Cicero'.

There has been speculation since the war that von Ribbentrop was right to have his suspicions because 'Cicero' was in fact a successful double agent working for the British. Convenient as it might be for the British to appear on top of the matter, it seems the conspiracy theory is probably only bunkum. Almost certainly, there was a criminal lack of security at the British embassy that endangered Allied activities throughout Europe. Sir Hughe was quietly moved to another diplomatic posting without appearing to suffer so much as a reprimand.

One of the greatest of the German security scoops during World War II came when they asserted full control over intelligence operations out of Holland. Their canny grasp of the system cost the lives of hundreds of Dutch and British agents.

They stole a march on Holland early in the war. Two accomplished Nazi agents posed as plotters against Hitler and made secret contact with Britain.

Two Britons, Major Richard Stevens and Captain Zigismund Payne Best, met the men claiming to be Captain Schaemmel of the transport corps and Captain Hausmann, an army medic, first in Arnhem and then in Venlo, on the Dutch-German border.

One of the Germans was in fact Walter Schellenberg, a notorious spy now being used to discover if the British were party to any genuine anti-Nazi plots. His carefully laid subterfuge went awry when a bomb exploded in a Munich beer cellar, clearly aimed at Hitler who narrowly escaped with his life. Believing it to be a British plot, Hitler wanted revenge.

So when Stevens, Best and a Dutch agent arrived for a rendezvous at Venlo, three carloads of armed SS men were waiting for them. The Dutch agent was shot dead while the Britons were bundled into a car and taken to Berlin for interrogation.

Talks that had been taking place through the Vatican were now

---

By the summer of 1940, the British secret service channels in Europe were in shreds

---

abandoned by the British who saw new security risks. And when the Germans marched into Holland and France in 1940, they seized details of the secret agent networks from the Allied embassies.

By summer 1940, the British secret service in Europe was in shreds. As one chief put it: 'We did not possess one single agent between the Balkans and the English Channel.'

Germany, meanwhile, was piling on the pressure. A team of agents was parachuted into Britain, but most of them were easily identified by their amateurish approach.

The Germans also used men like George Owens, a Welsh engineer, recruited as a subversive by the Abwehr to whip up domestic disharmony and promote the Nazi cause. When Owens was caught by the British, he switched allegiance and began sending fake messages to Berlin under the guidance of MI5. It was the first step on a long road for Britain in her attempt to win the secret war.

■ DOUBLE AGENT ■

Germany continued its attempts to undermine the British through the use of agents. One of their biggest coups was to recruit Christiaan Lindemans, thought to be a hero of the Dutch resistance but in fact a double agent in the pay of the Nazis.

Lindemans was arrested on 28 October 1944. Following an interrogation by MI5 in London he was returned to Dutch custody where he languished until July 1946 when he committed suicide.

Ex-wrestler Lindemans was a strapping man who went by the codename King Kong. He had offered his services to the British in 1944 to help Allied servicemen escape from the occupied territory.

He had no problem getting security clearance, and then he set about his task with enthusiasm.

D-Day was followed by the march through Europe and the battle for Antwerp. Britain's Field Marshal Bernard Montgomery hoped to break the battle deadlock with 'Operation Market Garden', in which parachute regiments were sent into Arnhem to capture key bridges from the Germans and assist the thrust forward. When the paras landed they found to their surprise and horror that the area was already held by crack German troops. One division was pinned down and suffered horrendous casualties.

> **It has been suggested that Lindemans was a double agent on the Allied side**

There was speculation that the plan had been betrayed, and the prime suspect was later thought to be Lindemans. This suggestion has largely been rejected on the grounds that the Wehrmacht could judge for itself that a major airborne operation was imminent simply by the weight of radio traffic that September. Also, it is thought unlikely that Lindemans was privy to the necessary information.

In Lindemans' defence, it has been suggested that he was in fact a double agent whose loyalties remained true to the Allies even while he was briefing the Germans. He was then sacrificed to expediency.

Whatever the facts of the Lindemans affair, it was certainly true that while Britain triumphed in the spying game elsewhere, in Holland they came a poor second.

Germany had its fair share of agents at work in the heart of the Allied war effort. Among them were Nazi sympathisers at the American embassy in London who spent their time copying Churchill's secret telegrams to Roosevelt. Spycatcher Joan Miller helped to stem this gushing leak.

Yet internal rivalry between the Abwehr, the military intelligence branch which considered Nazis to be thuggish and undesirable, and the SD, Hitler's own security machine, would ultimately hamper the effectiveness of operations.

■ BARBAROSSA ■

Russia, meanwhile, had a thriving network of spies most of whom were inspired to pass on what secrets they could through their loyalty to the communist cause.

It was thanks to this somewhat blind devotion that Stalin was so well-informed about the Nazi

Below: Sir Hughe Knatchbull-Hugessen with his wife and daughters. He was guilty of slack security when he was Britain's ambassador to Turkey.

◆ EYE WITNESS ◆

Edward Howe was a former foreign correspondent who was recruited for the Special Operations Executive in 1943 to cultivate contacts with the resistance movements of Hungary and Yugoslavia.

'Someone told our august military hierarchy that I knew Hungary quite well. I was asked if I would help. Would I put myself in their hands? Somehow, they said, they would get me into Hungary so that I could report on conditions there.

This meant changing the War Correspondent tabs on my shoulder for three pips. The change caused me one embarrassment. I found it hard to salute smartly. Fortunately, I was not in Cairo – the only place it mattered – very long.

After two months training in the winter of 1943 I was considered ready to drop into Yugoslavia whence Partisans would pass me on towards Hungary. That was the plan. Things turned out differently.

Bad weather and German activity delayed my drop into Yugoslavia for two months. It took five flights and about 40 operational flying hours before I touched down in the Majevica hills bordering the River Sava.

It is a nerve-wracking business waiting in the fuselage of the aeroplane before being dropped by parachute. You do not know where you are or what is happening and it is extremely uncomfortable.

The crew are too busy with their own jobs to take much interest in you and it is impossible to keep up a conversation in a warplane.

So you sit quietly and anxiously in the darkness. Or rather you crouch, for your only seat is the bundles of supplies destined to follow you to the ground. On your back you wear your parachute fitted before you enter. It must not be taken off until the operation is declared unsuccessful and the plane has turned back.

With 28lb of costly silk on your back, a comfortable position is hard to find. But the physical discomfort is nothing compared to the mental anguish.

My feelings when the missions were abandoned were mixed, disappointment, a little relief. There is always some relief in the postponement of danger. But then there is the thought that I should have to go through all this again.'

Left: **Walter Schellenberg was probably Germany's most accomplished spy. His covert activities helped control the intelligence network in Holland.**

'Operation Barbarossa'. Nevertheless, he chose to ignore the warnings that a Nazi invasion of Russia was imminent.

The German Richard Sorge was one of the communist sympathisers who betrayed his country to Russia. A clerk at the German embassy in Tokyo, he regularly passed on classified information to Moscow. With Japan having now joined with Germany and Italy in the Tripartite Pact, top grade security information was being processed through the embassy. Sorge ensured that the best of it was passed to the Kremlin. This impeccable source was silenced when Sorge was caught spying and killed.

Also working for Moscow was the Lucy Ring in Switzerland. This was a

---

For nearly two years, the Lucy Ring in Switzerland fed about 140 messages a month to Russia

---

cell made up of three committed communists who fed Stalin top-notch information from early 1942 until October 1943 when Swiss police, acting under pressure from Germany, broke up the network they knew as 'Rote Drei' (Red Three).

■ LUCY RING ■

The trio were Bavarian anti-Nazi Rudolf Roessler, Hungarian Sandor Rado and Englishman Alexander Foote. Foote was arrested as soon as he aroused suspicion. Roessler was taken into Swiss custody on 2 June 1944 and Rado went into hiding until the war ended.

It is still uncertain how and where this cell obtained its information.

At the height of its activity, the Lucy Ring was generating about 140 messages a month to Russia. So efficient was it that information was passed on sometimes within a matter of hours of crucial meetings held in Berlin. German Chief of General Staff Franz Halder later said: 'Almost every offensive operation of ours was betrayed to the enemy even before it appeared on my desk.'

The information passed to Russia during this period was so accurate

Above: **Mystery still surrounds the source of the information gathered by Rudolf Roessler and his associates in the so-called Lucy Ring.**

that even the Kremlin became suspicious about its provenance. Soviet spymasters continually pressed for the sources to be unmasked but they apparently were never divulged to the Kremlin. Time and time again, the codenames Werther, Teddy, Olga and Anna appeared as the informers.

Theories about their identities have been legion. One book claimed they were all friends made by Roessler in World War I in the army who had since achieved high rank in the Wehrmacht and were dismayed at the excesses of their Führer.

Another suggestion is that Swiss intelligence fed the Lucy Ring despite the country's fierce neutrality. There was fear that as Germany swept through Europe it would submerge little Switzerland, and it was in the interests of the independent Swiss state to ensure that Russia was given a fighting chance in the conflict so as to lessen the risk to its own security.

A third proposition is that the Lucy Ring was under the control of the British. Happily, Britain had virtually all the enemy's secrets thanks to the codecracking Ultra system. Although Stalin was distrusted despite being one of the Allies, Churchill wanted to give the Red Army every advantage in its fight against Hitler, so it may be that information gleaned from Ultra was funnelled directly to the Russians through the Lucy Ring.

Two teleprinter operators in Germany who were deeply involved in an anti-Nazi conspiracy also came under the spotlight. Rado himself endorsed this theory.

■ CANARIS ■

Foote, who was an agent for Moscow until he defected back to Britain in 1947, died in 1956. Despite the services he rendered, Rado spent 10 years in a labour camp in Russia following the war. With both Rado and Roessler now long dead too, it seems unlikely the mystery of Lucy's impeccable sources will ever be revealed.

The Allies became well practised in the art of espionage and won some notable successes. Perhaps their greatest coup was to receive help from Admiral Wilhelm Canaris, one-time head of the German Abwehr.

Canaris was a patriotic German who, like many people, was filled with disgust for Hitler and his abuses of power. That he was a leading figure in the German resistance which hoped to overthrow Hitler has long been established. By 1951, the

> ## Admiral Canaris was a patriotic German disgusted by Hitler's abuses of power

speculation about his role as an agent for Britain was rife.

Yet it was not until 40 years after the end of the war that MI6 officer Andrew King confirmed to the Sunday Times that Canaris had passed on secrets to London through an emissary.

His link was Halina Szymanski, wife of a Polish Colonel who lived out the war in Switzerland. Canaris met a grisly end, being strangled with piano wire by the vengeful SS in reprisal for the July 1944 bomb plot against Hitler.

American-born Eric Erickson, a Swedish citizen and international oil dealer, was one of the free world's most successful spies. It was his information about oil installations around the Third Reich that provided valuable assistance to the bombers of both Britain and America. Their repeated

LONG KNIVES

When Hitler won power as Reich Chancellor in 1933, he set about eradicating opposition not only among those of different ideologies but those that shared the same callous creed as himself. His targets were the Brownshirts, internal paramilitaries who had played no small part in promoting the cause of Nazism through their bully-boy tactics on the streets of Germany.

At their head was Ernst Roehm, an ageing soldier who fashioned the Brownshirts – otherwise known as the Sturmabteilung or SA – after himself. They were brutal, ruthless, sadistic and many were openly homosexual.

Hitler had a long-standing friendship with Roehm which he was loath to betray. But, wary of the increasing power of the Brownshirts and the excesses in their behaviour, he felt he had no choice in the matter. On 30 June 1934 he sparked the beginning of the Night of the Long Knives. An estimated 200 died in 48 hours after henchmen worked their way through a list of Reich 'enemies'. Gregor Strasser, Hitler's one-time rival for the leadership of the Nazi party and Roehm himself, were among the victims.

Rudolf Hess alone among Hitler's inner circle was appalled at the bloodshed and argued long and hard for reprieves for names on the list. Others, including Himmler and Göring, appeared to relish the massacre, and were confident that it was consolidating their own grip on power.

attacks finally helped to throttle the Fatherland which was unable to maintain its war effort without fuel.

Erickson had frequently travelled to Germany before the outbreak of war, spoke the language fluently and was a noted anti-Nazi. When he was offered

Right: Admiral Wilhelm Canaris was among the most high-ranking Germans to assist the Allied cause.

a chance to bring down Hitler by working undercover for Britain and, later, the Allies, he didn't hesitate.

It meant undergoing a public personality change. No longer did he attack Fascist policies at every opportunity. Now he trumpeted their cause and defended their actions.

■ ERIC ERICKSON ■

Although it cost him many of his friends, by September 1941 Erickson had won the permit he needed to enter Germany.

Once there, he had to undergo questioning from the Gestapo, a crucial test of his new pro-Nazi identity. Cool and collected, Erickson persuaded the grim-faced security men that his passion for Hitler was genuine. Soon he was being taken on a conducted tour of German oil fields

because he had convinced the Nazis that he was there to buy some for his own country.

Only two people in Sweden knew about his mission. One was his new wife Ingrid. The other was Prince Carl Gustav Bernadotte, nephew to the Swedish King. Erickson persuaded Bernadotte to wine and

> *Erickson persuaded the Germans he was a Nazi then went on a guided tour of their oil fields*

dine high-ranking Germans in Sweden – a neutral country in obvious danger of invasion – to smooth his perilous mission.

Above: Captain Eric Erickson and his wife leaving London's Surrey Commercial Docks aboard the liner *Ostrobotina* bound for Sweden.

Erickson put his superb memory into overdrive and took details of refineries and production plants home in his head. Once in Sweden, he committed the information to tape and sent it to American agents.

There was a backlash from his friends and relations and continued pressure from the Gestapo who remained suspicious of his American birthright. Nevertheless, Erickson managed to continue his tours of Germany and the occupied territories and dispatched the information he gathered to the Allies.

He recruited a network of agents and acted as a courier for at least one other Allied agent operating behind enemy lines, a svelte brunette named Marianne von Mollendorf. It was not long before Eric and Marianne became lovers.

By May 1944, German oil production was shattered by the Allied bombardments. Now there was no oil left for Erickson to purchase on his 'buying trips' so he concocted a story about building a synthetic fuel plant back in Sweden to aid the Nazis.

At the end of 1944 when he flew to Germany he was picked up by members of the SS and taken to the notorious Moabat jail. Believing the game was up, Erickson prepared himself for the worst. Then it became clear he was a privileged visitor there to watch some executions. He was not going to be killed – but to his horror he realised one of the victims was to be his lover Marianne.

■ LOVER SHOT ■

Barely more than a glance passed between the two intimate friends before a burst of machine gun fire ended her young life. Erickson knew that if he betrayed any emotion he too would be shot. So he kept the agonising grief he felt behind a facade of normality.

He embarked on another tour, this time with Himmler's personal blessing. By this time the atmosphere in Germany had become extremely tense. Erickson knew he was being tailed by the Gestapo. And, if that wasn't bad enough, he ran into an old acquaintance by the name of Franz Schroeder, himself a Nazi supporter who remembered Erickson as an enthusiastic anti-Fascist. It was a desperate situation that required a desperate remedy.

> **Erickson thought he was being put in prison, but he was only being invited to witness an execution**

Erickson threw off his Gestapo tail and followed Schroeder by taxi. As the German picked up a public payphone to confide his suspicions in an SS friend, Erickson produced a pocket knife and lunged at the back of his head. The super spy had now turned killer, a ghastly task made easier with the thought of beautiful, dead Marianne still fresh in his mind.

It was the last trip he made to Germany. Another was deemed too dangerous. But he had carried out his dual role brilliantly.

It wasn't until a month after the end of the war that Eric Erikson was revealed as a man of great courage. Still ostracised by his friends in Stockholm, the American ambassador smoothed Erikson's way back into society by holding a grand party with Erickson, his wife and Prince Carl as guests of honour. It was time to tell the truth about Erickson, the Nazi-lover who never was. At last he was received as a hero.

Ib Riis was recruited by the Germans as an agent when he lived in Denmark. When Britain occupied his native Iceland, he was sent back there to monitor troop movements. When his best friend in Denmark was murdered by the Nazis, Riis knew he

LIES

One of Churchill's famous quotes during the war was:

'In wartime, truth is so precious that she should always be attended by a bodyguard of lies.'

Below: **Prince Carl Bernadotte of Sweden appeared a Nazi sympathiser when he socialised with the Germans. In fact, he was a vital cover for a Swedish spy.**

must make different plans for the sake of the whole of Europe.

He was delivered to Iceland on 6 April 1942 by U-boat and went straight to the Allies to offer himself as a double agent. It was treacherous work. One whiff of suspicion would have brought about his death. But with the British convinced of his sincerity, his dual role began.

Codenamed 'Edda' by the Germans and 'Cobweb' by the British, Riis fed duff information to the Germans from Reykjavik. His greatest coup was to persuade the Germans that 250,000 Allied troops were poised to invade Norway, as a consequence of which two German armoured divisions were sent there, miles away from Normandy where the genuine invasion took place a few weeks later. His ruse involved the construction of dummy airfields and training camps in Iceland.

Riis survived the war but remained bitter about his heroism being 'forgotten' by the British.

■ GLAMOROUS SPY ■

It might have been a dangerous game but spying was not without glamour in World War II thanks to Canadian financier William Stevenson.

Stevenson became the head of British Security Co-ordination – an organisation established in New York before America had joined the war to link up with US secret services. This was a delicate operation in what was at the time a neutral country. Stevenson was given the appropriate codename 'Intrepid'.

> *Stevenson's information gatherers included the English playwright and wit Noel Coward*

Among many famous personalities from the world of show business who were members of his espionage ring was actor Leslie Howard, who was apparently on a mission for Stevenson when his plane was shot down over the Bay of Biscay in 1941 while returning from Spain.

Noel Coward, the playwright, wit and raconteur, also gathered information where he could and passed it on to Stevenson. It was years before he admitted his role as spy.

Above: From his US base, William Stevenson recruited many famous names from the world of show business to aid the Allied war effort.

Left: Debonair Leslie Howard, star of *Gone With The Wind,* worked for British Security Co-ordination before his death in a plane crash in 1941.

snapped Italian military posts on behalf of the Allies which helped in their invasion plans.

One of the most glamorous of all the spies from Stevenson's stable in action during the war was Amy Elizabeth Thorpe, an American beauty who married a British diplomat by the name of

■ GRETA GARBO ■

Greta Garbo, the screen goddess, manipulated contacts in her native Sweden from her home in Hollywood to keep the Allies up to date with important news and gossip.

Among other stars who played key roles in the secret war was David Niven, the suave British leading actor who became a commander in the Phantom Reconnaissance Regiment.

He disguised himself as a German officer and put his admirable grasp of the German language to good use, to provide a distraction while his men got to work on sabotage missions.

Jacques Cousteau, the diver who became famous for his fascinating underwater photography, took film of a different kind during the war. Apparently a casual diver, he took to the Mediterranean waters and

> **One of the most glamorous spies in Stevenson's stable was Amy Elizabeth Thorpe**

Arthur Pack. A dull man, he nevertheless won postings in glamorous locations like Chile, Spain and Poland. It was there in 1937 that she

Above: **Playwright and wit Noel Coward, pictured broadcasting for the BBC, secretly gathered information on behalf of William Stevenson, a.k.a. 'Intrepid'.**

was recruited as a spy by the British with the codename 'Cynthia'.

She shamelessly used her stunning looks and figure to woo important people and discovered their secrets between the sheets.

Her affair with an official at the Polish Foreign Ministry helped to elicit vital information about the development of the German Enigma cipher machine.

In 1941, when she was in New York, she courted Admiral Alberto Lais, Mussolini's naval attache, to learn Italian secret codes.

Then she moved on to the French embassy in order to crack their ciphers. France, once the ally of Britain was now part occupied and part ruled by a puppet government. The ambassador's press officer was Captain Charles Brousse with whom Cynthia fell in love. Together they rifled the embassy's secrets although they never found the cypher coding.

> ## 'Cynthia' shamelessly used her stunning looks and figure to discover important secrets

So, posing as illicit lovers, they persuaded a nightwatchman to let them use the embassy at night for a tryst. They offered the nightwatchman champagne which he gleefully accepted. It was drugged – and soon he slept like a baby. Meanwhile, Cynthia was showing an expert locksmith to the safe door and he was followed by a team who copied the secrets they found inside.

■ 'TREASURE' ■

After the war, Cynthia married Brousse and they lived happily together in the south of France until her death from cancer in 1963.

She was not the only provocative agent at work during the war. Double agent Lily Sergueiev, codenamed 'Treasure', prompted MI5 to employ its first women spy master, Gisella Ashley. 'Treasure', a Russian by birth who would only co-operate with the security services if her pet poodle was allowed to travel with her everywhere she went, was regarded as a

Right: Screen goddess Greta Garbo used contacts in her native Sweden to discover information for the Allied cause.
Below: Screen actor David Niven was an idol before he turned hero. He was one of many Hollywood stars to join the forces and even posed as a German in undercover operations.

'man-eater'. MI5 bosses feared for the innocence of any young male officer assigned to her case.

■ ODETTE SAMSOM ■

Odette Samsom was another woman who was placed at the sharp end of intelligence work by the Special Operations Executive. At thirty years old, she was a mother of three, French-born but married to an Englishman who was now fighting overseas for his country.

Willing to offer her services as a translator to the British, she was taken aback when they asked her to go on active service underground in her native France. However, full of anxiety about her mother and family in occupied France, she underwent the training course and was ultimately sent to Cannes in October 1942.

There she met Peter Churchill, the man liaising between London and the local resistance movements who was destined to become her second husband. She was a courier employed on desperately dangerous missions. Had she been stopped in southern France, which was at the time swarming with German soldiers, carrying such deeply incriminating evidence, she would have been shot.

When the Germans began closing in on the Cannes network, Odette and

Below: **Sea-life photographer Jacques Cousteau secretly snapped vital Italian waterside installations and relayed his pictures to the Allies.**

Peter fled to the safety of the mountains in Haute-Savoie, which was considered to be resistance territory. Then her knife-edge existence of carrying communications between key members of the resistance movement began again.

■ BETRAYAL ■

It was all destined to end with her arrest and incarceration in Ravensbruck concentration camp after her group was betrayed to the Germans by an infiltrator. Although sick and

SINGAPORE

A courageous commando unit made up of British and Australians sabotaged Japanese shipping in Singapore harbour until it was wiped out in 1944.

The men were taken to Singapore aboard a submarine and hid out on the Riouw archipelago in Indonesia from where they hoped to carry out their mission in 'Sleeping Beauties', or midget submarines. However, when they were spotted by local policemen, they were forced to scuttle their craft for fear the new technology would fall into enemy hands. Nevertheless, they continued their mission by paddling canoes into Singapore harbour and fixing mines to anchored cargo ships.

Relentlessly, the Japanese army hunted them down. Out of the 23-man squad, 10 were captured, beheaded and their heads impaled on spikes in the Singapore streets. Two bit on cyanide pills when they were cornered. The rest died fighting, taking many enemy soldiers to the grave in the process. The mission, branded 'a failure' despite the bravery and achievements of those involved, was kept secret for years after the end of the conflict. A campaign has returned most of the victims to graves in a war cemetery where they have been re-interred with full military honours.

subject to torture, Odette remained remarkably self-possessed during captivity. She explained later that she survived the long hours of solitary confinement because she had been

Odette was unafraid of the dark because she had been blind for over three years as a child

blind for three and half years when she was a young girl. It made her unafraid of the dark. She was finally released by the Americans in 1945.

Another woman spy who used her considerable talents for guile against the Germans was not so fortunate. Violette Szabo, the daughter of an English father and a French mother who was brought up in south London, did not return from the war.

Bold Violette was 18 years old at the outbreak of war and worked on the perfumery counter of a store in Brixton, south London. It was there following the fall of France that she met a handsome officer of the French Foreign Legion in a park.

Left: After the war, William Stevenson recounted his role as spymaster in a book. *Below:* In 1947 Odette Samsom, spy and concentration camp survivor, married another British undercover worker, Captain Peter Morland Churchill.

■ VIOLETTE SZABO ■

Good-looking Etienne Szabo, from Marseilles, was devoted to the liberation of his homeland. He had already fought in Norway, suffering frostbite and demoralising defeat, before meeting Violette. There was a whirlwind courtship in London before Etienne was moved to Aldershot. Thereafter, they wrote daily to one another, expressing their flourishing love. Soon they were wed in a service

◆ EYE WITNESS ◆

One British soldier who slipped through the fingers of the Germans after the round-up at Dunkirk stayed on the run in France until liberation came four years later in 1944.

❛ Len Arlington, one of those left behind following the evacuation, was being marched into captivity by German soldiers when he dived unseen into a ditch and emerged hours later when the files of dejected British men and their victorious Wehrmacht guards had disappeared.

It was the beginning of an adventure without parallel during the treacherous years of occupation when he was at risk of betrayal from all but the most loyal Resistance workers.

The man who grew up in a London orphanage used his Cockney common-sense to keep his freedom despite the fat rewards offered by the Germans to anyone who would give him up. Dressed as a French labourer, he once cycled past a parade of German soldiers being inspected by a high ranking officer – who made his troops stand back and saluted as the runaway went past.

On another occasion, the house where he was hiding was raided by the Gestapo. Alerted by the sound of jackboots, he escaped by the skin of his teeth by clambering through a skylight, crawling along a rooftop and then ducking past the soldiers, running barefoot to a friend's house some two miles distant.

Len proved an immense asset to the Resistance by being able to spot Nazi impostors attempting to break up escape rings organised for Allied airmen. He fell in love with Marcelle Faucomprez, the daughter of a family which sheltered him, and finally married her in 1946. Len's incredible story is told in the book 'The Man the Nazis Couldn't Catch' by John Laffin. ❜

Above: **Peter Churchill was a hero of the French Resistance and the Allied spy network after his astonishing survival in enemy territory during the war.**

at a register office that was interrupted by an air raid.

There was a brief, ecstatic honeymoon before Etienne was dispatched by sea to fight in East Africa. Following the successful campaign, he returned to Liverpool for just one week to be reunited with Violette before flying to Cairo.

When their daughter Tania was born, Etienne was holed up in the Western Desert under pressure from Rommel's army. Soon after, in the opening rounds of the Battle of El Alamein, he was fatally wounded.

It was weeks before Violette heard of his death. She was devastated for herself and for her baby who would now never know her courageous, handsome father. Yet Violette quickly found comfort after receiving a mysterious letter. Her talent for speaking French had been noted in her records when she worked for a while with the ATS. Now she was recruited as an agent to work behind enemy lines with the expanding French resistance.

■ STEN GUN FIRE ■

On her second mission behind enemy lines in the run up to D-Day Violette was captured after a shoot-out with German soldiers. She had pinned down a number of troops with fire from her sten gun allowing another Frenchman with her to escape.

She was taken to Fresnes – a prison outside Paris – to be interrogated, then on to the Gestapo

Violette was interrogated and tortured at Gestapo headquarters at Fresnes prison outside Paris

headquarters in Paris itself to face torture. She nevertheless refused to comply with the demands of the German officers to spill the beans on her fellow agents and their aims.

As the liberating forces approached Paris, Violette and other prisoners were transferred by train to Ravensbruck concentration camp. From there Violette was alternately sent to work outside the camp or detained in punishment blocks.

■ SHOT IN THE HEAD ■

When the war ended there was no news of her for months. Finally, a Ravensbruck camp commander confessed Violette and two other British women had been shot in January 1945. They were dispatched with a bullet to the back of the head, their thin, battered bodies still bearing the marks of torture, then incinerated in the camp crematorium. Violette was posthumously awarded the George Cross and the Croix de Guerre for her courage.

Below: Violette Szabo sought revenge on the Nazis when she joined British intelligence. Her exploits as a commando won her medals for her courage, posthumously given after the war.

PARTISAN RESISTANCE

'Whatever happens, the flame of French resistance must not be quenched and will not be quenched.' Those were the fiery words of Charles de Gaulle on 18 June 1940 in a BBC broadcast to his countrymen.

A little known French tank commander who fled to London when Hitler's forces overran France in 1940, Charles de Gaulle was to become the leader of a resistance movement which mushroomed over France.

Wherever Hitler's armies stormed in, a covert opposition would inevitably spring up. And as the extremes of Nazi behaviour became increasingly evident, sympathy towards and membership of resistance groups would flourish. Consequently, France, Belgium, Holland, Denmark, Norway, Greece, Yugoslavia and Czechoslovakia all had resistance movements, some of which were larger and naturally more successful than others.

Their role was to harry the Germans, sabotage their operations behind the lines, keep London informed of German army activity and assist escaped prisoners or crashed airmen to safety. Following the D-Day landings, the members of the resistance movements in Europe fought alongside the Allies to rid their countries of the Nazi menace once and for all.

Local people would go hungry while German officers sated themselves at the best restaurants

If the resistance groups burgeoned, then German troops had no one but themselves to blame.

As invaders, they took the best of everything for themselves, including food, accommodation and transport. Often local people would go hungry while German officers ate fine food at the best local restaurants. Prices escalated and decent clothing and footwear became outrageously expensive and out of reach to the ordinary folk of the region.

Opposite: German retribution against suspected Partisans was swift. The sight of a local woman or man hanged in the street as a warning to others in the occupied territories was common.
Above: A Moroccan freedom fighter wearing a steel helmet taken from a dead soldier prepares for night patrol.
Left: The weapons used by Partisans were often outdated. Their main advantage lay in local knowledge.

N.I. Slugachov fled a German train containing thousands of Soviet prisoners as it crossed Poland and went on to lead a partisan group.

'We started with small operations, concentrating mainly on hunting down agents provocateurs and Nazi spies and were the assault groups, as it were, of a party organisation.

A Pole of German origin whom the Nazis employed as an informer lived in the village of Srednie Lany. We marked him down for execution. We went to his house at night, tied him up and made him give us the names of the Nazi informers in the neighbouring villages and also of the people he had betrayed. After that we took him to the house of the elder, called the villagers together, read out the death sentence and carried it out on the spot. To safeguard the villagers against trouble, I left behind a note which read: 'This is what will happen to anybody who works for the Germans.'

At another time we went to a village in broad daylight and found the tax-collector there. He had with him a vice and iron tags which he hung in the ears of the pigs, calves and cows, thus marking them as German property which the peasants could neither sell nor slaughter. Our men called the villagers and in their presence hung the tags on the ears of the Nazi minion, giving the people a good laugh.

Then there was the raid made on the cashier's office at a railway station in front of the noses of the police and German gendarmerie. Our men got away with money that the party needed for organisational expenses.

Word of our operations spread through the region. We had the support of most of the population who invariably coloured up the truth about our operations and exaggerated our strength and armaments. The Gestapo and the police combed the villages and forests but could never find our trail.'

Furthermore, the German troops violated the personal liberty of those in the countries they occupied. Night curfews curtailed free movement and there were frequent identity checks, often at gunpoint.

Perhaps the biggest burden that was placed on the occupied peoples was the introduction of forced labour by the Germans. This would tear men and boys from their homes and loved ones. They were shipped off to Germany to work on undermanned farms or in factories, where they frequently had to face the hazards of Allied bombing raids, while the rest of the family was left to manage as best it could.

The introduction of forced labour tore men and boys away from their homes and loved ones

Thousands of young men went into hiding. They found a welcome in the ranks of the newly formed underground armies intent on disrupting Germany's grand plan. When America entered the war, it seemed to many in Europe that Hitler's days were numbered and they were encouraged more than ever before to fight back in any way possible.

■ GUERRILLAS ■

Of course, it was no soft option being part of a resistance group. The penalty on discovery was death. Not only resistance members but also their families and comrades were put in grave danger.

The activities of such groups often brought disaster down on the heads of many fellow countrymen. From 1941 it was common practice for the Germans to shoot 100 civilians in reprisal for the killing of every German officer.

While captured airmen or troops were protected by international law, no such umbrella existed for guerrilla fighters. The most gruesome tortures were earmarked for captured members of the underground in a bid

Left: **Those captured by the Germans and found guilty of assisting the Allies had little hope of survival.**

Right: General de Gaulle, here shaking hands with Free French Army General Leclerc, was the Resistance figurehead.
Below: The Resistance was a family affair with sons helping fathers dismantle pavements to build barricades in Paris.

to extract valuable information. Death almost always followed. Still, no amount of terror could quell the nationalist fire burning in the bosom of Europe's oppressed peoples.

> ## No terror could quell the nationalistic fervour in the bosom of Europe's oppressed peoples

One of the largest and most active resistance movements was in France. France had been divided after its conquest in 1940, and the resistance operated both in the nominally independent Vichy France and in the fully occupied territories. The outlawed group became known as the Maquis, a Corsican bandit word meaning brushland.

Figurehead of the movement was Charles de Gaulle. However, it was hero Jean Moulin who unified the different strands of the movement by forming a National Resistance Council (CNR). He was betrayed and murdered by the Gestapo in 1943.

■ FRENCH MAQUIS ■

The vast open areas of France, including mountains and forests, gave the Maquis plenty of scope for hiding itself away from the Germans to carry out its brief of causing havoc behind enemy lines.

Yet there were still more members of the resistance who lived normal lives in towns, rubbing shoulders every day with the hated Germans.

Most trusted cells of the resistance were in regular contact with Britain through MI9, an organisation cloaked in secrecy that had been set up specially to help stranded Allied servicemen out of hostile terrain. The

◆ EYE WITNESS ◆

Bill Crowell, from Nova Scotia, Canada, joined the army in the summer of 1943 and arrived in England aged 19 for the battle of Normandy.

'I was a private at the lead of our battalion one morning coming into a little village when a German jumped out of the ditch at me. I nearly pulled the trigger of my gun until I realised he had his hands up. He was surrendering. He was blubbering, terrified and couldn't really talk. It was my job to march him back as a prisoner of war.

I had been in trouble for being separated from my group before so I decided to take him only a little way. Some French people came out of their houses and lined the street, staring at us. A young French man with a commando knife leapt towards me, making for the German. He was going to slit his throat. When I gestured to him with my bayonet he threatened to slit my throat. I went ahead and left the German with some officers.

Back with my unit, we stopped at a crossroads and my corporal sent me down to the left to check for Germans. I came to another crossroads when I suddenly heard a shot being fired by my head. I crouched down and looked around. There was another shot. Behind me came three Frenchman including the one with a knife who I had seen earlier that day. Now he was carrying a sten gun. They signalled that there were some Germans in a farmhouse ahead. These Germans shoved an old lady outside the door so we couldn't shoot at them.

The Germans circled the house, crossed a small bridge behind it over a river and then blew up the bridge. One of the Germans popped up from behind a bush and waved to us before running off.

The Frenchman who had been so fierce lifted his lapel and showed me a pin bearing the cross of Lorraine, the symbol of the French underground. He took it off and gave it to me. He wanted someting in return but I had nothing to give him. I went back to my platoon soon afterwards but I never forgot the Maquis. So on the 50th anniversary of D-Day I took a plaque to the same spot where I spoke with him that day dedicated to the 'unknown Maquis'.

US had a resistance aid group called MIS-X that was similar to MI9.

Transmitting coded messages by radio maintained contact with London. As Germany's technology in detecting the source of unauthorised radio messages improved, this became increasingly risky. As often as possible, a heavily coded reply was broadcast on the BBC radio network.

For the members of the resistance, there was much organisational work to do, and messages between units were of paramount importance. Couriers were at constant risk from lightning German body searches which could lead to capture and jeopardise planned operations.

> *Secret messages were wrapped around needles which were then hidden in cigarette casings*

A favoured method of carrying information was to write down a short message and wrap it around a needle until it could be inserted into a cigarette casing. Not only was it cleverly hidden, it could be 'smoked' if the agents thought themselves in danger of discovery.

The French and Belgian resistance movements were crucial in helping crashed Allied airmen to escape from the occupying Germans. As there was a worrying shortage of pilots and trained air crew at one stage of the war, their actions were invaluable to both the Royal Air Force and, later, to the USAAF.

■ AVOIDING CAPTURE ■

To avoid capture, airmen who crashed badly needed civilian clothes in the local style to replace their telltale flying suits. It was also essential for them to put all their military training behind them if they came under the scrutiny of German soldiers and slouch instead of march, conceal their valuables and become

Left: **Gangs of anti-fascist fighters had none of the discipline or skill of regular troops but were consistently enthusiastic in their bid to rout the Germans.**

effectively indistinguishable from the local population.

Local people who were not members of the resistance were happy to help, in spite of the dangers. As the war progressed, the resistance became practised at spiriting airmen and sometimes escaped prisoners or key political figures out of danger. To locate local resistance groups, those evading the Nazis would first make contact with the local monastery or convent or the village priest.

■ SAFE HOUSES ■

The resistance could supply forged documents and all the necessary contacts from a safe house to transport and accommodation the length

Above: **Russian guerrilla fighters pore over a map and plan the best way to hit back at the superior forces of the German invaders.**

of southern Europe. While some fled to England straight across the Channel, most chose the safer, if considerably longer route, which took them via British-held Gibraltar.

Before assisting anyone, the resistance members would have to be convinced they had a genuine ally on their hands and not a German infiltrator. So there were a series of rigorous questions before the procedure of escape got underway.

Then the escapee would be coached in where to go, what to do and how to stay incognito.

> ## The Resistance had to make sure the people they were helping were not German infiltrators

One of the most well-used escape routes was the so-called Comet Line which ran across the Pyrenees into Spain. This was run by a young Belgian women called Andree de Jongh. Thanks to her team's efforts, more than 700 men reached freedom.

A different route, the Pat line, was masterminded by another Belgian,

Albert Guerisse, who also enjoyed a high success rate. Both de Jongh and Guerisse ended up in concentration camps for their courageous efforts, although happily neither perished before liberation came.

Before D-Day, the Allies airdropped supplies of arms to the Maquis so that, when the time came, they could at last fight openly against the Germans.

■ PARTISANS ■

One ambitious resistance group gathered a force of 3,000 and seized the Vercors plateau of southern France. Their mistake was choosing a site far from the front line which was impossible to hold long enough for the Allies to provide relief.

A substantial German force crushed the resistance despite aid dropped by the Allies. This demonstrated that the Maquis worked better as an underground organisation than as a fighting army.

Partisan groups soon got to work in Greece and Yugoslavia. The island

LORRAINE

One of Churchill's famous quotes during the war included:

'The heaviest cross I have had to bear during this war is de Gaulle's Cross of Lorraine.' (Reflecting the tensions felt between himself and the leader of the Free French.)

of Crete, from which Allied forces were compelled to make a hasty departure, was full of rabidly anti-German people who were only too happy to take up arms against them.

Yet Crete was occupied by German paratroopers who deeply resented

---

Crete was full of people who were only to happy to take up arms against the German invaders

---

the losses they had suffered during the taking of the island, when many of them had been shot as they descended to earth. They recalled the ninth of their mentor Karl Student's 'Ten Commandments': 'Against a regular enemy, fight with chivalry but give no quarter to guerrillas.'

Local people were also suspected of mutilating the bodies of German soldiers during the invasion. If this happened at all, it was on a tiny scale. Yet rumours of it spread like wildfire and the Germans eagerly sought revenge. Between the May invasion and September 1941, no fewer than 1,135 Cretans were killed.

It was against this background of savagery that the highly independent village and townsfolk organised a resistance which would show no mercy to German soldiers. Mountain villages quickly became no-go zones

for Germans who were already quite reasonably afraid of walking at night through the streets of Heraklion and the other fortified towns of Crete.

■ DEFENCE OF CRETE ■

It was only thanks to the enthusiasm of the local people for the Allied forces – which remained despite the debacle which had taken place in defence of Crete – that so many British, Australian and New Zealand servicemen survive the German occupation after being left stranded following the hasty evacuation.

There were so many stragglers from the forces that the submarine HMS Thrasher arrived on the island's south coast to remove as many fugitives as possible.

On Crete Britain's Special Operations Executive installed personnel to help organise the local fighters. One of them, Captain Guy Turrall, cut a curious figure as he insisted on wearing his British uniform complete with medals while trying to identify underground cells.

In Yugoslavia the most professional partisans were formed under the leadership of Josip Broz, otherwise known as Tito. A committed communist who fought with the Red Army in the Russian Civil War, he won the admiration of the Allies in his handling of the unwieldy collection of factions in his sphere.

By 1943 they were so convinced of his ability that the Allies awarded him official recognition at the expense of the Chetniks, a Serbian guerrilla group operating in the region. Embittered by this apparent betrayal, the Chetniks then began to co-operate with the Germans in a confusing volte-face. However, America's Office of Strategic Services remained in contact with the Chetniks even after they had made their own separate peace with Germany in 1943.

Below: Marshal Tito, pictured here signing the proclamation of Yugoslavia's independence, emerged among the most successful of underground leaders.

Left: Hitler shows his ally Mussolini the lucky escape he had after the assassination attempt at Rastenburg.

Yugoslavia, with its mountains, hidden valleys and extensive coastline, gave ample opportunity for the SOE to smuggle in supplies.

Partisans were so troublesome to the occupying Germans that in May 1943 some 100,000 German troops were committed to fighting the resistance movements in the region.

■ CROAT PARTISANS ■

Matters in Yugoslavia were further complicated by the activities of Croats who were pro-German and formed their own partisan groups which operated in support of the Axis powers.

On the Eastern front, anti-Nazi partisans were vehement in their opposition to German soldiers and exacted a terrible revenge for the barbarity of the Nazi invasion. Amply sheltered by the rocks, forests and mountains of western Russia, the partisans indulged less in the finer points of resistance and more in violent struggle. Their actions, often desperate and reckless, tied up German forces for days and weeks at a time, causing havoc behind the lines when the Wehrmacht was at its most stretched at the front. If they

were caught, these fighters were usually hanged publicly as a warning to others.

Resistance in Germany was on a much smaller scale. This is not at all surprising, given the barbarity of the Nazi regime. The Catholic Bavarian White Rose group – one of the main resistance movements within the Fatherland itself – was wiped out almost as soon as it formed in 1943.

There was, however, still a core of anti-Nazis who continually tried to undermine Hitler's rule, both before and during the war. They received woefully little support from the British and the Americans.

The German dissident movements routed their appeals for assistance through various neutral countries, including Sweden, Spain and Portugal. Indeed, although a shot was never fired in Lisbon, the Portuguese capital was a hotbed of intrigue involving all shades of subversives. Among them was the highly educated and eloquent Lufthansa lawyer Otto John, whose job took him out of the Third Reich regularly on business. His appeals for aid were made to MI6 in Lisbon through the English novelist Graham Greene, then a

counter-intelligence officer in charge of operations in Portugal.

Alas, Greene was subordinate to Kim Philby, who had already been recruited as a Soviet spy. Philby blocked all communications from the rebel Germans to the Allies. This was in accordance with his instructions from Moscow – Stalin hoped to see the Third Reich torn apart before peace broke out, and so if Germany remained intact, his plans for postwar empire-building might never have got off the ground.

■ STAUFFENBERG ■

So when the most tangible of resistance moves against Hitler occurred, with the bomb plot of 1944, the conspirators were isolated from the Allies and had to rely on their own wits in their daring attempt to pull off the assassination.

The plotters wanted to eliminate Göring and Himmler at the same time, and it was this overambition that ultimately caused them to fail. Behind the plot were Oberst Klaus Schenk von Stauffenberg, recently promoted to colonel and chief of staff General Fromm, the commander in

> ### The Portuguese capital was a hotbed of intrigue involving all shades of subversives

chief of the Home Army. Stauffenberg was frequently called in to report to Hitler about finding fresh reserves of men for the Eastern Front. In league with him were Generals Friedrich Olbricht and Ludwig Beck.

◆ EYE WITNESS ◆

Liepke Scheepstra, from Amersfoort, was a leading member of the Dutch resistance movement, called the LKP (de Landelijk Knok Ploegen). He recalls his feelings on D-day.

❛I heard about the D-Day invasion by radio – we followed all reports while moving around on foot. We were glad it had happened but we hardly had time to think about the landing. We were preparing a raid on a house guarding prisoners in Arnhem and it required every bit of our energy. There was a lot at stake – people were threatened with execution. We had already attempted to free them three times but had had no success so time was of the essence.

On 11 June, we finally carried out the raid. There were seven men and a woman called 'Little Peter'. We had guns although no idea if they worked so it came down to being smart and using the element of surprise.

It was a success and 53 people came out with us. One of the first things they asked was whether the English had arrived. As I waited in the cell corridors making sure that everyone got out, a woman asked me if she could look at freedom. I took her to the door and said: 'Go on, have a sniff at it'.❜

Right: **The judiciary showed no mercy to those found guilty of trying to kill Hitler. They were killed after first having being strung up with piano wire.**

■ GESTAPO ROUND-UP ■

Stauffenberg bravely carried a bomb to Hitler's Berchtesgaden headquarters on 11 July 1944 but decided against detonating it when Himmler failed to attend the meeting as scheduled. Four days later Stauffenberg attended another conference, again armed with a bomb. But Hitler abruptly left while Stauffenberg was on the phone to his co-conspirators.

Tension rose as the Gestapo rounded up suspected traitors, targeting members of the illicit group.

On 20 July Stauffenberg set off to see Hitler at Rastenburg in East Prussia with a bomb hidden inside his briefcase. Here was the 'Wolf's Lair', Hitler's bunker and alternative capital to Berlin.

At a high-level meeting in a reinforced hut, Stauffenberg placed the bomb as near to Hitler as he could before making his excuses and leaving. Assuming that Hitler would soon be dead, Stauffenberg made off in a car along a cobbled road through dense woods and bluffed his way past an aerodrome guard to board a Heinkel bomber for the three-hour journey back to Berlin.

Alas, a fellow officer inadvertently moved the briefcase again. At 12.42, when the bomb exploded, Hitler was screened by a stout wooden table. His hair was set alight in the explosion and his trousers were torn to shreds – but he was very much alive.

Following the blast, Keitel gathered the prone body of the stunned Führer into his arms. When he realised Hitler was still alive, he wept for joy.

Afterwards, Goebbels wrote: 'The assassination attempt was surrounded by the most dramatic circumstances and one can only repeat yet again that it is a miracle that the Führer was not maimed.'

Now the nuts and bolts of the plot which should have held it together snapped under pressure. Stauffenberg

> *Goebbels wrote: 'One can only repeat that it is a miracle that the Führer was not maimed'*

had instructed a sympathetic General to sever all communications from Rastenburg following the explosion. But lines remained open and news that Hitler was still alive winged its way to Berlin even while Stauffenberg was making his escape.

A German army major had been sent to arrest Goebbels but Hitler was able to personally countermand the order.

Stauffenberg soon came under suspicion and was shot with other leading lights in the plot shortly after midnight. The grisly work of the firing squad was lit by car headlights. Before he died, the noble Colonel shouted: 'Long live holy Germany'.

■ PIANO WIRE ■

A further 4,980 people also paid the ultimate price for the Stauffenberg conspiracy as Hitler called for savage wholesale reprisals. Other suspects were hanged by piano wire, their final agony being filmed for Hitler's delectation. It was a reel he loved to show to high ranking German military officers to illustrate the price of treachery to the Führer.

Whole families were wiped out or carted off to concentration camps. Franz-Ludwig Graf Stauffenberg was six when his father's ill-fated bomb plot occurred. He recalls the events which followed: 'The day after the

Above: **Partisans enjoyed some spectacular successes. The Germans who fell into their hands were either kept captive, handed to the Allies or killed.**
Right: **German officers mingled with the crowds to witness the hanging of a convicted partisan in Minsk.**

bomb my mother gathered us together and said: "Something terrible has happened – Papi is dead."

'I did not cry. Then we were told by a maid that my mother and great uncle had been taken away. Two days later my grandmother and her sister disappeared.

'Two men came to take charge of the house. I had never heard the word Gestapo before. They took us for a walk. There were six Stauffen-

berg children, the four of us and two cousins.

'We went to the village Catholic priest. He told us we were in bad trouble. We should always be proud of our father, he said, and gave us a blessing.'

The children were sent to a kindergarten with the children of other executed conspirators. Franz-Ludwig was finally reunited with his mother who had been kept alive as a possible

◆ EYE WITNESS ◆

Special Operations Executive agent Edward Howe parachuted into the Majevican hills to join Yugoslavian partisans.

'The Majevica hideout was tucked away high in the hills. The entire region was Moslem in religion and culture. The house I was in was comparatively clean and tidy but it contained little furniture. It was used as a headquarters by the Partisans and, as I entered, I met the Partisan leaders, about a dozen of them, all seated in a circle on the floor. Everyone was eager to hear the latest news from 'outside'.

From the moment their questions began I realised how well informed they were. They listened to the BBC from London and to the Free Yugoslav station that operated 'somewhere in Russia'. I could tell them little they did not already know.

While we talked, the British planes went on dropping their loads. For the Partisans this was a great occasion. They had been starved of supplies because of their inaccessibilitiy and constant harrassment by the Germans. This unfortunate state of affairs was to continue.

The Partisans had become most efficient at sorting out supplies dropped in the darkness. It was not an easy job for sometimes chutes were blown far from the target. Everything depended on the pilot. Under good conditions, with the moon to light the area and no strong winds, there was always a chance that the supplies would fall plumb on the fires.

On the ground the Partisans would stand and watch the planes come in. Usually the pilot flashed his signal lamp to indicate that the drop was beginning and then the Partisans counted the chutes as they opened out and teams were sent off to follow each one to the ground and bring the container to an assembly point.

Here they were sorted out and stacked in piles ready to be distributed at first daylight. The practice was to have everything completed and the dropping area cleared before the day was old enough for German aircraft to come nosing inquisitively around.

Each plane – and that night five planes dropped to our pinpoint brought as many as 40 containers and other packages. Supplies of boots, for example, were 'free drops'; they were made up in bulky parcels that fell without a chute and were extremely dangerous to everyone below.

All the chutes were collected and the local people often made clothes of the silk. It was a common sight to see peasant women in that part of Bosnia wearing bright red and blue blouses made from parachute silk. Clever seamstresses also made excellent underwear for the men. In many ways this silk and the linen chutes sometimes used for stores were as valuable to the Partisan as the stores.

After what seemed a long time the sound of aircraft overhead ceased. The last plane had 'shot us up' as the RAF used to say of the final dive they made over the target. It was their way of saying goodnight and goodbye.'

hostage in Ravensbruck concentration camp in August 1945.

Had the Stauffenberg bomb plot succeeded, countless Allied and German lives would have been saved and the obscene work of the extermination camps would have come to a

The Führer decided to exterminate root and branch the generals who were opposed to him

quicker end. Despite its failure, however, the enormous pride that Franz-Ludwig still takes in his father's actions is perfectly apparent. He echoes the very sentiments of his father when he says: 'Success, killing Hitler, was not that important. It was necessary to show our people and the world that there was another, an honourable, Germany.'

Goebbels recorded the bomb plot and its aftermath faithfully in his diaries and by doing so revealed that Hitler still maintained the core of his following even though the war was going badly:

'The Führer is exceptionally fed up with the generals, particularly the general staff. He is absolutely determined to make a bloody example of them and to exterminate this lodge of freemasons who have always been hostile to us and have simply waited for the moment where they could in the most critical hour of the Reich stab us in the back.

■ BLANKET POWERS ■

'... I asked the Führer in the future to give me blanket powers to command the guards battalion and the Führer agrees. The consequences of the plot will certainly be far-reaching.

'At first a cleansing has to take place and the Führer has decided to exterminate root and branch the whole clan of generals who were opposed to us and in this way to destroy the wall that had artifically been built by them between army and Party and people.

'... I will take charge of the State apparatus, wielding an iron hand to restore clear lines of command.

'What does cause me to have grave doubts is the fact that the Führer has got very old. Because of the pain he is suffering, he seems fragile. Yet his being is highlighted by exceptional goodness and I have never seen him exude such inner warmth than during these days.

'One simply has to love him. He is the greatest historical genius alive in our time and with him we will either gain victory or with him we will go under as heroes.'

In the far east, the villagers of Burma and other territories conquered by Japan were little worried about the occupation. It made no difference to them whether the

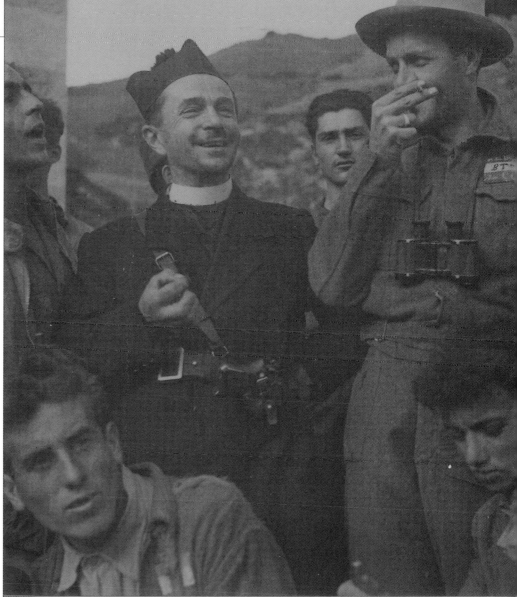

Left: French Resistance workers not only had the Germans to contend with. Vichy's internal police force, the Milice, also rounded up freedom fighters. *Below:* A band of Italian partisans, including a priest, a doctor, an engineer and a 13-year-old boy, await orders. Their leader is the brother of a man hanged by Germans.

Brave men and women passed information about Japanese military activity to the Allies

foreign forces on their land were Japanese or British so there was precious little by way of a resistance movement. But there were a troop of brave men and women in the far east who risked everything to provide details of Japanese soldier and ship movement to the Allies.

■ COAST WATCHERS ■

These were the coast watchers, civilian volunteers working for Australian naval intelligence who secreted themselves around the Pacific Islands to spy on the Japanese.

Coastwatchers had first been recruited in 1919 from traders who made their homes on these islands. Now they were overrun by Emperor Hirohito's men, but they had long since established the perfect cover from which to watch out for seaborne threats mounted against the Australian mainland.

The penalty for their actions was instant death at the hands of the brutal Japanese. Yet the information they gathered gave the Allies a jump start in their battles in the region.

ENIGMA CODES

Every day, Wehrmacht commanders in the field sent reports back to base. Their dispatches included details as mundane as the weather – and as crucial as troop movements, battle plans and supply shortages. Items like these were for the ears of Germany's top brass only.

Little did the operators realise as they punched out the reports on their portable transmitters that the Allies were eavesdropping each and every time. They were also monitoring U-boats and Luftwaffe aircraft.

Early in the war, Britain cracked the secret codes which the Germans used to communicate. It was a coup which they put to excellent use as the conflict progressed. For their part, the Germans maintained an unflinching faith in the ciphers they had so painstakingly developed and stayed blissfully unaware of the enormous security breach until years after the end of the war.

Of course, Britain's code-crackers did not win the war on their own. The information they gathered was used in conjunction with other intelligence from agents and diplomats as well as the forces in the field, sea and air. But their breakthrough saved lives and helped Churchill and the other Allied leaders plan a strategy that could only lead to victory. Only in 1972 was the secret of Ultra unveiled to an astonished world.

■ ENIGMA ON SALE ■

Germany made use of a machine that had been specially developed to send encoded messages. The first model appeared in 1919 in Holland where it was designed. Soon after, a German modified the original and named it the Enigma. At the time it was a commercially available machine that was on open sale in Britain.

Opposite: **At Pearl Harbour the backbone of the US Pacific Fleet was smashed. When the US cracked Japanese codes, surprise attacks like this were eliminated.** *Right:* **Code crackers use the latest machinery in pursuit of the correct keys.**

While tension mounted in Europe throughout the Thirties, Enigma was brought into use by the German army, navy and finally the air force in addition to the security services and the railways.

Modern warfare had rendered the telephone unreliable. As German units surged forward in their 'Blitzkreig', they went beyond the most outlying telephone cables and risked being out of touch with their

Messages could not be broadcast in everyday language; a coding machine was needed

command. Also, telephone lines were subject to bomb blasts or enemy sabotage. Radio was the favoured method of communication but messages could not be broadcast in

everyday language. A coding machine was necessary and Enigma was it.

Now the Enigma was a far cry from the basic model unveiled at the end of the Great War. The Germans prided themselves on a series of advances which would keep their secrets safe.

An Enigma machine, powered by an electric battery, had similar dimensions to a typewriter and also had a keyboard. But for each letter entered on the regular keyboard, another would appear on a second, rear keyboard that would duly become the coded message. The transposition was done by three or more wheels behind the keys whose role was to scramble each word automatically. Each wheel had a multitude of settings and the code was varied from day to day.

It was a two-man operation: as one man turned the report into code, the second took a note of the new set of letters appearing in code on the

rear keyboard and transmitted it, either by Morse code or by wireless. A machine which transmitted simultaneously and would require just one operator never came into use.

■ DAILY CHANGES ■

In theory, only the receiver of the message had the correct formula to turn the gobbledegook back into good sense. He knew the setting of the sender's machine, the correct order of the wheels and could vary his to the corresponding setting.

In its basic form alone, Enigma would have caused enough headaches for the decoders. However, there were further refinements added by the Germans as war approached. The

Below: **The three cogs of the Enigma machine were a vital security bar. Although it looked like a typewriter, Enigma had two keyboards to create its codes.**

codes were altered every day – or sometimes every eight hours – to protect its security. So one message successfully read could be followed by scores more in another, unintelligible code. Further security devices were added, too, including the coupling of letters through pairs of plugs.

The mathematical difficulties of resolving the code were mindboggling. For their success, the British owed a debt of gratitude to Poland and its security services.

The Poles had been reading German military messages for years before the advent of Enigma. By 1929 they had acquired a German Enigma machine and within four years made huge strides in understanding its workings and output.

The Poles in turn had the French to thank for their achievements.

When documents detailing the workings of the Enigma fell into

French hands via a German traitor, they were duly passed on to the Poles who put them to good use.

Although the French never cracked the German codes, the Poles were regularly translating messages generated by the Third Reich. These made alarming reading. Hitler's expansionist intentions were clear for all to see.

> ## Hitler's expansionism was abundantly apparent to those eavesdropping behind the scenes

To help in the task of deciphering, the Poles had invented a machine they called a 'bomba' which automatically crunched codes until it hit on the right one. This was later modified and developed by the British and

operated around the country by the women of the WRENS who waited patiently for results. It could take them a few moments, a few hours or even days. Then again, sometimes they failed completely to make any sort of translation.

■ BLETCHLEY PARK ■

In 1938, the Poles lost their advantage when the Germans introduced yet another complex Enigma safety system. By the time the invasion of Poland loomed in 1939, they were hopelessly at sea with the new codes.

Wisely the Poles saw a brick wall ahead of them and decided to salvage what they could of their labours. In July 1939 they met with counterparts from Britain and France and shared their knowledge of Enigma. The Poles went so far as to present each of their allies with an Enigma machine.

Although Poland was subsequently conquered, refugee decryptologists worked with the French until France too was overrun by Germany. A handful of Polish code crackers were

> **It is a tribute to all those involved that the work carried out at Bletchley Park remained secret**

snared by the Germans in France. Despite harsh conditions of captivity, they never once imparted the vital information about the Allied knowledge of the Enigma which would have prompted Germany to change its method of coding.

Now it was the responsibility of Britain alone to capitalise on the knowledge so arduously gained by their Polish and latterly by their French allies.

The Codes and Ciphers School was based at Bletchley Park, a

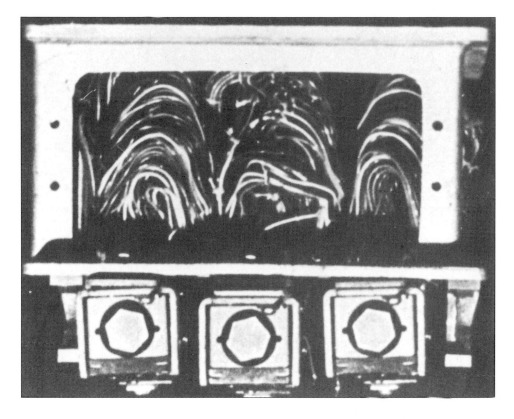

Above: **The machine used by the Americans to decipher 'Purple', the Japanese navy code.**

rambling mansion in Buckinghamshire that dated back some 50 years. Gathered here were fluent German speakers, outstanding mathematicians, radio experts, military tacticians and chess players.

Some came through the services, others were plucked from universities and colleges. Their shared aim was to listen in to the German secrets and relay the information as speedily as possible to Allied commanders to give them the upper hand in battle.

Secondly, it was their avowed duty to keep their activities cloaked in secrecy. A whisper about the project could have alerted the Germans and silenced Enigma forever. It is a tribute to all those involved that the valuable work carried out at Bletchley Park remained a closely guarded secret throughout the war.

The name given to information wrung from Enigma by the Allies was Ultra. Vitally important messages were called Top Secret Ultra.

Still, the task of reading the codes was a mighty one. First came the

problems in transmission. Broadcasts made over radio or wireless sets were often fogged by atmospheric conditions, leaving the eavesdropper short of chunks of the message. The installation of intercept stations to improve reception was made a priority.

Then there were difficulties in identifying the senders of various broadcasts and in differentiating between normal radio traffic and coded Enigma messages. Directional Finding or D/F was instrumental in pinpointing the locations.

British intelligence chiefs found that verbatim transcripts were not the only useful items to be gleaned from the work being done at Bletchley Park. For example, a surprise increase in the weight of traffic and a change in its locality indicated the likelihood of a fresh offensive.

To break the code itself, there was only one thing the listeners could be

◆ EYE WITNESS ◆

Earle Demone, of Halifax, Nova Scotia, served aboard HMCS Assinboine. Missions included patrolling waters off the French coast shortly after D-Day when there was concern that senior German officers might try to escape the Allied net by sea.

One night about 9.30pm our captain comes on the radio telling us not to get undressed or into our hammocks because we would be at action stations around 1am. They obviously had some good intelligence because around 1am we sighted five armed trawlers trying to sneak out of a small port.

We were part of a patrol of four destroyers and of course we opened up on them. Two of our ships rammed two of theirs and we had all of them ablaze. Yet they still kept firing back at us. We were amazed. We couldn't understand how anyone could have stayed on those boats, never mind continue the fight.

In the end we sank four of the five. The people aboard could have got to safety if they'd wanted because they were so close to the shore. We had no way of knowing how many of them made it, nor did we ever find out the nature of their mission.

sure about: Enigma never mirrored a letter in its transposition. So for example if the letter 'a' appeared in the encoded message, it certainly would not appear in that position in the translation. That left just 25 options per letter.

However, there were short cuts which the cryptographers looked out for. Many messages contained a weather report. By matching words likely to appear in that report, they could stumble on the key to the code if they were lucky.

Sometimes messages sent in a different cypher already known at Bletchley Park were translated onto the Enigma, thus providing eavesdroppers with a welcome clue.

■ GLARING SIGNALS ■

Also, German operators became slack through over-confidence and inadvertently gave themselves away. Instead of choosing a random three-letter security code, they picked the same letters day in, day out, with the result that the listeners were then able to translate them with considerable ease. Every piece of information

that was translated was kept stored at Bletchley Park for assessment by intelligence chiefs. Even the most innocent of messages was probed to see if it held a deeper meaning. As the

> *Even the most innocent of messages was probed to see if it held a deeper meaning*

skill in cracking the Enigma Code increased, so too did the volume of associated paperwork.

The first code to be broken by the listening ear at Bletchley Park was that used by the German Wehrkreise, Hitler's home command. It was labelled 'Green' and provided little by way of hard information.

Then at the time of the invasion of Norway in 1940 the British cracked the Enigma code used by the Supreme

Below: **Work at Bletchley Park, where vital German codes were read, was kept strictly secret. Only in 1972 did its story emerge.**

Command of the German Armed Forces, called 'Yellow'. For the first time the potential of Ultra was realised with operational details being read in Britain soon after they passed between German commanders. Although the translation of Yellow was by no means complete, it gave intelligence at Bletchley Park plenty to go on and masses of encouragement.

Next to be decoded were the Luftwaffe Enigma codes, branded 'Red'. Thereafter a handle on all German air force messages was maintained throughout the war.

Gradually, the extent to which codes were broken and the speed at which German messages were translated substantially improved. By 1944 the advantage of the system was beyond doubt.

A signal containing bombing schedules for the following day sent

Next to be cracked at Bletchley Park were the German Luftwaffe's Enigma codes

by German High Command at 21.40 hours on 26 October 1944 was transcribed and relayed to the relevant commanders soon after midnight. Hundreds of thousands such messages were dispatched from Bletchley Park during the war. The value of the insight they gave to Allied commanders was immeasurable.

By January 1941 Ultra gave clear indications about the German build-up for the invasion of Yugoslavia and Greece. There was little the British could do to prevent the attack, nor could it find sufficient troops to fend off the Germans. While the reading of codes failed to assist the Allies in Greece and Crete, it did help prompt

the evacuation of troops. In the same year the Italian codes which dealt with shipping in the Mediterranean were cracked. This meant that the Allies could target Rommel's supply ships with ease and it substantially decreased the speed with which the German commander could progress in North Africa.

■ NEW U-BOAT CODES ■

By the end of January 1942, Bletchley Park was decrypting the naval Enigma virtually simultaneously. Convoys were routed away from wolf packs and the anti-submarine squads were able to target their prey. Ultra is believed to have saved one and a half million tons of shipping, equivalent to 350 vessels, that year alone.

U-boats were temporarily withdrawn from the Atlantic at the close of 1942. When they returned they were communicating with a new and different code which Bletchley Park could not recognise. By now

Above: The rear of the Enigma machine revealed some of the refinements added by the Germans after its inception in the 1920s.

Germany had realised that U-boats were the ace in their naval pack and production had been stepped up to replace those sunk by the Allies and provide more besides.

Only when the new Enigma key was broken in March 1943 were the convoy routes offered adequate protection again. Ultra coupled with improved radar, high frequency direction finding and more powerful forces, enabled the Allies to take the offensive against U-boats with a vengeance. The previously secret German refuelling points were sunk and they could now be attacked even while they were on their way towards the busy shipping lanes of the North Atlantic Ocean.

Both the Allied victory in North Africa and their success against the

penetrate and the Gestapo code was never read even though it remained unchanged between 1939 and 1945.

Churchill knew that Ultra was a precious gift, not to be given away

> ### *Churchill knew that Ultra was a precious gift, not to be given away lightly*

lightly. It complicated issues for him and his commanders because they were unwilling to advertise its existence. Therefore, extensive use of

Above: Thanks to wartime code breakers, the first electronic digital computer was made in 1946. *Right:* Aircrews were saved by advance warnings from code readers.

U-boats were key factors in the final outcome of the war. Had Rommel triumphed in Africa it would have cost the Allies dearly in terms of a vastly extended campaign. Britain, meanwhile, could have found itself besieged on the home front had the U-boats done their worst. At the very least, 'Overlord', the invasion which finally liberated Europe, would have been delayed.

The invasions of both Sicily and France were significantly assisted by the knowledge gleaned from Ultra. The decrypting of codes enabled the

Allies to determine the exact whereabouts of German troops, their battle formations, the effect that air-strikes were having and all their weaknesses and strengths.

■ GEHEIMSCHREIBER ■

Not all Enigma codes were broken. While the Luftwaffe key remained in the hands of the Allies virtually throughout the war, both the army and navy keys were harder to

the information gleaned from Ultra was pretty well prohibited. Only the choicest items were utilised in order that no pattern was established in the use of such high-grade intelligence. Had the Germans suspected that their codes were being widely read, they would naturally have changed them immediately.

In fact, the Germans already had the Geheimschreiber, an alternative machine to Enigma used only at the highest level, which was never cracked by the decoders at Bletchley Park. There was widespread alarm that the Germans would use this for all communications, bringing Ultra to an end once and for all. Fortunately for the Allies, they never did nor did they realise the extent to which their code system had been infiltrated.

■ COVENTRY RAID ■

It led to accusations years after the war that Churchill had known in advance about the devastating air raid planned for Coventry in November 1940 and done nothing to stop it. Certainly, British intelligence did know that a city other than London was being targeted in a raid the Germans codenamed 'Moonlight Sonata', and they believed it to be either Birmingham or Coventry.

British scientists had been working on bending navigation beams used by the Luftwaffe to guide them to their targets, and thus lead them astray. On the night of 'Moonlight Sonata', 14 November, the procedure failed.

It was a clear night. This aided the German pilots, while the defensive fighter planes and barrage balloons this time claimed only one casualty between them. In a single night's work German bombers caused the deaths of 568 civilians. A further 863 were injured and the city of Coventry was gutted.

Germany, of course, listened to British and Allied messages where it could. One of its major success stories was the reading of the cipher used by the US military attache in

> ### By 1940, B-Dienst was reading up to half of the British Royal Navy's communications

Cairo which let them into untold secrets about British troop movements in the desert.

By 1940 the Führer's observation service B-Dienst was reading about 50% of Royal Navy communications,

a situation that persisted until 1943 when new codes at last began to be used. This was another major contribution to turning the tide of the U-boat war in the Allies' favour.

■ BATTLE OF MIDWAY ■

Nevertheless, on balance Britain won the radio war. Likewise, American intelligence was ahead of the Japanese. The US broke the Japanese naval code and diplomatic cipher, known as 'Purple', before the fighting began thanks to the 'Magic' organisation.

Perhaps the most telling use of the US 'listening ear' was in the Battle of Midway. Admiral Nimitz was in possession of much of the Japanese battle plan days before it began. That knowledge enabled him to place some of his fleet in the Pacific where the Japanese were least expecting to find it. The Battle of Midway has since been widely acknowledged as a turning point in the war with Japan.

Below: **Some of America's top men assembled to successfully breach the Japanese radio codes.**

PROPAGANDA WAR

As the age of Hitler dawned, Hollywood, its moguls, its movies and its glamorous stars already wielded a mighty power.

Thousands of people flocked to the pictures every week to hang on the every word of their idols and absorb every nuance of the finely-spun tales. Yet as storm clouds of war gathered over Europe, the good and the great of the film-making capital were reluctant to put their talents to use in the fight against fascism.

They were not only reflecting the isolationist fervour prevalent in America during the Thirties. There were sound financial reasons for their neutral stance in that lost revenues from box offices in Germany and Italy would have hit their pockets hard.

The first film-making company to break out of the mould was Warners with its Confessions of a Nazi Spy, made in 1939 and starring Edward G. Robinson and George Sanders. Overtly anti-Nazi, it had the popular Robinson featuring as a G-man rooting out traitors who had gone to ground in America. It even contained footage of meetings of the German-American Bund, an organisation of expatriate Germans which flourished in America's Mid-West and was avowedly pro-Hitler.

Warners had good reason for antipathy to Hitler – its German agent had been kicked to death

Warners had good reason for its antipathy to Hitler. Its German agent, Joe Kaufman, had been kicked to death in Berlin in 1936 by Nazis. Now its abhorrence of the creed received yet more justification. Several Polish projectionists were hanged in their cinemas for showing the movie.

There followed a collection of films, either overtly propagandist or morality tales following little England's brave stand in the face of overwhelming odds. Few found great favour a the box office, however.

It became the crusade of a dedicated band of Jewish and other anti-Nazi writers to keep the message alive. Fortunately, their numbers grew and began to include people of real influence in politics.

Now it would only be a matter of time before film stars and makers fully grasped the

Opposite: The Olympics in 1936 held in Germany gave Goebbels a golden chance to trumpet the Fascist cause.
Below: A scene from the anti-Nazi film *Confessions of a Nazi Spy* starring Edward G. Robinson. *Bottom:* Greer Garson and Walter Pidgeon in *Mrs Miniver.*

medium at their disposal to aid the Allied cause.

In 1940, Charlie Chaplin – playing for the last time the little tramp figure for which he was so loved – made The Great Dictator. Chaplin played two roles – a humble Jewish

Hollywood helped to undermine isolationism and bring the USA into the war on Britain's side

barber and a Hitleresque dictator called Adenoid Hynkel, who bore a striking resemblance to one another. Needless to say, there is confusion between the two and the persecuted

Jewish man ends up making an impassioned speech to a Nazi rally about freedom and the rights of man. Basic in its theme, the film was nevertheless stirring.

Now the messages in the movies became bolder. From MGM came Escape in which the dashing Robert Taylor rescued his mother, played by silent movie star Alla Nazimova, from a German concentration camp followed by The Mortal Storm, which also illustrated the dangers to hearth and home of Nazism.

The same year, 1940, also saw the general release of Alfred Hitchcock's Foreign Correspondent with Joel McCrea as a spy-ring buster who in the film's finale makes an emotional appeal for stepping up the war effort in the States.

At last the stage was set with Roosevelt clearly indicating his preference for Britain and the isolationists losing credibility by the month. The key was in persuading the American public that some causes were worth fighting for and it looked as if this was beginning to filter through.

■ MRS MINIVER ■

There were a number of anti-German films before America was brought into the war, none quite as accomplished as Mrs Miniver.

Made in 1941 and starring Greer Garson and Walter Pidgeon, it was

Below: Charlie Chaplin played two roles in his satirical and poignant film *The Great Dictator* which ridiculed both the Nazi and the Italian Fascist systems.

an out-and-out tribute to Britain's home front which scooped a clutch of Academy Awards. Little could have done more to drive home the message. Audiences up and down America wept with Mrs Miniver over one woman's tenacity and tragedy in the conflict. They barely had time to recover when they were crying on their own account. Pearl Harbor brought America into the war at the end of 1941 with the deaths of thousands of their own servicemen.

■ CASABLANCA ■

Hollywood studios were vacated by the cream of their stars who either volunteered for military service or joined troop entertainment facilities. Among those who went were Clark Gable, James Stewart, Mickey Rooney, Tyrone Power and John Ford. British stars who donned a uniform included David Niven and Laurence Olivier.

Right: Josef Goebbels, the accomplished Nazi propagandist to whom Hitler owed much of his staying power.

Women stars sold war bonds, toured the Pacific and Europe to brighten up the lives of the troops or served refreshments in canteens.

Now the film-makers who remained behind channelled all their energies into winning the propaganda war against Hitler.

Out of this era came what is possibly one of the greatest films of all time, Casablanca. Humphrey Bogart was mean and moody while Ingrid Bergman was as delicate as a rose. The lovelorn pair forced apart by the war in Europe captivated the free world then and continue to do so even today.

Satire and parody had their place too. The swipes taken at Nazis in the enduring To Be Or Not To Be kept the audiences entertained while leaving them with the clear impression that all German men in uniform were humourless dimwits. Many came away with the impression that SS stood for Stuffed Shirt.

Apart from films with a barely hidden message, many others were made with a 'feel good' factor, escapist stories designed to keep morale high on the home front, particularly musicals.

Besides making the box office blockbusters, Hollywood's fount of talent contributed to the war effort by making documentaries and stirring series demonstrating the value of American-style democracy.

So thanks to Hollywood film, perhaps the most popular medium of the age, the message of the Allies was presented to the receptive British, American and Australian publics, who flocked to the cinema.

Masterly though Hollywood became at manipulating messages for

the benefit of the Allies, it was competing with the best.

Germany had a master in its upper ranks in Josef Goebbels, who took charge of all forms of public expression when the Nazis came to power.

Born in 1897 of devoutly Catholic lower middle-class parents in the

Germany's master of media manipulation was Propaganda Minister Josef Goebbels

Rhineland, Josef Goebbels was psychologically inhibited in his childhood by a disfiguring club foot. In adulthood he hardly topped five feet in height and barely tipped seven stones on the scales.

Nevertheless, he had a quick and able mind which won him a place at university. He was able to take up the opportunity thanks to financial support from a Catholic fund. The loan gave him a certain obligation to the church. But when the money ran out, so did his faith. The charity eventually sued him for the money.

Below: Goebbels had the common touch and knew the way to the hearts of the Reich's soldiers.

From there, Goebbels turned his hand to writing books and plays. None was successful and he blamed the 'Jewish literary mafia' for that rather than looking for his own

Goebbels was a writer who blamed his lack of success on 'the Jewish literary mafia'

shortcomings in style and ability. In 1925 he joined the Nazi party which appeared to reflect much of what he thought and felt at the time. He was

at first a devotee of Gregor Strasser, a radical revolutionary who ran a branch of the party at odds with that that of Hitler. Goebbels once even demanded the expulsion from the Nazi party of 'the petit bourgeois Adolf Hitler'.

Ambition, however, moderated his extremism. He finally recognised Hitler was the man who would take the party to great heights.

By 1928 Goebbels was the party's leader in Berlin and five years later, when Hitler came to power, he became Minister of Propaganda and Entertainment in the new Reich.

He was himself an accomplished public speaker, well able to rouse the passions of his audience with an apt quip, taunt or compliment until they were putty in his hands.

It wasn't long before this gift for assessing the public mood got to work on a larger canvas. Under his expert eye, all press articles, radio broadcasts, exhibitions, posters, feature films and news reels were given a pro-Nazi slant, often with a blatant disregard for the truth.

■ PRO-NAZI SLANT ■

News and entertainment programmes made by the Allies were imported then shamelessly cut to 'expose' the population as degenerate and their leaders as teetering icons.

Perhaps his greatest talent was for never allowing dogma to interfere in his work. Historians have since accused him of lacking ideals and inner substance. Certainly, he was never blinded to reality by fascist

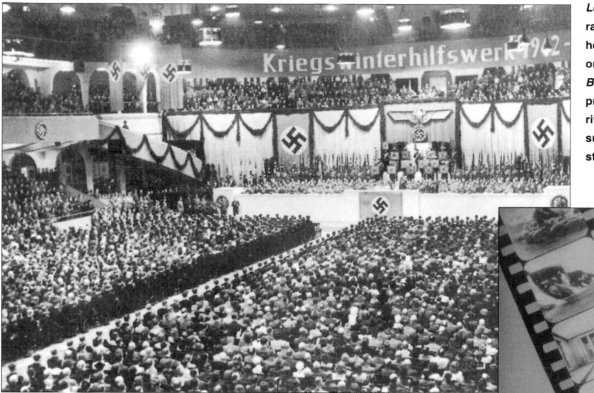

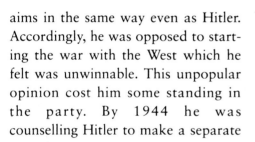

aims in the same way even as Hitler. Accordingly, he was opposed to starting the war with the West which he felt was unwinnable. This unpopular opinion cost him some standing in the party. By 1944 he was counselling Hitler to make a separate

> **Goebbels was opposed to starting the war with the West which he felt was unwinnable**

peace with Russia to save Germany from annihilation. The hated adversary could become a valued ally once more, he argued, to push back the advance from the West.

Yet this lack of restraint was in itself a strength. His ideas were always fluid, allowing him to plot a sure and certain course to success rather than be hidebound by the conventions of fascist beliefs. His gestures were always calculated and

to get him what he wanted – they were never from the heart.

His personal contradictions were manifold. He dressed smartly in expensive suits and was a notorious womaniser. Yet at the same time he possessed a puritanical streak which baulked at extravagance and had him sneer at the lavish lifestyle of rival Hermann Göring. He remained aloof from other members of the Nazi hierarchy whom he regarded as little better than contemptible, swaggering beer cellar bullies.

Hitler came to rely on the faithful Goebbels to translate his unsavoury messages into a form that would be readily and eagerly devoured by the German public. Although he himself didn't invent the lies of Nazism, Goebbels certainly played a major part in propagating them. He skilfully manufactured a myth of infallibility which even survived Hitler's death. Without Goebbels in tow, it is questionable whether Hitler would have maintained his hold over the German people for a dozen years.

The relationship between the two men was never personally close, although Hitler was a witness to Goebbels' marriage to Magda in 1931. When his wife later sought divorce on account of the runtish Goebbels' string of ill-concealed love affairs, Hitler intervened to effect a reconciliation between them.

■ UNDER THE SPELL ■

Yet Goebbels and Hitler were lost in mutual admiration. Goebbels fell under the spell of Hitler's magnetic power in those early days of Nazism and never looked back. For his part, Hitler saw Goebbels as something of an intellectual who shared the same artistic aspirations. Of course, Goebbels wasn't an intellectual. He would burn books of great worth because they were written by Jews or contained left wing philosphies, along with the rest of the Nazi thugs. He did this even if he admired the content of the book, so detached was he from his inner feelings.

■ RABBLE-ROUSER ■

In fact, Goebbels steered clear of addressing himself to the great thinkers of the day on the basis that they could never be converted to Nazism if they weren't already. His work was consequently directed at the man in the street whom he saw as much more malleable.

While Hitler undoubtedly had a fascinating charisma, only a fraction of the population got to meet him personally. It was for Goebbels to project this image and recruit loyal servants throughout the Reich. His aim was to bring a radio into every German household, because that way the words of the master could be brought to all the population.

His control of cinema became a legendary example of how to sway the minds of the masses. Films containing messages contrary to the Nazi cause were banned. New films bore the Goebbels hallmark of artistic uniformity. By the time the film industry was nationalised in 1942, many of its brightest talents had quit Germany in disgust, unable to find an outlet for dissenting opinions.

> ## *Goebbels quickly realised that to hammer away at the Jews could provoke a backlash*

Goebbels quickly realised that to hammer away at a theme like the hatred of Jews could provoke a backlash. So the messages in the works he liked best were subtle. Only a few films diminishing the Jewish race were produced while historical spectacles recalling the triumphs of Bismarck and Frederick the Great, containing possibly one Jewish villain, were favoured instead.

In fact, much of the output of the state-controlled industry was devoted

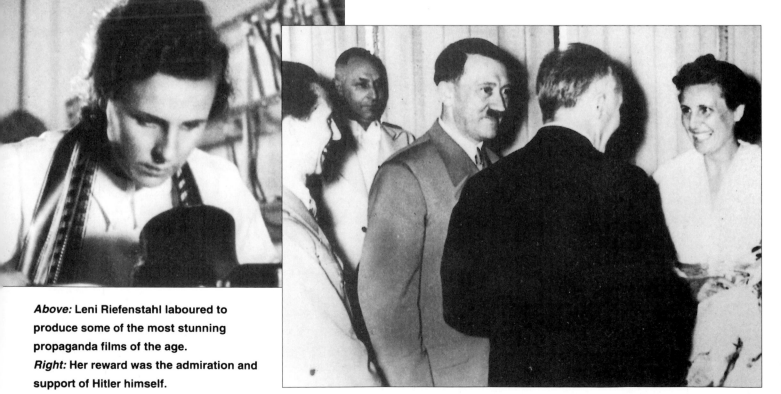

Above: Leni Riefenstahl laboured to produce some of the most stunning propaganda films of the age.
Right: Her reward was the admiration and support of Hitler himself.

to comedies and fantasy giving the German people their quota of escapist movies to relieve them of the pressures of the war.

■ LENI RIEFENSTAHL ■

The two outstanding propaganda films made in the era were Triumph of the Will, capturing the Nazi party Nuremberg Convention of 1934, and Olympia, a tribute to the 1936 Berlin Olympics. Both were made by Leni Riefenstahl, an actress and dancer turned film-maker who embarked on her new career during the ascent of Hitler in Germany.

Her copious talents won her the accolade of Hitler's favourite film-maker – and with good reason. She

---

He killed his wife and six children with cyanide and then took the same poison himself

---

had an uncanny knack of promoting the Nazi cause with scarcely a mention of it by name.

Allegedly, she became a mistress to the Führer – a charge she constantly denied. Following the war, she was jailed by the French for peddling

Nazi propaganda and spent nearly four years behind bars before being freed. All attempts to revive her film career failed and she worked instead as a stills photographer in magazines.

As the war continued and Germany's fortunes declined, Goebbels became increasingly extreme, his speeches more and more outrageous. It appears he began to believe the propaganda that he was distributing – that, against all odds, Germany could win the war after all. He even believed that if only he had been Chancellor the war could have ended in victory. His faith in his own talent never wavered.

On 22 March 1945 Goebbels records in his diary: 'My war propaganda is now being eulogised quite openly in London. It is being said that it is the most exemplary of all the war efforts being made anywhere today and that it is primarily responsible for the fact that German resistance is so much in evidence, even though on a reduced and enfeebled scale.'

Both he and Hitler were convinced that America would pull out of the war on the death of Roosevelt. When their gleeful prophecy proved wrong, both had to face the inevitability of defeat. After presiding over the funeral of his master Hitler in May 1945, he

killed his wife and his six children, aged between four and 12, with cyanide and then poisoned himself in the besieged Berlin bunker which had become his final shelter.

In contrast, Britain's propaganda was hopelessly awry when the war broke out. It was amateurish, condescending and ineffective, and one of the first suggestions to emerge from Churchill's publicity department was the necessity to provide tea following an air raid.

Britain always shied away from the use of propaganda. Its ham-fisted attempts to blacken the name of 'the Hun' during World War I backfired when they were quickly exposed to be nothing but a pack of lies.

Now there was a reluctance to use such measures, no matter how extreme the international situation. Government advisor Horace Wilson was outraged at the suggestion by Eden in 1938 that the BBC, press and British Council should get their heads together and produce a unified output to help combat the menace

---

◆ EYE WITNESS ◆

On 1 May 1943, Goebbels made the following entry in his diary.

❛ The Soviets at the moment are extremely insolent and arrogant. They are quite conscious of the security of their position. They have no consideration whatever for their Anglo-Saxon allies. The men in power in the Kremlin know exactly how far they can go. There is a great bitterness in London and Washington about it which nobody seeks to disguise. The Anglo-Saxon camp is in a blue funk about the fact that our propaganda has succeeded in driving so deep a wedge into the enemy coalition. ❜

posed by Germany. In a memorandum to Prime Minister Neville Chamberlain, Wilson wrote: 'Having been old-fashioned for very many years, I find myself unable to show enthusiasm for propaganda by this country and I still cannot bring myself to believe that it is a good substitute for calmly getting on with the business of government, including a rational foreign policy.

'... I do not believe that any propaganda is really harmless. Even if you are careful, in praising yourself, not to decry others, the unflattering implication is always there. Ten days ago, the British press acclaimed our diplomatic efforts in the cause of peace. That could be read as implying that Germany was on the point of an act of aggression. It was so read in Germany and bitterly resented. The example is worth quoting as showing how easily the most harmless publicity may give offence.'

This feeling that propaganda somehow wasn't quite cricket infected the launch of the service charged with producing information for the public. Its staff, though well meaning, had no training in the art and lacked the common touch.

Consequently, the Ministry of Information was soon publicly scorned for its inadequate efforts. Comedians like Tommy Handley and satirists like Evelyn Waugh had a field day.

■ GAS MASKS ■

There were numerous posters issued offering advice on how to put on a gas mask. Yet attack by the enemy did not come for months. The posters appeared pointless.

They were accompanied by a volley of 'do's and don'ts' from the government which even tried to close down cinemas for the duration of hostilities – until they realised the extent of the potential of film for entertainment and the dissemination of propaganda. The Ministry of Information constantly referred to the public as 'you', making ordinary people feel like underlings. The patronising tone of posters aimed at raising spirits on the home front merely succeeded in irritating people.

Above: American Jesse Owens swept the board at the Berlin Olympics – and was promptly ignored by the Führer. *Left:* The Führer hoped the Olympics would be dominated by Aryans.

There were hoardings galore advocating the wisdom of evacuation, showing a mother shielding her children from bombs falling from the sky. But bombs had not fallen from the sky as expected. Bureaucracy had

British attempts to smear Germany during World War I had backfired when exposed as a pack of lies

gone mad. At this stage of the war, Hitler had done little to inconvenience the masses while the government had done a great deal.

Rationing itself was not resented by the majority. They were keen to see signs that the war was affecting rich and poor alike and across-the-board measures did just that.

Another weakness in the information channels quickly came to light. The service ministries were happily dispensing information to news organisations without reference to the MOI, an error which Goebbels would never have made.

■ DUNKIRK ■

As Britain's fortunes of war declined, so the MOI feared a threat to morale. It came as something of a shock following Dunkirk and the Battle of Britain to find that, in spite of the government, the populace was keeping chirpy. Still, they kept back information about the war for fear of inspiring defeatism. It was hard facts that the public desperately wanted.

The vast majority were merely frustrated by the bumbling efforts of the Ministry of Information. A stock phrase on the radio following reports of an RAF action was 'all our planes returned safely'. It was widely disbelieved and rightly so.

Above: Humphrey Bogart and Ingrid Bergman are still best remembered today for their roles in *Casablanca*.

Less derogatory and more effective were straightforward slogans like 'Dig for Victory' and 'Save Fuel for Battle', to which everyone could relate. The most useful and well-received of all posters were those

Britons tuned into broadcasts from Germany by William Joyce, better known as Lord Haw-Haw

As the British government's obsession with secrecy took an iron grip and few details were released about the war effort in general and troop movements in particular, people tuned in to the propaganda broadcasts made from Germany by traitor William Joyce, better known as 'Lord Haw-Haw' because of his plummy voice. After listening to his version of events and discounting the obvious German slant, British listeners at least felt they had an inkling of what was going on.

During the Blitz, the Ministry happily handed out pictures of a housewife clearing up her broken windows with the incredible caption: 'Well, there's one thing about this Blitz. It keeps you busy and you forget the war.'

While the people of London were stoical, they were far from delighted at seeing their houses blasted. Reports claimed that the air raids had made little impact – these were designed to undermine the German effort, but they inflamed the British, too. It denigrated their efforts. And later, when other British cities were flattened in bombing raids – and then

they were not even mentioned on the national news – there was further justified upset.

Gradually, the officials learned that lack of information adversely effected enthusiasm for the war effort. The Germans knew exactly where they had bombed even if they didn't know the extent of the damage they had inflicted. So there was little point in suppressing the whereabouts of the latest raids.

Posters which exhorted the population to work harder when they were already doing their utmost also caused a widespread negative effect.

used in the 'Careless Talk Costs Lives' campaign, simple in message and beautifully drawn by Fougasse, and the recipes for rationed food, even if some contained expensive ingredients not found in many working-class kitchens.

■ **THE TIDE TURNS** ■

After the Allied victories in 1942, the Ministry of Information's job became much simpler. News of victory in North Africa had a far greater effect on public morale and production figures than any poster or radio message ever could.

FILMS

The top money-spinning films in the UK during the war years were:

1939: *Pygmalion;* Forerunner of the musical *My Fair Lady* in which a professor tries to turn a flower girl into a 'duchess' within six months, starring Leslie Howard and Wendy Hiller.
1940: *Convoy;* A story of sacrifice as a British merchant ship goes under to save a vital convoy. Unknowns Clive Brook and John Clements starred while the acclaimed director Pen Tennyson was later killed in action.
1941: *49th Parallel;* Eric Portman, Laurence Olivier, Leslie Howard and Raymond Massey were the stars of this drama set in Canada about five U-boat crewmen attempting to escape to the US.
1942: *The First of the Few;* Called *Spitfire* in the US, it was the story of the plane's creator R. J. Mitchell and once again starred Leslie Howard.
1943: *In Which We Serve;* A host of stars including director Noel Coward, John Mills, Richard Attenborough and Celia Johnson peppered this flag-waving epic about the survivors of a torpedoed destroyer who remember their recent pasts.
1944: *This Happy Breed;* A portrait of family life in the London suburbs between the wars, from a play by Noel Coward.
1945: *The Seventh Veil;* Polished romantic drama starring James Mason and Ann Todd about a talented concert pianist suffering from divided loyalties.

TRAITORS

Among the grey apartments of a Parisian suburb, gaunt-faced Jews were herded from their homes in terror for their lives. Sour-faced guards, quick to administer a powerful kick or stinging punch to the stragglers, knew the fate of their prisoners well enough.

These quiet, clean-living Jews were bidding a desolate final farewell to the country where they were born and bred. Stinking, airless carriages were ready to ferry them into Germany and its appalling concentration camps where sickness, starvation and death were almost inevitable.

The guards who relished the unsavoury task of committing these helpless folk to their doom were no rabid Nazis, however. They had not sworn allegiance to Hitler nor were they even German nationals.

Here were French people who enthusiastically seized the opportunity to carry out the Reich's dirty work. Without apparently turning a hair, they set about the task of ridding occupied France of its Jewish population with alacrity. Neighbours, colleagues and even friends were no longer safe, so eager were certain members of the French population to do their duty, as they saw it. Members of the French police force were joined by civilians for the effort to rid all France of Jews.

> **They set about the task of ridding occupied France of its Jewish population with alacrity**

In every land that fell into German hands, there were a good number of collaborators who would do the Nazis' bidding. For them, the chance of power and aggrandisement from the invader was worth more than any loyalty to their own country's flag. In France the actions against the Jewish people were even sanctioned by the government who introduced two rounds of anti-Semitic laws to exclude all Jews from public life. Those people who carried out the grim work of the Nazis were traitors, no more, no less.

■ BLACK THURSDAY ■

On 16 July 1942 came Black Thursday, the biggest anti-Jewish operation since the Fall of France. In all, 12,884 people, including 4,051 children, were taken to transit camps or the notorious Drancy concentration camp in France before being transported to Germany where virtually all died.

This reflected a rich vein of anti-Semitism rife in French society even before the outbreak of World War II. The influx of Jewish refugees from Germany and, later, Poland had done nothing to abate feelings which were running high. By 1939, there were upwards of 150,000 Jews in Paris – although that figure was only a fraction of the number of foreigners

Opposite: **French Jews rounded up by neighbours bound for Drancy concentration camp.** *Below:* **Marshal Pétain co-operated with the invading Germans.**

◆ EYE WITNESS ◆

Dirk Bruggeman was 17 and en route to the German higher school in Arnhem when he heard about D-Day. His parents were members of the NSB (Nationale Socialistische Bund), a pro-Hitler group in the Netherlands. Now a priest in the Hague, he is associated with the 'Stichting Werkgroep Herkenning', the Foundation of Recognition, an organisation for children of parents with mistaken beliefs.

'On the way I saw a group of people by a newspaper office where a bulletin read that the Allies had landed in the Seine Bay and I wondered how this could be possible, believing it to be in Paris.

I didn't have my uniform on that day. Strangely enough, I had mixed feelings. On the one hand, I found the news threatening, and on the other hand, exciting. Real war was getting closer.

The atmosphere at school was uneasy. The teachers remained courageous but I believe that in their hearts they were working out how to save their own skin. On the outside there was an air of: "Oh, we will contain them." For months afterwards we believed we would contain them and didn't want to believe in the destruction of our ideal.

I never doubted my father's ideals. The Nazi songs were impressive, so was the marching, and so were the special uniforms of the Hitler Youth to which I belonged. You felt exceptional and strong.

However, I was a delicate and vulnerable lad and not at all sporty. I didn't actually fit in to this showy atmosphere but I couldn't tell anybody this.

It is still a major question for me: Could I be to blame? Should I have acted differently? If I could change things then I gladly would but I understand that my fate now is to live with the past.'

living there at the time. Already, the Jews were under pressure from expulsion orders and police harassment.

When the invasion came, Paul Reynaud was Prime Minister with Marshal Philippe Pétain his deputy. Pétain was a key rallying point, in Reynaud's eyes. He had won victories

Despite his great age, Marshal Pétain was a hero figure to many French people

in the field against Germany during World War I and helped to steer France from defeat to triumph. Despite his advancing years – he was 84 years old – he was a hero figure to many French people.

It was Pétain who signed the armistice with Hitler that left one third of France unoccupied. He assumed control of that free state from a base at Vichy. Despite his willing subservience to the German invaders, many French people still admired Pétain as the man who delivered France from a costly and protracted war with Germany.

■ PIERRE LAVAL ■

Alongside him was so-called socialist Pierre Laval, an experienced statesman and confirmed pacifist who won the patronage of Hitler, so much so that when he was sacked by Pétain, his reinstatement was ordered by the Führer himself.

Although Pétain and Laval were far from being friends, they co-operated together to assist the

Left: **In court after the war Pierre Laval denied he was a tool of the Nazis even though he had Hitler's personal support for his actions during the Occupation.**

Germans and finally even allowed them to cross Vichy territory, destroying any illusion of independence. Ironically, neighbouring Italy – which was run by the Fascist Mussolini, an ally of Hitler's – actively provided a bolt hole for Jews forced to flee from Vichy France.

■ OBEYING ORDERS ■

Pétain, Laval and their cohorts at grass roots level denied responsiblity for what happened to the French Jews. Those in command professed ignorance of the real purpose of the deportations. Those carrying out the commands insisted that they were only doing their job.

The French branch of the Gestapo ran its own torture chambers. The Milice, Pétain's paramilitary force, used methods whose barbarity rivalled those of the SS.

Following the war, Pétain was tried as a collaborator and sentenced to death but reprieved by de Gaulle on account of his great age. He lived until 1951. Laval fled to Germany following the liberation of France but was finally persuaded to return. After a trial he received the death penalty and was executed by firing squad.

There were even rumours of a more sinister collaboration in France, that of tacit assistance given to the Germans by the Union Générale des

> **There were rumours of a pact between the occupying Germans and French Jews**

Israelites de France. It was feared that the organisation, run by established French Jews, contributed towards the deportation schemes at the expense of poor immigrants in a bid to save the native Jewish population. After the war it was cleared by a jury of the charge not once but twice. The rumours probably arose because the unpopular UGIF allowed itself to be manipulated by the Germans and French and became responsible for tax collection and administration of aid, which was sorely lacking.

> **After the war the French took a terrible vengeance on Nazi collaborators during the Occupation**

■ QUISLING ■

Collaborators in France were to suffer the vengeance of the Resistance. More than 9,600 were executed without trial following the liberation of France. In later trials a further 7,000 were sentenced to death, although only 767 were killed. In all, about 40,000 people received jail terms for aiding the Germans.

In Holland, there were similar sympathies for the Nazis in sectors of

◆ EYE WITNESS ◆

Madeleine Tomin, from Le Havre, northern France, fell in love with a German soldier and had his baby. When France was liberated, her neighbours sought revenge.

❝When they came for me I thought they would break down the door. Luckily my boy, now two, was asleep. I was frog-marched into the street where men and women held me down. Their faces were twisted with hate. They were calling me *putain* (whore) and *traitre* (traitor). At least three pairs of hands pushed me down on to the pavement then somebody else grabbed a handful of my hair and started hacking away with a pair of scissors. I breathed deeply to hide my fear. But I could have choked when a razor flashed before my eyes. It was scraped across my scalp so painfully. The crowd were whooping and baying. They daubed swastikas on my forehead using mud from the gutter. I never felt more wretched before or since.❞

Below: Vidkun Quisling (*centre*), the Norwegian whose name became a byword for treachery, stands under armed guard after the war.

the population. The Nationale Social-istische Bund was formed for Nazi supporters. They donned uniforms and helpfully carried out the wishes of the

Vidkun Quisling was head of the puppet government set up in Norway by the Nazis

invader, particularly with regard to the rounding up of Jews and communists.

In Norway, Vidkun Quisling actively courted the Germans even before they invaded. His name has since become a byword internationally for all traitors and fifth columnists, those who work within a country to secure its downfall.

Quisling led the National Union Party in Norway and was rewarded for his devotion to the Fatherland by being made 'minister president' of the puppet government set up there by the Germans. Arrested in 1945, he was found guilty of war crimes,

RESISTANCE

The first Aryan German to be executed for showing signs of resistance died at Sachsenhausen concentration camp. He was a communist working in the Junker factory at Dachau. When he refused to carry out air raid protection work he was reported by the works police, arrested and sent to be quizzed by the Gestapo in Berlin. It was Heinrich Himmler who ordered his death, intolerant of even the most token element of resistance against the Third Reich. Even today, the name of the hero resister is unknown.

German communists continued to carry out acts of sabotage during the war. They also tried to help prisoners of war and slave labourers when they could. The best known are Bernhard Bastlein, Franz Jacob and Theodor Neubauer who set up an underground network spanning a dozen towns. All were killed by the Gestapo in the last year of the war.

Although German resistance was notoriously small-scale, Gestapo records in August 1942 reveal that 1,761 Germans were arrested for striking; 1,583 were detained for having contact with imported workers or POW's; 1,210 were held as suspected anti-Nazis and 1,007 were branded resisters.

having sent countless numbers to their deaths in the gas chambers of extermination camps in Germany, and executed.

■ LORD HAW-HAW ■

Perhaps the traitor who was best known to British people was William Joyce, otherwise known as 'Lord Haw-Haw'. Born in America of Irish parents, he was a devotee of British fascist Oswald Mosley. He arrived in Germany in 1939 on a British passport and happily broadcast propaganda for the Nazis throughout the hostilities. British families crowded around their radio sets to hear his news and views, not because they believed what he was telling them – on the contrary – but because they were starved of

Left: **William Joyce, popularly known as 'Lord Haw-Haw', broadcast pro-German propaganda to the British throughout the war. His messages were treated as comical.**

information about the war effort by the Ministry of Information.

After the war, Joyce tried to escape capture by blending in with the refugees in Germany but his voice – the hallmark of his life of treachery – gave him away. He was arrested, tried for treason and executed.

Other British traitors included a motley crew of about 200 who fought for Hitler in the 'British Free Corps'. The Corps was primarily established for Nazi propaganda purposes although it did see action on the Eastern front.

Some of those in its ranks were motivated by ideology, some were on the run from British justice and others had been persuaded to change sides after being taken prisoner by the Germans. At least one corps member, Thomas Cooper, is almost certainly responsible for slaughtering many Jews in Poland. He was never brought to trial.

The Corps was founded by John Amery, son of Leo Amery, one of Prime Minister Churchill's cabinet colleagues. John Amery, declared bankrupt in 1937 aged just 24, became embroiled in politics by

disinformation throughout the Resistance networks.

As D-Day approached, air chiefs were unwilling to spare aircraft for further raids. Thus the secret weapon programme was then left unharried.

Pressure was brought to bear on the German scientists, still not happy with the launching of the flying bombs, to initiate a strike against England soon after D-Day.

Confusion reigned at the launch sites as the prescribed date drew near. Although there were plenty of missiles and adequate fuel, none of the sites had its full quota of safety equipment. Thus German commanders risked substantial numbers of crewmen in order to comply with the order to start the flying bomb offensive immediately. They appealed for a postponement but they were allowed just one hour.

In the end, the expected salvo did not materialise. Only ten missiles were launched, five of which crashed at once. A sixth disappeared, probably coming down in the sea, while the remaining four reached England.

The bomb could travel at up to 400 miles per hour and as high as 3,000 feet. Inside the nose of its streamlined fuselage was packed one ton of explosive. Behind the warhead was a tank with a capacity of 150 gallons, sufficient for a journey of

---

The bomb could travel at 400 mph at a height of 3,000 feet; it had a range of about 130 miles

---

about 130 miles. For steering, it relied on a magnetic compass and a pre-set automatic pilot. It had small wings and a tail.

As its journey ended, the propulsion unit would cut out. Thereafter, it nose-dived towards the earth, silent except for the rushing sound made by a heavy object travelling at speed through the air. Its effect was usually more devastating than that of a bomb because it exploded before it hit the ground.

Vigilant members of the British Royal Observers Corps were the first to spot the bombs as they split the night air. They noted 'a swishing

sound' and spotted a bright red glow firing from the rear end of the missiles.

Soon many people living in south-east England, especially residents of the so-called 'Doodlebug Alley' along the path taken from France towards London, came to recognise the sinister outline of a pilotless aircraft in the sky. And they knew from bitter experience the terror inspired at the moment the noisy motor cut out just before the bomb fell to earth.

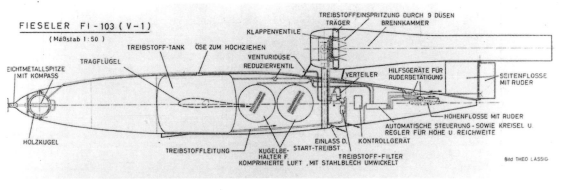

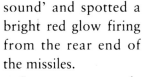

Above: Designer's blueprint for the V-1. *Left:* The ominous outline of a V-1 bomb in flight brought a chill to the hearts of the British people.

The introduction of doodlebugs into the war brought unprecedented terror to London. People were far more frightened by a robotic weapon

Within a matter of seconds, 121 were killed and a further 80 injured in the Guards Chapel

launched at London from some distant spot than they were of even the worst nights of the Blitz.

■ EVACUATIONS ■

There was a new wave of evacuations organised by the government. And for the first time citizens who endured the privations of living in London in its darkest hour dug deep into their own pockets to finance refuge for themselves in the country.

The City of London, Penge, Bermondsey, Deptford, Greenwich,

Camberwell, Lewisham, Stepney, Mitcham, Croydon and Chiselhurst were among the most badly affected areas of the metropolis.

Churchill succinctly expressed the effect that the secret weapons had on the people of London:

'This new form of attack imposed upon the people of London a burden perhaps even heavier than the air raids of 1940 and 1941. Suspense and strain were more prolonged. Dawn brought no relief and cloud no comfort.

'The man going home in the evening never knew what he would find; his wife, alone all day or with

the children, could not be certain of his safe return. The blind, impersonal nature of the missile made the individual on the ground feel helpless. There was little that he could do, no human enemy that he could see shot down.'

■ GUARDS CHAPEL ■

At first the new bombs caused little loss of life. But one bomb landed by fluke in central London and changed all that. On Sunday, 18 June 1944 a bomb cut out over Birdcage Walk and dived into the Guards Chapel at Wellington Barracks.

Right: A prototype of a piloted bomb given the name V-3 but never launched.
Below: When its engine cut out, this V-1 bomb descended silently upon Piccadilly in the heart of London.

Another method sometimes employed was for the pilot to come alongside the V-1 and carefully nudge its wingtip against that of his own plane, sending the V-1 into freefall and sparking its destruction.

Perhaps the most dangerous technique of all was to fly in front of the bomb so that the manned plane's slipstream would throw the bomb out of control.

Fighter planes operated both out at sea, avoiding the gun belt, and inland.

The barrage balloon network on the outskirts of London also played an important role and netted 232 V-1 bombs during the war.

Bomber Command continued to do what it could to combat the V-1 threat and kept up attacks on launch sites in France even though Churchill refused to release aircraft for these

---

About 8,000 V-1 bombs were launched against London, 2,400 of which reached their target

---

missions if they were needed for battle operations in Normandy. In the event, attacks against the launch sites yielded disappointing results, and the main storage depots for the flying bombs in France proved much more rewarding targets.

In July 1944 British bombers attacked and largely destroyed the natural caverns at St Leu d'Esserent in the Oise valley where 2,000 German bombs were stored. At about the same time, another similar storage station was reduced to ruins by American bombers.

Right: A cross-section of the V-2 rocket reveals how much of its capacity was devoted to the storage of high-octane fuel.

Yet despite all these Allied efforts, it wasn't until the invasion forces overran the launching bases in the first week of September 1944 that the flying bomb campaign finally came to an end.

About 8,000 V-1 bombs were launched against London, with 1,000 crashing immediately after take-off and about 2,400 reaching their

target. Civilian casualties amounted to 6,184 with 17,981 injured. Germany attempted to maintain its assault by launching V-1s from planes and from long-range sites in Holland but with little success.

But it was not quite over yet. Hitler still had the long-range rocket or V-2 with which he planned to avenge the invasion of France.

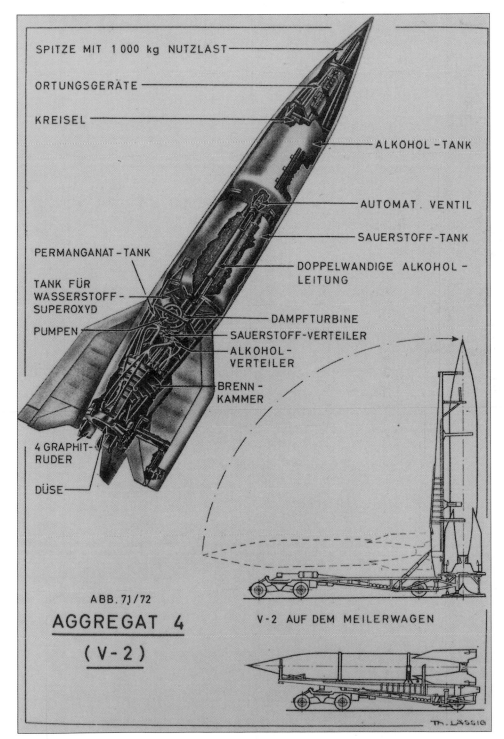

SPITZE MIT 1 000 kg NUTZLAST
ORTUNGSGERÄTE
KREISEL
ALKOHOL-TANK
AUTOMAT. VENTIL
SAUERSTOFF-TANK
DOPPELWANDIGE ALKOHOL-LEITUNG
PERMANGANAT-TANK
TANK FÜR WASSERSTOFF-SUPEROXYD
PUMPEN
DAMPFTURBINE
SAUERSTOFF-VERTEILER
ALKOHOL-VERTEILER
BRENN-KAMMER
4 GRAPHIT-RUDER
DÜSE

ABB. 71/72
AGGREGAT 4
(V-2)

V-2 AUF DEM MEILERWAGEN

Th. LASSIG

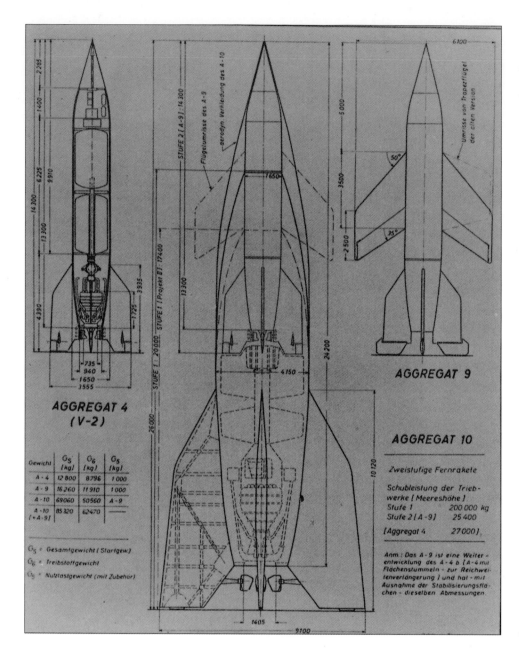

AGGREGAT 4 (V-2)

AGGREGAT 9

AGGREGAT 10

Left: **Hitler believed his new breed of rockets would force the Allies back from the borders of the Fatherland.**

ground. Cherwell swayed Prime Minister Churchill and thereafter little credence was given to the dissenting views of other scientists.

The existence of rockets was slowly proved beyond doubt thanks to British intelligence. A bugged telephone conversation between two high ranking German prisoners caught them wondering why no loud explosions had been heard around their London cell when the imminent arrival of rockets had been promised while they were still in Germany.

Once again Peenemunde was the base for development. More concrete information came on 13 June 1944 when a rocket landed on Swedish soil and was shipped to Britain for further investigation.

■ TURBINE-DRIVEN ■

How had this rocket got to Sweden? The story was that a German expert in glider bombers had been invited to witness a rocket trial. So overawed was he by the sight of the rocket rising into the air that he pushed the control lever he was holding to the left and held it there, throwing the rocket well off course.

British investigators marvelled at the rocket with its jet fired by alcohol

> ***Nearly four tons of alcohol and five tons of liquid oxygen were consumed each minute***

and liquid oxygen. Nearly four tons of alcohol and five tons of liquid oxygen were consumed in each minute of flight. A special thousand

Rockets have been in existence for thousands of years. They were used as long ago as 1232 by the Chinese against marauding Mongols. By the 19th century, rockets rivalled artillery in popularity with armed forces but their technology stayed in the backwoods while that of artillery leapt ahead.

■ ROCKET SCIENCE ■

Following World War I, Germany experimented long and hard with rockets, convinced that they were working on the key weapon of the future. The major breakthrough

came when scientists realised that instead of powering rockets with cumbersome and limited explosives, the answer lay in liquid fuels. It took them years to perfect their weapon, even though they were amply funded by Hitler's regime.

Rumours of a new German aerial weapon reached London in 1939 when a crowing Hitler gave a speech that all but gave the game away.

Yet scorn was poured on the idea of a rocket when a British expert, Lord Cherwell, pronounced that because it would need to weigh some 80 tons it would never get off the

horsepower pump forced the fuel into the jet chamber, which was worked by a turbine.

■ FUEL CUT OUT ■

The V-2 rose vertically for six miles and then, guided by its automatic controls, turned to an angle of 45 degrees. At the end of its range, the fuel cut out and the missile fell to earth. With a maximum speed of about 4,000 miles per hour, it took only a few minutes to reach a target anywhere in Europe.

In July, a courageous Pole was spirited to England with evidence of

Little could be done to bring down the rocket once it started on its inexorable path

the rocket. Germany had pulled back its research into the heart of Poland following damaging RAF raids. Although German patrols raced to retrieve experimental rockets, one that fell was pounced on by Polish underground workers, hidden in a river until the Germans gave up their search and then dismantled by night. The Polish engineer/messenger carried technical documents and more than 100 pounds of parts to a rendezvous with an RAF Dakota on 25 July 1944. Selfless and patriotic, he returned to Poland, to be executed by the Gestapo in Warsaw on 13 August.

On 8 September the expected bomb arrived. One fell in Chiswick and within 17 seconds, another struck at Epping. Now a different bogey haunted the British people. For while there was a decent warning with the buzz bomb, there was nothing to indicate the imminence of a rocket explosion.

H. E. Bates called it 'an ingenious and diabolical robot. It came without sound, without warning and without discrimination. Its inaccuracies were so vast that it became a weapon of monstrous chance.'

More than 1,300 were fired at London from The Hague and an estimated 500 hits were made. On average, each killed twice as many as its predecessor, the flying bomb. In all, 2,724 people were killed and a further 6,476 were injured.

Little could be done to bring down the rocket once it had started on its inexorable path. The best hope for civilians in Britain was that the Allied advance in Europe would reach the launch centres and knock them out before further damage was done.

Not only Britain was under threat. Antwerp was the target for 8,696 flying bombs and 1,610 rockets. Only recently freed from German occupation, the Belgians did not have the benefit of anti-aircraft guns and fighter aircraft to protect them.

■ RETALIATION ■

The tally of death amounted to 3,470 civilians and 682 Allied servicemen. Hitler and Göring were enthusiastic supporters of these 'retaliation

Above: Dr Todt and General Olbricht were two of the leading lights in Germany's 'retaliation weapons' project. Although initial trials were disappointing, they were convinced the bombs would devastate Britain.

weapons', certain that they would inflict immense casualties on the enemy and could reverse the fortunes of Germany. The fact that mass production of the new weapons was virtually impossible under the regular Allied bombing raids appeared to have escaped them.

Speer, meanwhile, had grave doubts. He saw cash and resources being poured into rockets and flying bombs to the detriment of other arms for the military, particularly the Luftwaffe. He declared that it took as long to produce each rocket as it would to build six or seven conventional fighters and that each one cost the same as 20 flying bombs.

Britain continued to use Mosquitoes, approximately the same price as a rocket, each of which could drop about 125 tons of bombs within a mile of its target, while a German rocket could drop only one ton of explosives with an imprecise target margin of 15 miles.

ATOMIC BREAKTHROUGH

Even before the outbreak of war, the race was on to construct an atomic bomb. It was German scientists making the running, too, as they probed the mysterious world of nuclear fission.

In January 1939 Otto Hahn and his colleagues had achieved the first stage of the process by which the weapons of tomorrow's world were made.

Eminent physicist Albert Einstein was among many to sign a letter voicing concern about the headway being made by Germany when the nation was in the hands of the mad Hitler.

Nobel prize-winning Einstein was a confirmed pacifist. But being a German-born Jew, he had refused to return to Europe following Hitler's rise to power in 1933 and knew more than most about the menace which now loomed. It was his justified fear of fascism that persuaded him to write his letter of warning to President Franklin D. Roosevelt.

'A single bomb of this type, carried by boat and exploded in a port, might very well destroy the whole port

Opposite: The Norsk-Hydro plant was key to Germany's bid for atomic weaponry.

Above: A mushroom cloud from the A-bomb dropped on Nagasaki, Japan.

Right: The awesome power of the A-bomb on impact.

together with some of the surrounding territory,' the letter warned.

It was Einstein's theory of relativity published in 1905 that had enabled physicists to embark on the trail of the nuclear bomb.

■ ADVISORY BODY ■

After receiving the warning in August 1939, even before the outbreak of hostilities in Europe, Roosevelt decided to appoint an Advisory Committee on Uranium that year. Its report made worrying reading. A bomb of the nature and power predicted by Einstein was indeed a possibility and, in the wrong hands, it could bring unprecedented devastation to the world.

> ## Albert Einstein's 1905 theory of relativity set physicists on the trail of the nuclear bomb

Even so, the Western nations were slow to make a concerted response to the issue. It wasn't until May 1941 that the US government set up an Office of Scientific Research and Development under the leadership of Dr Vannevar Bush. His brief was to channel all available resources into the field of nuclear research.

A report by Bush in March 1942 was sufficient to convince Roosevelt to launch a programme which would result in the construction of the first atomic bomb. It was called the

Below: The men of the University of Chicago research group gathered from all over the free world. These were the scientists who finally found the key to the nuclear age.

Manhattan Project and its very existence was kept as secret as any spy or security network.

At this stage, scientists knew little about the properties of uranium and its derivatives, the isotope U235 and plutonium. One of the biggest problems was finally solved by Italian professor Enrico Fermi in December 1942.

Fermi led a group of scientists who managed at last to control a nuclear chain reaction. They did it by using an atomic pile, another term for a nuclear reactor, built of layers of graphite and uranium on the football field of the University of Chicago.

A uranium nucleus was split when it was bombarded with a neutron. The resulting surge of nuclear energy was accompanied by free neutrons. These in turn split the nuclei and the process was repeated. It was the first man-made self-sustaining chain reaction of its kind in history.

The experiment was a triumph. Mindful of the secrecy surrounding the project, Nobel prize-winning physicist Arthur Compton sent the

> **Many nuclear scientists had been forced to leave Germany because they were Jewish or anti-Nazi**

following cable to colleague James B. Conant: 'The Italian Navigator has just landed in the New World. The Natives are friendly.'

By now the Allies had decided to pool their scientific resources and all scientists of repute from the assembled countries were combining their brain power to produce the first atomic bomb.

Ironically, many were Germans who had been squeezed out of their homeland because they were Jewish or were suspected of having anti-Nazi sympathies.

Meanwhile in Germany scientists were still striving to gain the upper hand in the nuclear race. The invasion of Norway had provided them with the leg-up they needed.

■ HEAVY WATER ■

In France physicists working under Frederic Joliot-Curie had been experimenting with atomics using 'heavy water'. With the chemical name of D20, 'heavy water' is deuterium oxide, a form of water that has been infused with hydrogen with a boiling point of 101.42 degrees Centigrade. Nowadays it is used as a moderator and coolant in some nuclear reactors. Back then, it was produced only at the Rjukan dam in Norway.

As Germans closed in, Joiliot-Curie dispatched his close aide Hans von Halban to England with the French stocks of heavy water. A team of British and French scientists continued his work at Cambridge University until the centre of nuclear research moved to America.

With the heavy water plant, called Norsk-Hydro, in German hands, the British realised the threat. There was even more concern when the plant's production target for heavy water was raised from 3,000 pounds a year in 1942 to 10,000 pounds. It was a cue for action.

The plant nestled in the mountains of southern Norway amid dense forest. An initial plan to put it out of action with a team of commandos flown in by glider was thwarted when the light planes crashed.

As it was thought to be too difficult to bomb, six Norwegians were trained by Britain's Special Operations Executive to attack the dam.

The team, codenamed 'Gunnerside', was dropped into a remote region of Norway where they were greeted by a three-man advance party, 'Swallow'.

Clad in white camouflage suits, they skied cross-country to the dam to embark on their mission.

With great difficulty they scaled the plant, broke into the key installation and planted their explosives. They narrowly escaped before the

Above: **Physicist Dr Ernest Orlando Lawrence, of America, was one of the men who probed the workings of the atom in the development of the A-bomb.**

PATTON

US General George Patton won his reputation for revelling in warfare after making comments like: 'Compared to war, all other forms of human endeavour shrink to insignificance. God, how I love it.' He also wrote to his wife: 'Peace is going to be hell on me.'

Below: **Norsk-Hydro, the Norwegian centre of production for heavy water, was comprehensively bombed to put an end to its activities.**

blast which wrecked the tanks containing the precious heavy water. With the exception of two men left as a rearguard, the two teams fled to neutral Sweden.

On 16 November 1943 the dam came under attack from USAF B-17 Flying Fortresses

Despite this setback, the Germans were not finished yet. It took them months but they recovered and again stockpiled heavy water.

With a second sabotage operation deemed too dangerous, it was down

to Allied bombers to wipe out the target. On 16 November 1943, the dam came under attack from a host of B-17 Flying Fortresses which showered it with heavy bombs.

■ BLOWN UP ON LAKE ■

While much of the site was wrecked, the last stocks of heavy water remained intact in specially built heavy duty concrete bunkers.

Scientists decided to move these remaining supplies to the comparative safety of Germany. The journey included a ferry crossing over one of Norway's deep lakes. The two men who had remained in Norway following the commando expedition earlier in the year were able to lead a team which put explosive charges in the bowels of the boat.

It was another flawless operation. As the ferry approached the deepest

point of the lake, the bombs went off and the ferry capsized. Although 26 passengers were killed, the Norwegian Resistance had nevertheless managed to end Hitler's foray into the field of nuclear weapons.

■ VON BRAUN ■

Frustrated by Allied action, Hitler lost interest in the nuclear race and concentrated all technical resources on his other secret weapons, the V-bombs. It left German scientists like Werner Heisenberg and Wernher von Braun tantalisingly close to cracking the nuclear code – but thankfully not quite close enough.

In America, unhindered by enemy operations and with considerably more cash at their disposal, Allied scientists were making great strides.

Even so, it wasn't until 16 July 1945 that the plutonium bomb 'Fat Man' was detonated at Los Alamos in New Mexico and the assembled scientists knew they were ready to enter the nuclear age. In charge of the project was Dr J. Robert Oppenheimer.

Above: **The Rjukan dam in southern Norway.**
Right: **The US plutonium bomb 'Fat Man' was tested here in the desert at Los Alamos, New Mexico.**

It was too late to have any effect in the war in Europe. That had ended in May 1945 shortly after the suicide of Hitler. But it was to have telling consequences on the conflict in the Pacific. Japan would not surrender, and the Allies feared a huge loss of life if the war dragged on for much longer while the Japanese mainland was liberated.

Tokyo finally agreed to a surrender with terms acceptable to the Allies after two atomic bombs had been dropped, one on Hiroshima and another on Nagasaki.

The secrets of the bomb were closely guarded to preserve world security. Yet although none of its nationals were working on the Manhattan Project, Russia was soon in possession of its ingredients and construction method.

No one gave the Russians more atomic secrets than German refugee Emil Klaus Julius Fuchs, a communist who had sought asylum in Britain when Hitler came to power in 1933. He gained a doctorate at Edinburgh University and afterwards worked in scientific research.

Like other German nationals in Britain when war broke out, Fuchs was interned as an 'alien' and shipped to Canada. On the way there his boat was torpedoed by a roaming U-boat and he was lucky to escape with his life.

Above: **After his release from a British jail, Fuchs flew to East Berlin where he was greeted by nephew Klaus Kittowski (*right*), and later reunited with his father Emil.**

By 1941 the British authorities were convinced he posed no threat and Fuchs returned to a job in the war effort. Poorly paid, it nevertheless required him to be vetted by security chiefs – this caused no difficulties.

On 7 August 1942 Fuchs became a British citizen. Yet he was already betraying the nation he swore allegiance to by passing information to the Russians.

He stepped up his efforts on behalf of Stalin when he was posted to the US to work on the nuclear devices.

■ LOS ALAMOS ■

Now his spymaster was the notorious Russian vice-consul Anatoli Yakovlev and his main regular contact a respected biochemist by the name of Harry Gold.

Fuchs was one of the privileged few to witness the Los Alamos test as he now worked alongside the man known as the father of the atom bomb, Dr Robert Oppenheimer.

Afterwards, Fuchs had a fat dossier of facts to hand over to his Soviet friends, including details of the new bomb's design and the components necessary for its construction.

At the end of World War II, Fuchs came home to work at Harwell on Britain's nuclear initiative. He even represented Britain at a 1947 conference in Washington, arguing that information about the nuclear industry given out to the Western public should be restricted.

In the same year he first accepted money from the Soviets for the nuggets he passed on. He was paid £100 for inside information on Windscale, Britain's new nuclear reactor plant in the north-west.

Little did he know his treachery had at last been detected. The clues left by Russian negotiators and in radio messages intercepted by America identified the traitor as someone who came from Britain and had witnessed the testing at Los Alamos. Fuchs was chief suspect but

◆ EYE WITNESS ◆

Following the atomic bomb blasts Emperor Hirohito broadcast on the radio for the first time to his people.

‘We, the Emperor, have ordered the Imperial Government to notify the four countries, the United States, Great Britain, China and the Soviet Union, that We accept their Joint Declaration. To ensure the tranquility of the subjects of the Empire and share with all the countries of the world the joys of co-prosperity, such is the rule that was left to Us by the Founder of the Empire of Our Illustrious Ancestors which We have endeavoured to follow. Today, however, the military situation can no longer take a favourable turn and the general tendencies of the world are not to our advantage either. What is worse, the enemy, who has recently made use of an inhuman bomb, is incessantly subjecting innocent people to grievous wounds and massacre. The devastation is taking on incalculable proportions. To continue the war under these conditions would not only lead to the annihilation of Our Nation but the destruction of human civilisation as well.’

security investigators didn't have sufficient grounds to nail him.

■ FUCHS CONFESSES ■

In October 1949 Fuchs made an appointment with Harwell's security officer, Wing Commander Henry Arnold, with a 'personal problem'. Clearly troubled by his treachery, he said he was worried that he might became a target for Russian espionage attempts and was prepared to resign. It was the signal that the security chief had been waiting for.

An accomplished interrogator was dispatched to Harwell and, during the third interview, Fuchs admitted to his links with the Russians. His confession ultimately led him to the dock of the infamous No 1 Court at the Old Bailey where he admitted breaching the Official Secrets Act.

Judge Lord Chief Justice Goddard had a tough rebuke for Fuchs:

'You took advantage of the privilege of asylum which has always been the boast of this country to people persecuted in their own country for

Fuchs was jailed for 14 years. On 12 February 1951 he was stripped of his British citizenship

their political opinions. You betrayed the hospitality and protection given to you by the greatest treachery.'

Fuchs was jailed for 14 years. On 12 February 1951 he was stripped of

Right: **The A-bomb which was later to devastate Nagasaki, shown here in preparation on the island of Tinian the day before it was dispatched.**

◆ EYE WITNESS ◆

In the general election of 26 July 1945, Churchill was defeated in favour of Labour's Clement Attlee. Although wounded by the blow, Churchill spoke these words, alluding to the existence of the atomic bomb.

❝ The decision of the British people has been recorded in the votes counted today. I have therefore laid down the charge which was placed upon me in darker times. I regret that I have not been permitted to finish the work against Japan. For this, however, all plans and preparations have been made and the results may come much quicker than we have hitherto been entitled to expect. Immense responsibilities abroad and at home fall upon the new Government and we must all hope that they will be successful in bearing them. ❞

his British citizenship. Eight years later when he was released from Wakefield jail, he chose to leave Britain for East Berlin. Ultimately, he became director of the East German Central Institute for Nuclear Physics at Rossendorf, near Dresden.

His seven-year betrayal of Britain and the USA undoubtedly did a great deal to advance Russia's knowledge of nuclear weaponry. Yet Fuchs was not the only scientist in the West who betrayed nuclear secrets to Stalin.

Soviet spy chief General Pavel Sudoplatov has alleged in his memoirs that Dr Oppenheimer himself, the man who led the Allied atomic bomb programme, was also guilty of spilling closely guarded secrets to the Russians.

Sudoplatov, the man who organised Trotsky's murder, recalls how Oppenheimer condoned the exchange of information with Russian scientists before the end of the war. Following the war, Oppenheimer opposed the development of the hydrogen bomb. In 1954 he was branded a security risk by Senator Joseph McCarthy, the US politician who conducted a witch hunt against suspected left-wingers.

Given the world order at the time, it is not altogether surprising that both Fuchs and Oppenheimer were prepared to assist Stalin.

■ PRO-COMMUNISTS ■

The pre-war prejudices against Communism had been cast aside in 1941 when Russia became one of the Allies and fought so bravely to repel the Nazis from its soil. And the Red Army played no small part in the downfall of Hitler, suffering millions of casualties in the process.

Those who harboured socialist sympathies were delighted to see communist Russia and capitalist America pulling together to achieve a common goal. This rose-tinted view was even shared by President Roosevelt who sincerely believed the end of the war would mark a new era of co-operation between the victors.

These were the days before the Iron Curtain when Stalin's empire-building was not entirely obvious. The men who handed over atomic secrets almost certainly never considered the gravity of their actions until the full extent of Stalin's brutal imperialism became clear.

AFTERMATH OF WAR

World War II had brought with it widespread death, starvation, homelessness, unmitigated misery and horror for millions. When peace broke out, none of that changed overnight.

For all the fighting nations, there was no time to lick their wounds. The immediate priority was to revive and reorganise in haste to lay the foundations for the future. It was to be a haphazard path to peace, however.

An estimated 50 million people had perished. Some countries suffered far more deaths than others. The Soviet Union was left mourning no fewer than 14 million people, only half of whom were fighting men – the other half were non-combatant civilians.

Poland had incurred grievous losses – approximately six million, around a fifth of her pre-war population. France lost half a million, Italy 330,000 and Holland was bereft of 200,000, most of whom were civilians killed in bombing raids or through deportation.

Britain lost 244,000 servicemen, and 60,000 civilians on the home front. America emerged unscathed on the home front but lost 292,000 servicemen overseas.

Britain lost 244,000 servicemen and an additional 60,000 people on the home front

Commonwealth countries had thousands of troops killed in action. Canada lost 37,000 men, India 24,000, Australia 23,000, New Zealand 10,000 and South Africa 6,000. Chinese losses were incalcuably high and continued as a civil war which had been raging before Japanese involvement in 1931 resumed.

Aggressors Germany and Japan had been severely battered. Four million German servicemen died for

their Führer while 593,000 civilians were fatally wounded in Allied air attacks. Japanese casualties in the field alone amounted to 1.2 million. In addition, their countries were left with perhaps the worst battle scars and were now under occupation.

■ REFUGEES ■

In Europe the problem of homelessness was particularly acute. Air raids had accounted for many houses and flats, leaving the native populations in difficulty.

Also, there were refugees released from labour camps which had been set up throughout the Reich who now had no place to go. Many wished to avoid returning to the East for fear of coming into Stalin's clutches. The dispossessed were hungry and desperate people. There were many who were seeking personal revenge against the defeated Germans. They became a major security consideration for the occupying forces.

The situation was exacerbated in Germany by the flight of its population in the east when the Red Army approached. As many as a million died during the early months of 1945 when the flight from Stalin's vengeful troops began in earnest.

More Germans were expelled from eastern Europe and unceremoniously dumped in the British zone when peace broke out. The German population east of the Elbe was forcibly reduced from 17 million to 2,600,000. The number of displaced persons within the British zone of Germany was judged to top 2,460,000. That included 464,000 French people, 219,000 Belgians and 151,000 Dutch people all heading

Opposite: **Some children study the small print ahead of the signing of the United Nations Charter in San Francisco in 1945.** *Below:* **Less than five years after the end of World War II, trouble flared between the super powers in Korea.**

◆ THE BATTLE OF BERLIN, APRIL 1945

In April 1945 Marshall Zhukov began preparations for the Red Army's final push on Berlin. Konev's 1st Ukrainian Front made for the Neisse River, Rokossovsky's 2nd Belorussian Front went to the northern bank of the River Oder, while Zhukov's own 1st Belorussians held the line along the Oder opposite Berlin. Together the three Soviet Fronts comprised no fewer than 2,500,000 men, 6,250 tanks, 7,500 aircraft and 41,600 artillery pieces. Berlin had already been bombed almost every night since 1 February, and then at dawn on 16 April the attack began in earnest. On 19 April the 1st Belorussian Front broke through the German defences and reached the outskirts of Berlin on the following day.

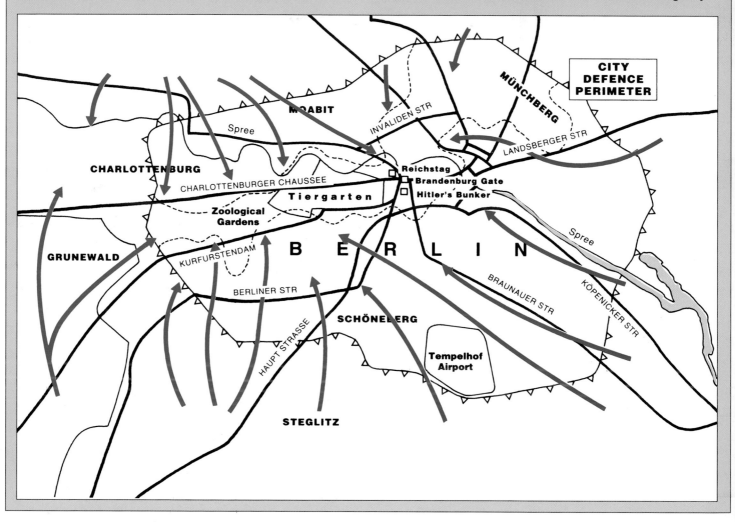

west and 580,000 Poles, 121,000 Russians and 422,000 Czechs destined to travel east.

■ UNITED NATIONS ■

Given the mighty bulge in population which had occurred in a country with a devastated economy, there was immense difficulty in feeding everyone. The aim was to give the Germans smaller rations so that those who had been starved for months and years at their hands could get better. Consequently, Germans were allowed about 12 ounces of bread a day, 10 ounces of potatoes but less than one ounce of meat and only one half ounce of fat and sugar. Also, the onus was put on the German people to supply the food needed for themselves and the displaced people inside their borders.

Fortunately the United Nations was already up and running although it wasn't formally launched until 24 October 1945. It had been started in 1944 after a series of conferences in Washington which resulted in a governing charter, and hoped to succeed where its predecessor, the League of Nations, had failed in preserving peace and fostering co-operation between nations. There were 51 founder member states.

From its Relief and Rehabilitation Administration came clothing, food and medical supplies which averted a crisis that could have enveloped Europe in its first few faltering months of peace.

As the victors prepared for peace, they looked towards the agreements drawn up at the Yalta conference held before the end of hostilities which had been duly ratified in Potsdam.

At Yalta were Churchill, Roosevelt and Stalin, the trio of leaders who had seen through the war

---

Even between the two conferences, held only months apart, the tensions between the Allies had perceptibly increased. At Yalta were Churchill, Roosevelt and Stalin, the trio of Allied leaders who had seen through the war.

■ POTSDAM ■

Before Potsdam, which was held in July 1945, Churchill had been replaced as British prime minister by Clement Attlee. Roosevelt had died, so President Truman represented America. The accord that existed between the original three seemed to have been diminished, not only because the new leaders were far less accommodating towards Stalin but also because of a growing intransigence in the Russian leader.

Stalin broadly mistrusted the intentions of Britain and France as the hostilities drew to a close. Throughout the conflict, he had felt that they were dragging their feet on military obligations in order to let

Right: **Churchill, Roosevelt and Stalin mapped out the defeat of Germany and Japan and much of the future of the world when they met at Yalta in February 1945.**

NAZI WEALTH

Hitler's own attempts to dabble in the world of art were doomed to failure. He was twice turned down for Vienna's Academy of Fine Arts on account of the poor quality of his drawings. Yet his aspirations did not change. Now he decided, as Führer, to become a patron of the arts. Those fine pieces that he gathered around himself were looted from homes, galleries and museums all over the world.

His lieutenants also took their cue from Hitler. Through the ranks there was wholesale theft from the cities, towns and villages swallowed up by the Reich. When it became clear Germany was going to lose the war, much of the prized art was spirited out of the country to languish in the bank vaults of South America, Switzerland and the Arab countries. The proceeds from the plunder were used by ODESSA, the organisation which helped SS men evade justice and which still operates to this day.

Of course, many items have been recovered. In caches around Europe, the Allies discovered treasures worth millions of pounds. As recently as 1983 60 tonnes of gold taken from Rome Central Bank were discovered down the well of a monastery in northern Italy.

However, experts still believe there is some £50 billion worth of bullion and other valuables secreted away. The knowledge of much of its whereabouts died with those who were killed in the final months and weeks of the war. The rest continues to finance the existence of war criminals in hiding. Not a single German was charged after the hostilities. They got away with daylight robbery.

Russia bear the main brunt of the German war machine.

Given the agonies inflicted by Germany on Russia, he was in no mood to compromise. He wanted enormous reparations levied against

Germany of a type that would make it impossible for the country to be viable again for years. But President Truman wouldn't hear of this, because he was determined that the vanquished countries should have

their part to play in the future of a safe and secure world.

Nevertheless, the spheres of influence for each of the victorious countries had been previously agreed and would be kept to.

The countries in the East were to fall under Russian domination, this being rubber stamped by the Allies

> ## Under the Yalta treaty the countries in the East were to fall under Russian domination

even though it meant an ardently anti-Communist country like Poland being put into the hands of Stalin.

Germany was sectioned off into four, one piece each to America, Britain, France and Russia. A similar arrangement was made for the

capital, Berlin. The Western nations decided Russia was behaving furtively and posed a threat to the rest of Europe. In 1946, Churchill spoke about the seriously deteriorating relations with Stalin on a visit to the US:

'Nobody knows what Soviet Russia and its Communist International organisation intends to do in the immediate future or what are the limits, if any, of their expansive and proselytizing tendencies. From Stettin on the Baltic to Trieste on the Adriatic, an iron curtain has descended across the continent.'

■ IRON CURTAIN ■

With the weight of Russia on one side, America determined to counter the balance to halt the suspected spread of communism. A civil war was raging in Greece between the Royalists, who had been receiving British aid, and the Communists. It caused appalling misery for civilians

Left: **After the defeat of Germany there were a few months in Berlin when the Allied leaders were all hailed as heroes. But acrimony between them soon set in.**

still reeling from the atrocities committed against the Jewish and partisan populations by the Germans. In 1947 when Britain could no longer

George Marshall believed only a strong Europe could resist the tide of communism

afford to maintain a presence in Greece, America stepped in with troops and cash.

George Marshall, US Secretary of State, believed only a strong Europe could resist the tide of communism. Accordingly, he set in motion a plan

to give food, fuel, raw materials and machinery to all European countries struggling to get on their feet once more. To distribute this aid the Organisation for European Economic Co-operation was formed in 1948. It comprised 16 member countries.

■ MARSHALL AID ■

The Marshall Aid plan was viewed by the Russians as empire building of the worst order by America and they in turn exerted pressure on countries in their own sphere of influence to turn down US offers of assistance. Only Yugoslavia defied Russian wishes and took advantage of the Marshall Plan, its leader Tito thus carving for himself an independence unknown in the Communist world.

Already it was clear that a vast gulf had opened up between the former allies. In March 1948 when the Western Allies decided to unite the divided zones of Germany, Russia reacted with menace. West Berlin, in the heart of East Germany, was suddenly isolated as Russia barricaded roads and railways into parts of the city under British, American and French control. Refusing to back down, the Western nations airlifted supplies to West Berlin daily for more than a year. It wasn't until secret negotiations in the spring of 1949

Below: **Allied planes flew in essential supplies to West Berlin for almost a year after the Soviet Union cut off land access routes to the western part of the city.**

Daily Worker
FRIDAY, JULY 27, 1945.

THE PEOPLE SWEEP LABOUR TO POWER

Big Majority Over All Other Parties: Tories Are Routed

IN THE MOST SENSATIONAL ELECTION IN BRITAIN'S WHOLE HISTORY, THE PEOPLE HAVE SWEPT LABOUR TO GOVERNMENTAL POWER WITH A CLEAR MAJORITY OVER ALL OTHER PARTIES.

Victory in Figures

Two Communists In the New House

Above: **British politics changed when Churchill was ousted and the Labour Party won the July 1945 general election.**

that the stalemate was broken though Germany remained in two parts with a Western enclave in Berlin in the middle of the communist East.

Out of this crisis grew the North Atlantic Treaty Organisation, a defensive grouping including America, Britain, France, Canada

> ## The Cold War began after the Berlin Airlift in 1948 and continued right up until 1990

and other European and Scandinavian countries. Other countries sought membership during its history and agreed to abide by its main rule, that they would come to the aid of any member state which was attacked. Russia saw this as a direct threat and set up its own military agreement with other communist countries, called the Warsaw Pact.

This crisis, coupled with an arms build-up during which each side stockpiled deterrent weapons, led to the Cold War between Russia and the East and America and the West being frozen into place. This stand-off between the superpowers lasted until Mikhail Gorbachev came to power in Russia in 1985, after which he actively supported the Strategic Arms Limitation Talks (SALT) which were already in progress and instituted further measures of his own to scale down hostilities.

The Cold War finally came to a close in 1990 following the momentous political changes made in the Eastern bloc.

Despite the depths to which Germany had plummeted in those dark days straight after the armistice, it wasn't long before at least part of the defeated nation was back on its feet. Thanks to the American aid package, which had been lent in no small part to make West Germany a strong buffer between communist Eastern Europe and the free West, production levels by 1950 matched those of 1938. From that point, West Germany built a strong economy and

developed an enviable track record for its industry.

As if to emphasise the division, in 1961 the communist leaders built a wall between East and West Berlin to cage its people in. In the years that followed, many East Berliners perished attempting to cross to the free West. It stood as a sorry tribute to the grimy side of communism for nearly 30 years until Germany reunited in 1990 and the wall was torn down.

■ POSTWAR EUROPE ■

Postwar Italy struggled to keep an even keel. King Umberto II was ousted by referendum in 1946. Yet successive republican Italian governments have been unable to find a reliable formula for stability. Amid unending allegations of corruption, Italy's economy has remained unstable while socially the country has suffered from bombs, kidnapping and other forms of terrorism.

France, meanwhile, had its own problems. Torn by a wartime record of honour and shame in almost equal measures, there was clearly going to be difficulty in restoring national pride.

Leader of the Free French, General Charles de Gaulle was determined to instil that sense of greatness back into France. However, he left power in 1946 and didn't return until 1958 when he set himself on a collision course with Britain and America, the two powers which had treated him with great caution and suspicion during war time.

> ## Now under a Labour government, Britain nationalised industry and launched a welfare state

Yet despite de Gaulle's hostility to the USA, it was American help which enabled France to become a modern and viable state by the mid-1950s.

Now under a Labour government, Britain set about nationalising many of its services and industries and launched a welfare state. Still, it did not enjoy the same speedy rate of recovery as its fellow European nations. Food rationing remained in place for some years and there was a shortage of quality housing. Most people found their existences dreary.

■ SUEZ CRISIS ■

Winston Churchill was at the helm again following the 1951 election and remained in charge until 1954 when Anthony Eden took over. Eden was compelled to resign after sending the British army into Suez when the canal was nationalised by Egyptian leader Nasser in 1956. The move, made in tandem with the French, earned international rebuke.

Like France, Britain gave independence to many of its colonies, primarily India which won its status in 1947 after a protracted campaign. This was perhaps the more successful side to post-war foreign policy.

Britain had supported the Jewish demand for a home nation in Palestine. Yet, as administrator of Palestine, it had sympathy with the anxious Arab population too. Consequently, Britain refused to raise the limit set on Jewish immigration into the area following the war for fear of sparking an Arab uprising.

Instead, it was the Jews who rebelled with a terrorist campaign which began in October 1945. By the following year some 80,000 British troops were tied down in Palestine attempting to keep the peace.

In 1947 the UN proposed to run the area as two separate states, one Jewish, the other Arab. Consequently, the state of Israel was created in 1948 with the rest of Palestine being divided between Jordan and Eygpt. The disaffection thereby created among Palestinian Arabs festered until it finally erupted into violence which manifested itself throughout the following decades. Only at the start of the 1990s did the problem appear to have a resolution.

Troops were also sent into action in Malaya, Indo-China and Indonesia as Britain policed trouble spots which flared around the world.

In 1973 Britain at last signed its name to the European Economic Community which was created in 1957 following the Treaty of Rome. At the start the Community involved the Benelux countries, France, Italy and West Germany who, under the umbrella of the EEC or Common Market, aspired to closer co-operation and increased economic activity. By the time Britain joined, it was called the European Community. Since then several more countries in the region have joined the EC.

■ POSTWAR USSR ■

The Union of Soviet Socialist Republics remained under Stalin's control until his death in 1953. His ambition to extinguish Germany was thwarted and he was forced to

Below: **Trouble between Israelis and Arabs occurred for years after the creation of the Jewish state in 1948. In 1973 came the Yom Kippur War.**

content himself with looting industrial machinery from the regions his armies overran.

The dictator fostered imperialist aims and exerted an iron grip on the countries under the communist umbrella. Although many of his harsh internal measures were condemned by later Soviet regimes, at the time no one dared raise a voice of criticism.

■ GLASNOST ■

The Soviet government used its military might to crush the Hungarian Revolution of 1956 and the Czechoslovak steps towards liberation in 1968 went the same way. Following the policy of 'Glasnost' or 'openness' installed by Mikhail Gorbachev, the communist systems in the USSR and surrounding countries collapsed and were replaced by democracies. The USSR itself ceased to exist in December 1991. Most of the former Soviet republics became known as the Commonwealth of Independent States – the exceptions were Georgia and the three Baltic states.

Seeds were sown in World War II which were to have tragic consequences some 45 years later. When the Germans marched into Yugoslavia, they granted rule to the nationalistic Croatians called Ustashi. After themselves feeling marginalised since Yugoslavia was created at the end of World War I, they now chose to seek vengeance. Atrocities were committed by the Ustashi against Serbs, Jews and other races that made up the state.

Opposing the Germans and Ustashi were the Serbian Chetniks and communists led by Tito. Following the war, Tito seized control and operated a less restrictive version of communism in a united Yugoslavia, maintaining its position as a non-aligned country.

On Tito's death in 1980, the threads that held the country together began to unravel with individual groups setting up their own power bases. A decade after the death of the dictator, Yugoslavia split up into five republics. However, memories of wartime injustices emerged and, coupled with dissatisfaction about new frontiers, these bubbled up into civil war. There followed one of the bloodiest and most vicious civil conflicts of modern times with reprisal following hot on the heels of attack, involving Serbians, Croats and the minority Muslim population. All attempts by the international community to make peace seemed doomed to failure.

America emerged from World War II as the

Left: **Mao Tse-Tung won the civil war in 1949 and isolated China from the world.**

wealthiest of the participating nations and was thus able to lend assistance to many others. During the Cold War years, its policies were mostly marked by a strident opposition to communism, encapsulated in Joe McCarthy's Un-American Activities Committee which harassed suspected left-wingers from all parts of American society. This American abhorrence of communism led them to intervene in Korea in 1950, in Cuba in 1961 and most protractedly and disastrously in Vietnam in 1961.

> *Japan has emerged as one of the most successful postwar industrial nations*

Japan remained under US occupation until 1951 when the Emperor renounced his claims of divinity. Welcomed back into the international fold when it joined the UN in 1956, Japan has emerged as one of the most successful postwar industrial nations.

Fighting continued in China where a civil war – suspended following the Japanese invasion – began once more. Chiang Kai-Shek, the Chinese nationalist, was pitted against communist Mao Tse-Tung. Mao triumphed in 1949 and then ruled until his death in 1976. Afterwards there were alternate periods of liberalisation and repression, the most noted example of the latter being the massacre of thousands of students in Tiananmen Square in Beijing in 1989.

So World War II was not a war to end all wars. But while the world has been peppered with conflicts since 1945, it is a tribute to all those who died between 1939 and 1945 that no all-consuming conflict has since engulfed the globe.

Horrors of War

NANKING MASSACRE

On the pretext that the Chinese had kidnapped a Japanese soldier, a momentous conflict between two brother nations was sparked in 1937.

China and Japan shared much by way of culture and history. Yet when hostilities broke out in 1937 each country fought the other with a tenacity and barbarity scarcely witnessed on a battlefield. The missing soldier at the heart of the dispute turned up some hours later, by the way, and was thought to have been biding his time in a brothel.

In the ensuing violence one of the worst atrocities ever committed by uniformed soldiers took place in an incident over which tensions still run high even today.

The scene of the horror was Nanking, a Chinese city serving as a makeshift capital following the fall of Beijing, whose population of some 200,000 was swollen with refugees trying to escape the onslaught of the Japanese army.

■ NANKING ATTACK ■

It was five months after the first shots of the war were fired that the Japanese army came within sight of Nanking. The government, led by Generalissimo Jiang Jieshi, evacuated leaving a determined Chinese army to fend off the invaders.

The first bombardment of the city walls came on 9 December 1937 after Chinese military leaders ignored a call for surrender. Within four days the Japanese with their superior mechanised weapons had blasted their way into the city. An estimated 40,000 Chinese had perished in the battle – yet that was only the start of the population's suffering.

First, there was turmoil as the desperate Chinese tried to flee through a rear city wall. Inside the 70ft tunnel which led to the gate, two vehicles had collided and burst into flames. There was chaos as a surge of

Chinese people turned to run from the flames and faced a tide of incoming city residents who were themselves followed by machine-gun toting Japanese soldiers. Countless scores died in the melee, suffocated, trampled under foot or fatally wounded by Japanese bullets.

Doubtless Nanking's refusal to surrender was an irritant to the Japanese. Yet nothing could explain the appalling acts which took place after the fall of the city.

In the words of one Swedish observer: 'With a blindness and absence of psychological judgement that astonishes the westerner who is at all familiar with Chinese mentality, the Japanese soldiers sullied their march to victory with repeated acts of cruelty, ruthlessness and bloodshed on innocent people.

'[These were] actions unparalleled in modern times and perpetrated by no civilised nation.'

During their approach to the city gates, two Japanese officers had a competition to see who could kill the most Chinese. It was a race to reach 100 but when confusion reigned over

the body count, they amicably decided to make their final target 150. Later, it was reported: 'Mukai's blade was slightly damaged in the competition. He explained that this was the result of cutting a Chinese in half, helmet and all. The contest was "fun", he declared...'

The Japanese officers had a competition to see who could kill the most Chinese

Any Chinese who turned and ran from the Japanese was doomed to die. While observing the rights of the international community, the Japanese then embarked on their debauched and disgusting campaign against the locals.

Where they could, the European doctors, welfare workers and writers

Left: **Chinese refugees fleeing Japanese troops.** *Below*: **Cities like Chungking were left in ruins by Japanese bombs.**

Above: Chinese army supremo Chiang Kai Shek lectures officers at a training camp. He was destined never to rule China.

roasted over a fire and still more killed in a bath of industrial acid. There were cases of soldiers being tied up and then blown up by hand grenades. Ferocious dogs were also used to kill Chinese prisoners and wild stories circulated about Japanese soldiers sating themselves on the hearts and livers of dead Chinese.

Official estimates for the number of dead vary between 155,000 and 300,000. The orgy of raping and killing last for seven long weeks.

General Matsui admitted 'the Japanese army is... the most undisciplined in the world'

In charge of the men was General Matsui who was himself apparently devastated at the conduct of his men. Matsui, who once admitted that 'the Japanese army is probably the most undisciplined in the world today', reserved a tirade of abuse for the officers under his command who had permitted their troops to run riot. In common with other Japanese generals, he considered the rank and file men to be uneducated, illiterate and akin to barbarians.

sheltered the Chinese and pleaded for tolerance on their behalf. Without this moderating presence, even more would have died.

■ MULTIPLE RAPE ■

For seven weeks, the women and girls of Nanking were subject to repeated rape by the rampaging Japanese soldiers, often many times in a single night. The soldiers knew no bounds and picked on pregnant women, the elderly and children as young as ten. Degrading sexual assaults were also carried out in broad daylight, by ordinary soldiers and officers alike. Although women were the main victims, there were also cases of attacks on young boys.

Anyone who tried to intervene was stabbed or shot. There were frequent

cases of civilians being used for bayonet practice. Others were disembowelled for sport.

There were many massacres in which the victims first had to dig their own grave. They were then lined up at the edge of the pit and shot or bayonetted or both.

At least 2,000 Chinese were buried alive in Nanking, several were

◆ EYE WITNESS ◆

In 1994, Prince Mikasa, brother of Emperor Hirohito, recalled what he described as 'truly horrible' scenes while he was a cavalry officer serving in China during the war. In an interview with the 'Yomiuri' newspaper, he described seeing film of Chinese prisoners being gassed and shot.

That could only be described as a massacre. I was shocked at one battlefront when a young officer told me: "The best way to train new recruits is to have them undergo bayonet practice using prisoners of war. It helps them acquire guts." The issue is not about the numbers killed but killing people in a cruel manner. The prime factors contributing to the tragic consequences were China's geographical proximity to Japan... also the strong disdain that Japanese held towards the Chinese.

Above: Bodies litter the streets after the Japanese army made gains in the key Chinese city of Shanghai.

After the scandal of Nanking General Matsui was recalled to Tokyo. Soon afterwards, he retired and devoted himself to building a temple in which to atone for the misdeeds of the army in Nanking.

Two missionaries from Nanking had a very different view of the dilemma. 'The common soldiers are all right if they are not drunk. The Japanese, in general, are very easily intoxicated, however, and then the trouble begins.'

Japanese people have since tried to excuse the actions of the army in those dark days. There were cases of Chinese mutilations of Japanese soldiers both before and after death in the war but none to match the terrorism which took place in Nanking.

For years, the formula explanation for Japan's actions was that it was 'liberating' its neighbours from Western influence. This explanation has been accompanied by a marked reluctance to apologise or reparate for the events which took place in the name of the Emperor.

Even as late as 1994, a Japanese government minister, Mr Shigeto Nagano, denied the war against China had begun through his country's aggression and denied the Rape of Nanking had even taken place. In a newspaper interview, he said: 'It's a mistake to call [the Pacific War] a war of aggression. It's not true that [it] was carried out with invasion as an objective. We sincerely believed in liberating the colonies.'

■ MILLIONS DEAD ■

Although he retracted his remarks and resigned, there is little doubt his opinion reflects a body of thought still widely believed in Japan today.

Naturally, such blunders inspire fury and resentment in those neighbouring countries which suffered under dominance of the Rising Sun. Abuse of Chinese prisoners particularly occurred all over the country, not just in Nanking.

Before the end of the Sino-Japanese war in 1945, at least two and a half million soldiers on both sides had died and there were many million more civilian deaths, particularly in China.

Whether the Japanese warmongers sincerely believed they were freeing Asia from its colonial ties or not, their commitment to war with China was ultimately a disastrous one. It kept an enormous number of troops tied up for years as they tried to conquer a land that proved to be unconquerable.

Left: Captured Chinese soldiers were ruthlessly slaughtered by the score by blood-thirsty Japanese invaders. Killings took place all over China.

THE WARSAW GHETTO

The clampdown on Jews in Poland began almost as soon as the first shots of World War II were fired.

Following the brief conflict, occupying German soldiers at first contented themselves with ritually humiliating any Jews they encountered on the street.

A punch was thrown here, a beating administered there. Crowds gathered as the crowing, cocksure military men publicly shaved off the whiskers which marked out an orthodox Jew. Few Jews fought back. The punishment for striking a German officer was torture and frequently death. And not just for the perpetrator of the alleged crime. The concept of mass punishments for one single misdemeanour soon brought the population to heel.

Laws were hastily introduced to formalise the new official attitude to Jews. They were forbidden to work in certain jobs, to bake bread, for example, or sit at the desk of a government office. No Jewish worker was allowed to earn more than 500 zloty a month – at a time when the price of bread was as high as 40 zloty per loaf.

All Jewish wealth was confiscated and no longer could they ride on trains, trams, wear gold jewellery or leave their own district without official permission. From 12 November 1939, every Jew aged 12 years and above was compelled to wear a white arm band with a blue Star of David displayed on it.

■ EASTER POGROMS ■

From this the situation deteriorated. During the Easter holidays of 1940, old-fashioned pogroms took place with Polish thugs in the pay of the Nazis wreaking havoc in the Jewish quarter of Warsaw. For the first time, the Jews retaliated. There was a collection of Jewish militants who refused to tolerate any further

subservience to the aggressor. They gave a good account of themselves in the ensuing street battles.

However, this token resistance could do litttle to halt the German roller-coaster in Warsaw. In November 1940 the Germans finally established the Warsaw Ghetto. Now the entire Jewish population numbering some 300,000 was confined to a specially designated area. Poles who lived within its boundaries were compelled to move out.

Walls were built around it and security was made even tighter with vicious barbed wire. By the middle of the month the Warsaw Ghetto had been entirely isolated from the outside world.

Inside, the existence was a sordid and miserable one. Now there was little opportunity to earn even a crust. Jews had already been brought to the depths of poverty by the actions of the Nazis, and they had nothing left to fall back on.

Jews were transported from all over Poland into the Warsaw Ghetto

Daily, the population of the Warsaw Ghetto increased with the arrival of more Jews deported from other cities and towns around Poland. There to greet them were the malnutrition, disease and hopelessness that were all mirrored in the bleak faces of the inhabitants.

To the people of the Ghetto, the war was now a distant issue. The effect of the segregation on their minds together with their physical hardships left them able to focus only on the day-to-day survival of themselves and their closest family.

Ghetto dwellers for the most part relied on soup kitchens and a meagre ration of bread, plus whatever they could scavenge or beg. Six-year-old boys were dispatched by their parents through holes in the barbed wire to steal food from other areas of the

Left: Bleak-faced German soldiers taken prisoner by the Polish Home Army.
Below: Poland's Home Army attracted enthusiastic recruits.

city. Occasionally they were shot in the process. If they returned, their haul was seized on by starving siblings and parents.

Food was smuggled in from the Ayran sections of the city by the burgeoning numbers of black marketeers who preyed on the snared Jews. Jewish businessman seeking to make a living were equally at the mercy of these rogues. The final vestiges of wealth remaining among the Jews were spent in this way during the first few months.

Within months people began to die of hunger in the streets. Corpses were covered over with paper which was weighted with stones until the daily round of the burial cart. Desperate families would dump their own dead in the streets to save the cost of a funeral. Often, the bodies were naked, stripped of rags which had now become a valuable commodity.

Disease was raging through the over-crowded and squalid conditions, with admissions to the hopsital exceeding 150 a day.

Below: Polish children ready to risk their lives to deliver underground newspapers around the occupied capital.

Instead of feeling pity or self-disgust in the face of this unmitigated horror, the delusion of the Germans continued. A German major who witnessed what was happening in the Warsaw Ghetto put the blame on Jewish barbarism:

■ CORPSE CARTS ■

'The conditions in the ghetto can hardly be described . . . The Jew does business here with the others also on the street. In the morning, as I drove through in my car, I saw numerous corpses, among them those of

Above: Starving Poles reach for Red Cross bread as it is distributed across the divide in occupied Warsaw.

children, covered anyhow with paper weighed down with stones. The other Jews pass by them indifferently, the primitive "corpse carts" come and take away these "remainders" with which no more business can be done.

The Germans claimed the Jews had brought the horrors of the Ghetto on themselves

The ghetto is blocked by walls, barbed-wire and so forth... Dirt, stench and noise are the main signs of the ghetto.'

There were continuous executions carried out on real or fanciful notions by the Germans. Those who worked on underground newspapers, for example, were targeted as were those whose illegal trading came to the notice of the authorities. Anyone found on the Aryan side of the divide without the necessary papers was returned and shot.

Yet there were also examples of killing without the remotest provocation. Three children sitting outside the hospital were slaughtered and a pregnant women who tripped and fell was continually kicked down by a German soldier who finally shot her. Every resident of the ghetto knew of horror stories such as these.

■ MASS DEPORTATION ■

In July 1942 events took an even more sinister turn with the start of mass deportations, with a German quota of 6,000 people per day. Their destination was the extermination camp at Treblinka in Poland. There was panic among the ghetto dwellers. Their options for escaping the round-ups taking place were limited. Each house and street targeted for the expulsions was thoroughly searched by German-sponsored officials who would shoot anyone they found cowering inside.

The spate of deportations eventually slashed the population of the ghetto to an estimated 60,000. Many of those that remained either worked for the Germans or the Jewish Council. Their conditions were barely improved by the reduction in

> **When mass deportation to Treblinka began, the Jews finally decided to fight back**

population but there began a subtle change of mood among the ghetto Jews. They decided to fight back. Covertly, they gathered together what arms they could, various

Below: Men and women from the Ghetto are marched off to camps. Their destination was probably Treblinka.

Leo Heiman was a young Jew rounded up in Russia who later wrote a book about his wartime experiences.

❝ On that morning Janek and I walked once again down the main street when we saw a big crowd of Byelorussians and Poles surrounding something. Naturally, we pushed right throught the crowd and saw three Germans kicking an old Jew in his belly and pulling him up by his beard each time he fell down. I recognised the Jew who was a cantor at one of the local synagogues. His two sons, both rabbinical students, were being hanged from a nearby lampost, the crowd applauding and cheering the Germans.

'What did the dirty Jew do?' I asked a Polish kid standing nearby. The kid laughed and told us that the Germans tried to take the Jew's two daughters away to a military brothel and the Jew was arrogant enough to slap one of the Germans. ❞

Above: During the Warsaw uprising members of the Home Army, two carrying flame-throwers, seek the enemy in the wrecked city.

ancient guns from bygone conflicts and a few more modern models that had been smuggled in by Polish freedom fighters on the German side. A system of underground tunnels was dug to aid Jewish resistance.

By 1943, it was no longer safe for Germans to enter the ghetto. Lone Germans or those in twos and threes found in the streets of the ghetto were killed. Terrible retribution was also wreaked on those Jews who collaborated with the Gestapo to save their own skins.

On 19 April 1943 the Germans decided to 'liquidate' the ghetto once and for all. In charge of the operation was General Jurgen Stroop who had been promised honour and accolades for his men if the operation was carried out quickly and efficiently.

■ GHETTO UPRISING ■

Stroop dispatched 2,000 troops from local garrisons, dressed as if for battle. They went in on armoured cars with grenade launchers and flame throwers. It was their aim to flatten the ghetto and kill all those who got in the way.

The Jewish resistance had been tipped off and was waiting.

Short of guns and ammunition, the determined fighters still halted the German advance and even stymied the tanks with their home-made grenades. The ghetto which was once a prison now became a fortress.

The bold action of the Jews took Stroop by surprise. He had branded them 'sub-humans and natural cowards'. Every day, increasing numbers of Germans were sent into the ghetto. They found a canny and determined opposition inspired by its

The Jews decided that it would be better to die fighting than to die in Treblinka

leaders, fighting with the conviction that death by defence was far better than death at the hands of the Germans in an extermination camp.

When all their buildings were flattened or burnt out, the resistance took to the sewers – until they were flooded by the Germans.

It took six weeks and thousands of German troops to quell the Warsaw uprising. German casualties were put at 1,200. Most of the Jewish fighters died in action. In the middle of May, when all hope had finally gone, 55,000 Jews remaining in the ghetto surrendered. More than 7,000 were shot immediately. A further 15,000 were sent to Majdanek camp and 7,000 to Treblinka where they were

Left: Following its initial success the Polish Army proudly flies its flag from the back of a captured German vehicle.

Above: A casualty is tended by his comrades. Despite their dedication, the Poles could not crush the German enemy.

killed in the gas chambers. Only a few hundred of the total population of the Ghetto escaped to the safety of 'Aryan' Warsaw.

But this was not the last time that the people of Warsaw gave vent to their anger against the Germans. In August 1944 the Polish Home Army under the command of General Bor-Komorowski seized the Old City

The Polish Home Army seized the Old City of Warsaw which was shelled by German tanks

which was subsequently shelled by the Germans using Tiger tanks.

Numbering an estimated 40,000, the Polish soldiers fought determinedly for each building and every street. They were doubtless bucked by the

sound of gunfire from the approaching Russians and with pride and optimism raised the Polish flag over the city for the first time in six years.

The cause was a hopeless one. Assistance from the Russians failed to materialise and the Germans, better equipped and in greater numbers, fought back tenaciously. For two months the battle raged, once again inflicting immense hardships on the residents of Warsaw who were confronted with starvation. But by October Warsaw was once again under German control, its population decimated by the revolt.

Nevertheless, the Poles were defeated in the knowledge that they had proved a costly diversion for the Germans. The Red Army was indeed close by, ready to press ahead once more against the Third Reich. That Russia

Right: Heavy-hearted Bor Komorowski surrenders to German SS commander Erich von dem Bach-Zelewski.

stood by and did nothing to aid the beleaguered Poles gave rise to accusations later that the Polish Home Army was sacrificed by Stalin. He had chosen his own men to lead Poland – and the fighting men were not among them.

In the event, Warsaw didn't fall to Soviet and Polish troops until mid-January 1945.

THE CAMPS

Internment has long been used to curtail the activities of so-called 'undesirables' by countries across the globe.

In this respect, concentration camps – although the very name now chills the heart – were nothing new in the Thirties. Unsavoury though the idea appears, they were to pen people without trial on account of their race or beliefs.

Indeed, during World War II both Britain and the US used similar devices to curb the movements of potential enemies on the home front. In Britain those with German ancestry or Fascist sympathy were targeted while in America the residents of Japanese descent were rounded up. In Russia, dissidents were put in Gulags.

The argument for such action in times of war is that of national security and it is a valid one. Concentration camps in Germany were different entirely because of the barbarity that became inextricably associated with them.

Concentration camps became a covert fact of life in Germany soon after Hitler came to power. The first was Dachau which opened on 22 March 1933 just 12 miles outside the centre of Munich.

■ ANTI-SEMITISM ■

Their main purpose was to cage 'enemies of the state'. Into this category fell Communists, Socialists, homosexuals, gypsies, pacifists, opposing politicians and intellectuals – and just about anyone else conceivably opposed to the Nazi regime. They were to become most notorious for housing Jews.

Anti-semitism was not invented by Hitler. He merely made a stake in a middle Europe movement which flourished among the ignorant and was expounded in pamphlets.

Some have suggested that Hitler's own vociferous brand of Jew-hating

was inspired by him having caught venereal disease from some dubious sexual relations with a Jewess.

The theory has never been proven. But certainly there is not a single fact contained in 'Mein Kampf' and his anti-semitic rantings which give the remotest credibility to his arguments. His depictions of Jewish people were so far-fetched as to be laughable. Perhaps it was this very extremism that captured the imagination of his supporters, who were tunnel-visioned people looking for a scapegoat in society on which to vent their otherwise aimless fury.

In 'Mein Kampf' Hitler wrote of his hatred of Jews: 'Thus I finally discovered who were the evil spirits leading our people astray... My love for my own people increased correspondingly. Considering the satanic skill which these evil counsellors

Hitler claimed that the German people had been tricked by the Jews in World War I

displayed, how could their unfortunate victims be blamed?'

So Hitler sought to excuse the weaknesses as he saw them of the Social Democrats and trade unionists, whom he had previously despised, at the expense of the longtime scapegoats, the Jews.

The steps taken against Jews increased gradually from 1933 and did so with the full force of law. By the time the 1935 Nuremberg Laws were passed, German Jews were

Left: Russian children, parted from their parents, were among those caged by the Nazis. **Right:** A prisoner at Buchenwald after liberation by the Americans.

stripped of their citizenship and the many still remaining at liberty endured a precarious existence.

■ NAZI SADISM ■

Following 1933, violence against minorities and dissidents became an accepted part of German society. The government itself was not beyond imposing law by terror and intimidation. There was a wide range of potential targets and many of the acts of thuggery carried out by Nazi bully-boys were pure acts of revenge or sadism. Too many people in the battered and buffeted state of Germany construed this to be a hallmark of strong government and favoured it.

Above: Britain also had its concentration camps, like this one at Ramsey on the Isle of Man.

Below: Himmler (*second right*) visits Dachau. He personally engineered much of the suffering.

◆ **EYE WITNESS** ◆

Alf Toombs was a German prisoner of war for five years after he survived the Normandy barn massacre of British troops shortly before Dunkirk.

'For the first two and a half years the treatment was really bad. After that we got Red Cross parcels. If it hadn't have been for them, many of us would not be alive today.

All we got was a cup of coffee in the morning. For lunch there was a loaf of brown bread between five of us. We had to take it in turns to have the small end of the loaf. We worked until 6pm when we were given soup, usually potato. Once we had cods' heads which was disgusting. The cooks were German and they didn't give them much to do.

The Poles were very good to us. Women took bits of bread and food to us while we worked. But when we got back we were searched so we had to be careful.'

When they could, German Jews fled. In the Thirties some 250,000 Jews left Germany, abandoning all hope of a peaceable existence when daily they read slogans and posters bearing the messages 'Let Judah perish' and 'Jews not wanted here'.

Inmates worked from morning till night, usually on futile tasks, always at jogging pace

Sooner or later, those who remained were destined to be sent to a concentration camp. Joining them were the much-despised Slavs, particularly the intelligentsia.

The first inspector of concentration camps was SS recruit Theodor Eicke who made it his business to breed out any signs of compassion in his men

Top right: Hitler's 'Mein Kampf', heralded around Germany, was full of anti-semitic rantings without a shred of fact.

who would be guarding the camp prisoners. Cruelty and sadism became a matter of professional pride. SS men involved in the running of camps boasted of their work and named themselves Death's Head units.

Helping the SS to run the camps were German criminal prisoners dressed in blue and white striped uniforms and just as willing to mete out beatings as their legal overlords. In fact, they were frequently more vindictive to impress their SS masters and avoid a beating themselves.

Names were dispensed with as each detainee was given a number for identification purposes. There was little attempt at pretence by the prison guards who would happily reveal the life expectancy for each prisoner was but three months.

■ BUCHENWALD ■

Between 1937 and 1945 Buchenwald concentration camp received 238,980 prisoners out of which 33,462 died. A grim note of reality comes in a letter written in December 1942 by an SS official which complained that out of 136,870 new arrivals in concentration camps between June and November, more than half were already dead.

Bottom right: Jews were marked out by a yellow star in Germany, one of the milder measures taken against them.

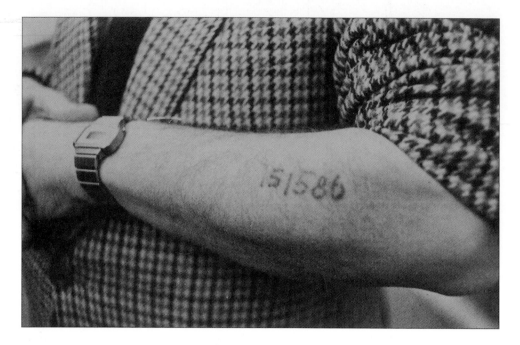

Above: Concentration camp survivor Maurice Goldstein reveals the number he was identified by as an inmate.

Discipline was harsh and the beatings regular, particularly for the old or infirm. Frequently the sadistic lashings carried out by the guards were enough to kill. Medical treatment for those who survived was a case of make-do-and-mend by fellow prisoners with a modicum of training.

Inside the wooden huts that housed the prisoners, beds were made of straw and their occupants were crammed together, forbidden to speak. In the summer the huts were acrid and airless, in the winter, damp and cold.

For inmates, the days were filled, morning until night, with unrelenting work. The tasks chosen by their captors were frequently pointless or futile. Nevertheless, all the jobs had to be done at a jogging pace.

In addition to all this, there were regular singing lessons in German complete with beatings for those who were judged to have performed poorly because they were too tired, too scared or because they couldn't speak sufficiently good German.

Inmates were colour-coded to denote the reason for their incarceration. Jews wore yellow stars. The others wore tags which were coloured pink for homosexuals, orange for political prisoners, purple for pacifists, green for criminals and black for those found guilty of anti-social behaviour.

Escape was rare – which was fortunate for the prisoners, because the retribution dished out to those left behind was terrible and merciless. For a single escape, hundreds of prisoners might be made to stand in the compound naked and still for an entire night, summer or winter. It was enough to claim the lives of those growing increasingly frail with the everyday rigours of camp life.

■ HEINRICH HIMMLER ■

The atmosphere bred tension, fear and despair. The terrorised inhabitants forced to witness the punishment of others and suffer the endless, undeserved beatings themselves felt their spirits crumble. Many had never seen a dead body before going into a concentration camp. Now they were seeing many each day who gave up the fight for survival.

There were those who collaborated with the Germans in a bid to save their own skins. At first they were despised and killed by the guards or exposed and slaughtered by fellow prisoners. Finally, the guards relied on such assistance and the inmates had no energy to strike back at the traitors.

Now inmates dreamed of dying a peaceful death in a comfortable hospital bed rather than be killed in such sordid surroundings. There seemed little hope of this small dream coming true.

Amid the despondency were a few glimmers of hope. Working parties sent outside the boundaries of the camp sometimes found local people bearing food and drink for them. When the residents of local towns were in evidence, the harsh treatment from the guards usually diminished for a while.

In 1942 Himmler drew labour from the camps to prop up German

'We Germans are the only people in the world who have a decent attitude towards animals'

---

industry. Some prisoners, he maintained, could be worked to death.

'Whether 10,000 Russian females fall down from exhaustion while digging an anti-tank ditch interests me only in so far as the anti-tank ditch for Germany is finished. We shall never be rough and heartless when it is not necessary, that is clear.

'We Germans, who are the only people in the world who have a decent attitude towards animals, will also assume a decent attitude towards these human animals. But it is a crime against our own blood to worry about them and give them ideals thus causing our sons and grandsons to have a more difficult time with them.

'When someone comes to me and says: "I cannot dig the anti-tank ditch with women and children, it is inhuman, for it would kill them",

'If the anti-tank ditch is not dug German soldiers will die and they are the sons of German mothers'

then I have to say "you are the murderer of your own blood because if the anti-tank ditch is not dug German soldiers will die and they are the sons of German mothers. They are our own blood." We can be indifferent to everything else.'

■ FINAL SOLUTION ■

By the end of September 1944 there were a staggering 7,500,000 civilian foreigners in harness for the Reich alongside two million prisoners of war. Often, the civilians who had been rounded up, herded on to insanitary railway trucks and shipped miles from their homes and families, were housed in concentration camps.

As the numbers deemed suitable fodder for concentration camps grew, so did the number of camps across Germany, Austria and, later, occupied Poland. The tentacles of the Reich spread still further, across the Low Countries, France and Norway, bringing in ever larger crowds of prisoners. When the camps could hardly cope with the daily influx, there seemed little option for the authorities. Tough measures were needed to deal with a tough situation. A systematical extermination would be necessary.

◆ EYE WITNESS ◆

Ron Tansley, a pacifist volunteer doing humanitarian work with the Friends Ambulance Unit, helped to clear Belsen and Neuengamme concentration camps.

We took the victims from there to various hospitals. It really was shocking. The atmosphere, the stench of death, the dead bodies, the poor victims on their last legs. The barbarity of it all was in each person who existed there. When we had cleared Belsen we were sent to Hamburg.

The worst people I met the entire time I was in Germany were in the Gestapo. They were not all Germans, there were Rumanians, Latvians, Hungarians and all nationalities. They couldn't care less about what had happened in the concentration camps.

From Hamburg we went past Lubeck to Neuengamme concentration camp. All the victims had gone but there were still piles of bones 10ft high and bones left partly in the furnace.

We had to get the camp ready for 5,000 Russian labourers on their way back to their homeland. I went down to the nearest town and asked for the mayor. He had run off so I spoke to the priest instead. I wanted 100 local people to help clear out this camp.

I told him: 'I'm surprised that you, a man of God, could allow that (the events at the camp) to happen'.

He turned up his sleeve and there was a concentration camp number tattooed on his arm. He had spoken out against it and a few days later he was inside the gates himself.

Then he turned to me and asked: 'What would you have done?' I have often thought about that since.

The Russians duly arrived. We fed them as best we could on cabbage and potatoes. On the day we had order papers saying the Russians were to go back, we posted notices and prepared them. The next day half of them had disappeared. They knew they would be killed in Stalin's Russia. All the Allied leaders knew it too.

NAZI MURDER SQUADS

A ruthless, merciless, murdering maniac. That's a description not of Hitler but of Joseph Stalin which might well have been levelled at the Russian despot by his own people.

For years they had suffered under his harsh and barbaric rule. Thousands had died as the 'man of steel' had sought both forcibly to improve Russian industry and eliminate possible opposition. Crude Gulags, state-run labour camps which were the forerunners of Germany's own concentration camps, housed thousands of dissidents.

All the passion so evident in the Russian Revolution of 1917 had evaporated. Society had been dulled by fear and repression together with a sense of helplessness.

A clever man determined to invade Russia might have made capital out of this, portraying himself as a liberator and winning the support of the downtrodden masses. Given the vast area to conquer, widespread support of the people would have made the task considerably easier.

■ NAPOLEONIC PLAN ■

Hitler wasn't smart enough to see the golden opportunities he was passing up. Blinded by his rabid racism which extended to Slavs, he ignored the easy path in favour of the outright hostility necessary for an ideological war of destruction.

> **The Führer considered Russia a stronghold of Jewry and Bolshevism, his twin loathings**

His plan was to incorporate the Crimea into the Reich along with the Baltic states. Further mineral-rich areas were ear-marked for the Fatherland. Germany would dominate Russia as far as the Urals and would

tolerate no armed resistance in the entire area. It was an ambitious plan, one which the Emperor Napoleon had found impossible to achieve. Much taken with the pint-sized despot of the previous century, Hitler was determined to retrace his steps but emerge as victor.

Left: **Partisans were usually hanged as an example. Above: These starving Russian soldiers were later executed.**

The Führer considered Russia a stronghold of Jewry and Bolshevism, his twin loathings. There is even a school of thought which says he

◆ EYE WITNESS ◆

Vera Inber, trapped inside Leningrad when it was under siege by the German army, kept a diary of the city's sufferings.

25 Jan 1942
Our position is catastrophic. Just now a crowd destroyed the wooden fence of the hospital grounds and carried it away for firewood. There is no water and if the bakery stops even for a single day, what happens? We have no soup, only porridge. In the morning there was coffee but there won't be any more to drink.

26 Jan 1942
For the first time I cried from grief and fury. Inadvertently I overturned the saucepan of porridge on the stove. We nevertheless swallowed a few spoonfuls mixed with the ashes. There is still no bread.

27 Jan 1942
The bakery did not stop work after all as we were afraid it would. When the water mains packed up, eight thousand Young Communist League members – weakened like everyone else from starvation and chilled to the bone – formed a chain from the Neva to the bakery tables and passed to them the water from hand to hand.
  Yesterday there were enormous queues at the baker's shops. Bread wasn't delivered till the evening but still it was there.

Above: Russian citizens were murdered in cold blood by rabid Nazis as they forged through following Barbarossa.

◆ EYE WITNESS ◆

Russian schoolmistress Genia Demmianova tried to negotiate with invading Germans who were in search of food when they occupied her home village of Povsk in August 1941. Her attempts to speak for an old man found herding his calf on the outskirts of the village were frustrated.

❛ I was seized by two soldiers. I fought to get free but I could not even move. I was screaming all the time but suddenly I stopped. It flashed into my mind that this was just a nightmare and that I should wake up in a minute. My eyes fixed on old Serge. He looked horrible. One of his eyes looked terribly big and staring and he was whimpering just like a young puppy dog. His face was one mass of blood and there was blood dripping from the gnarled hands he was holding up in front of it.

Two Germans tore the shirt off Serge's back, pulled down his trousers and topboots and left him standing half naked with is bloody hand covering the staring eye. The sergeant picked up a short whip from the table and stepping up to the old man he bawled: 'For the last time, where is the food depot?'

The interpreter quickly translated this. The old man tried to speak but only brought out a hoarse grunt.

All the Germans stepped aside. They knew what was coming. The sergeant raised the whip and brough it down on the old man's back with terrible force. It made Serge's dirty shirt split. The next blow and the next cut it to ribbons which were dyed crimson at the same time. The old man fell to one knee, with on bare bloody arm held in front of his face then he just collapsed on the floor.

The sergeant kept repeating with horrible gentleness: 'Where is the food?'

Two soldiers entered with a tub of water. They flung the water over old Serge. He made a faint movement and moaned once or twice but that was all.

'Take him out,' ordered the sergeant, 'and hang him on that tree.' He spoke casually without the slightest expression in his voice and asked the interpreter to explain why.

The sergeant forced me to look out of the window. The interpreter said old Serge was charged with food smuggling and would be hanged unless the people revealed where the food was hidden. I saw people being driven along to the school by soldiers from all directions. The interpreter kept talking on and on but I knew that the people did not quite understand him not only because his Russian was bad but also because they were dazed. They only began to understand when a German soldier came out with a long rope and tied it on a branch of the chestnut tree.

Immediately poor Serge was brought out. I do not think he was conscious. When people saw his battered bloody old body there was a murmur, then an old woman gave a scream, an old man shook his fist at the Germans and someone threw a stone. The old man was at least ninety.

The stone thrower could only have been a boy. But the Germans responded like beasts. They used their rifles blindly hitting out right and left like mad dogs. It all happened in a few seconds. The air was full of screams, groans, brutal curses. The people ran in all directions. ❜

carried out 'Barbarossa' not to provide 'Lebensraum' or 'living space' for his people as he professed but merely as a major thrust in his policy to rid Europe of Judaism. The diabolical excesses of Hitler and his forces surely saved Stalin's bacon.

Russia's vast Jewish population which in its history had already known so much about bully boy authorities was to be subjugated again. Although the task was immense, it became a military consideration for Hitler. The Slav people were equally unworthy and were to be extinguished as necessary.

■ KILLING SQUADS ■

Hitler gave his troops an amnesty for atrocities committed on the Eastern front before they even left German soil. Soldiers – and not just SS troops – were encouraged to treat Russian people, prisoners and Jews as nothing better than vermin. However, there was a special role for the SS.

Almost immediately after invasion, more Einsatzgruppen were formed, special killing squads which had cut their teeth in occupied Poland. They moved eastwards in the wake of the front line rounding up Jews and Bolseheviks and shooting them. Those Jews involved in the state or party machine were most at risk.

One Einsatzgruppe leader Otto Ohlendorff estimated that his unit alone killed 90,000 men, women and children in southern Russia in a year. Later, at the War Crimes Trials at Nuremberg, he explained his orders: 'The instructions were that Jews and Soviet political commissars were to be liquidated; the Jewish population should be totally exterminated.'

In the north, another Einsatzgruppe boasted of killing 135,000 victims in just four months. Adolf Eichmann once said that over the course of the war these killing squads claimed two million lives, probably a slightly exaggerated estimate but nevertheless a shocking one.

Above: **SS men didn't hesitate to mete out summary justice to those suspected of anti-German activities.**

As the idea of efficient extermination in order to achieve the Final Solution gripped the Nazis, mobile gas vans were eventually supplied for use around Russia.

■ THE WINTER WAR ■

For the first time, German soldiers became involved in atrocities which in the west had been the preserve of the Gestapo and the SS. At first, the army were simply encouraged to

> ## In White Russia, the German 707th Infantry Division shot 10,431 prisoners out of 10,940

trigger action by the local communities against their leaders. This was soon set aside. Although commanders feared individual action by

soldiers against the Russians would result in a catastrophic break-down in discipline, they did little to curtail the killings.

The invading German soldiers themselves were experiencing trying conditions, which were to become more acute in the winter months.

CHURCHILL

One of Churchill's famous quotes during the war was:

'If Hitler were to invade hell, I should find occasion to make a favourable reference to the devil.'

They found Russia to be a primitive country compared to their own. And they found actions by the rapidly expanding partisan movement which claimed many German lives almost intolerable. Before long, German soldiers were no longer able to tell the difference between partisans, Jews and communists.

In White Russia the 707th Infantry Division shot 10,431 people in one month, out of a total of 10,940 taken prisoner. Partisan action had inflicted just two dead on the division and five more men were wounded.

Below: **Russian citizens standing before a deep pit are gunned down by a German army firing squad.**

◆ EYE WITNESS ◆

Herman Graebe, a German civilian engineer building roads in the Ukraine, witnessed the modus operandi of an Einsatzgruppe. His account to a rapt courtroom at Nuremberg portrays the misery brought about at the whim of the 'master race'.

'Armed Ukrainian militia were making people get out, under the surveillance of SS soldiers... The people in the trucks wore the regulation yellow pieces of cloth that identified them as Jews. I went straight toward the ditches without being stopped.

When we neared the mound I heard a series of rifle shots close by. The people from the trucks – men, women and children – were forced to undress under the supervision of an SS soldier with a whip in his hand. They were obliged to put their effects in certain spots, shoes, clothing and underwear separately.

I saw a pile of shoes, about 800 to 1,000 pairs, great heaps of underwear and clothing.

Without screaming or weeping, these people undressed, stood around in family groups, kissed each other, said farewells and waited for the sign from the SS man who stood beside the pit with a whip in his hand.

During the 14 minutes I stood near I heard no complaint or plea for mercy. I watched a family . . . . an old woman with snow-white hair was holding a child of about one in her arms, singing to it and tickling it. The child was cooing with delight.

The parents were looking on with tears in their eyes. The father was holding the hand of a boy about ten years old and speaking to him softly: the boy was fighting back tears. The father pointed to the sky, stroked his head and seemed to explain something to him.

At that moment the SS man at the pit started shouting something to his comrade. The comrade counted off about 20 people and instructed them to go behind the earth mound. Among them was the family I have just mentioned.

I well remember a slim girl with black hair who, as she passed me, pointed to herself and said : 'Twenty-three'.

I walked around the mound and stood in front of a tremendous grave. People were closely wedged together and lying on top of each other so that only their heads were visible. Nearly all had blood running over their shoulders from their heads.

Some were lifting their heads and moving their arms to show that they were still alive. The pit was nearly two thirds full and I estimated that it contained about 1,000 people.

I looked at the man who did the shooting. He was an SS man who sat at the edge of the narrow end of the pit, his feet dangling into it. He had a tommy-gun on his knees and was smoking a cigarette.

The people, completely naked, went down some steps which were cut in the clay wall of the pit and clambered over the heads of the people lying there to the place to which the SS man directed them. Some caressed those who were still alive and spoke to them in low voices.'

The SS Cavalry Brigade clearing the Prypiat Marshes in August 1941 shot 699 Russian soldiers, 1,001 partisans and 14,178 Jews. All this killing was in retaliation for 17 dead and 36 wounded Germans. A report from the Second Army revealed it shot 1,179 people out of the 1,836 arrested between August and October 1941.

German soldiers readily believed tales of Jewish and Bolshevik barbarity. One story circulated about innocent Lithuanians having their homes burned, their hands and feet chopped off, their tongues torn out and their children nailed to the walls.

■ RACIST SENTIMENT ■

In letters home, the German soldiers who were anyway programmed by years of Nazi propaganda revealed their racist sentiments.

German Captain Hans Kondruss wrote: 'Here clearly a whole people has systematically been reared into subhumanity. This is clearly the most Satanic educational plan of all times which only Jewish sadism could have constructed and carried through.'

Lance-Corporal Hans Fleischauer wrote: 'The Jew is a real master in murdering, burning and massacring...

Left: On Wulecka Hill in Lvov, eminent scientists were shot by the Nazis.

These bandits deserve the worst and toughest punishment conceivable. We all cannot be thankful enough to our Führer who had protected us from such brutalities and only for that we must follow him through thick and thin, wherever that might be.'

Another soldier described Russian prisoners of war. 'Hardly ever do you see the face of a person who seems rational and intelligent. They all look emaciated and the wild, half-crazy look in their eyes makes them look like imbeciles.'

He went on: '[It is] almost insulting when you consider that drunken Russian criminals have been set loose against us. They are scoundrels, the scum of the earth!'

It wasn't until after the war that many soldiers questioned the brutality which occurred on the Eastern front.

'The Russian fights today... for nothing more or less than... his human dignity'

One junior officer who had served in Poland and Russia explained: 'Well, of course, what they [the Nazis] did to the Jews was revolting. But we were told over and over again that it was a necessary evil. No, I must admit, at the time I had no idea we had fallen into the hands of criminals. I didn't realise that until much later, after it was all over.'

One man in Germany spoke out about the folly of the campaign. Dr Otto Brautigam, a diplomat who became deputy leader of the Political Department of the Ministry for the Occupied Eastern Territories, pinpointed the mistakes being made in a 13-page memo written in October 1942. 'In the Soviet Union

we found on our arrival a population weary of Bolshevism which waited longingly for new slogans holding out the prospect of a better future for them. It was Germany's duty to find such slogans but they remained unuttered. The population greeted us with joy as liberators and placed themselves at our disposal.

'...The worker and peasant soon perceived that Germany did not regard them as partners of equal rights but considered them only as the instrument of her political and economic aims...

'...Our policy has forced both Bolshevists and Russian nationalists into a common front against us. The Russian fights today with exceptional bravery and self-sacrifice for nothing more or less than recognition of his human dignity.'

■ NAZI INVASION ■

The invasion of the Nazis wasn't entirely unwelcome. Ethnic Ukrainians, Lithuanians, Latvians and Estonians were thrilled to be free of Stalin's choking communist yoke. They even held parades and sported the Swastika. At least for them the German slogan of 'Liberation from Bolshevism' had some credibility.

Above: After liberation, women work to identify bodies.

Their young men rushed to volunteer for the SS and became in many cases some of its most ardent and hardline members.

Predictions that the Red Army would be beaten in ten weeks turned out to be wildly optimistic. Although it took two years, Stalin's men got the upper hand against the invaders and began pushing them back into their own territory and beyond. Here was their opportunity to pay back in kind the treatment their own people had endured.

German troops were now faced with the appalling prospect of giving themselves up to the Red Army and went to elaborate lengths to surrender to American and British forces instead.

British soldiers released from prison camps by the Russians were appalled at the behaviour the liberators displayed towards German civilians, little realising the horrors that had gone before on the Eastern front.

The horror inspired by senseless Nazi doctrine that had taken place in Russia makes up yet another shameful chapter in history from which neither side could easily recover.

FINAL SOLUTION

June 1941 did not only spell disaster for Russia, which was invaded by Hitler. It also marked a turning point in the treatment of European Jews.

The drive against Jews had escalated with dynamism. As each new European territory was incorporated into the Reich, there were thousands more shipped in cattle trucks to the concentration camps of Germany, Austria and Poland.

As they saw the countryside race by through the slits and cracks in the uncomfortable carriages, they knew they were facing their doom. The existence of concentration camps where only the supremely fit could survive was now no secret. Yet few could have been prepared for the state-sponsored horror which awaited them.

The death squads in Russia went about their task with the fervour of the zealot

Concentration camps and ghettos which by now had become the chosen route to 'free' Europe of Jews were both haphazard methods which took time to win results. The emigration of Jews to freedom, both voluntary and forced, had been curtailed in Palestine and was occurring at little more than a dribble. (It was finally brought to an end by the Germans themselves.)

Now the sheer volume of 'Untermenschen' or 'sub-humans' being deported into the Reich was multiplied many fold. The satellite death squads which went into Russia went about their task with the fervour of the zealot. Although as many as half a million died in total, it wasn't sufficient for the barbaric regime. Ideas of the 'Final Solution' were formulating in the heads of the most ardent Nazis; that is, the wholesale extermination of the Jewish people in Europe.

There is no exact date for the start of the Final Solution, though operations against the Jews were stepped up after the end of July 1941.

To that end, a range of experiments were tried. The first guinea pigs at Auschwitz were the much-despised Russian prisoners of war, who, alongside 300 Poles, were herded into a sealed cellar one night in September 1941. Through a grating, the callous guards pumped poison gas, oblivious to the screams of the men inside. It took hours for the cries and groans to stop. At dawn, other camp inmates were ordered to carry the bodies from the chamber to the crematorium.

In November 1941 another experiment in mass killing took place, this time in Berlin. The victims were Jewish slave labourers taken from Buchenwald concentration camp whose destination was the infamous Euthanasia Institute where they were gassed to death. The experiment was once again deemed a success. The answer to the Nazi problem was by now apparent.

On 8 December 1941 several hundred Jews were taken from three Polish towns to a wood outside the village of Chelmno and gassed in a specially constructed building.

The Wannsee Conference scheduled for 9 December 1941 was a top level debate on what to do with Jews in the Third Reich. It was sponsored by SS-Obergruppenführer Reinhard Heydrich, one of the authors of Nazi policy against the Jews.

■ WANNSEE ■

In fact, the conference was postponed after Japan's attack on Pearl Harbor. It didn't take place until 20 January 1942 when the representatives of seven high offices – including the Ministry of the Occupied Eastern Territories, the Interior Ministry, the Ministry of Justice, the Foreign Ministry and SS departments – gathered to hear about the Final Solution.

Heydrich made no secret of his desire to deport the entire Jewish

Left: Hopeless and helpless, inmates at Auschwitz concentration camp wait for the end. *Below:* Windowless huts in the Auschwitz camp housed thousands.

Left: **Reinhard Heydrich, known as the 'Butcher of Moravia', was one of the authors of the 'Final Solution' along with Himmler and Eichmann.**

Historians have since debated long and hard the significance of the Wannsee Conference. Today it is regarded as little more than a platform sought by Heydrich to broadcast his radical views. It was, nevertheless, the precursor to genocide and the holocaust for which

---

Mass murder was now sanctioned as an official Third Reich policy

---

population into the east where they would be quite literally worked to death. Those who remained would be 'dealt with'. Here, the policy on procreation was acidly clear. It was the germ that led to the sterilisation programme later brought in by the Nazis to stop the spread of the Jewish population. Among those present at the Wannsee Conference were Himmler, Adolf Eichmann and Ernst Kaltenbrunner.

the Nazis are best remembered today. The mainly localised examples of mass murder carried out on the initiative of individuals was now sanctioned as a Reich policy.

In a speech given by Hitler at the end of January 1942, he told the German people the war could only end when the Jews had been 'uprooted' from Europe.

Hitler said: '...The war will not end as the Jew imagines it will, with the uprooting of the Aryans, but the result of this war will be the complete annihilation of the Jews. 'Now for the first time they will not bleed other people to death but for the first time the old Jewish law of "an eye for an eye, a tooth for a tooth" will be applied.'

Left: **In Auschwitz camp the inscription on the main gate read 'Work brings freedom'.**

It seems clear, therefore, that not only the Nazi officials but also the general public knew of Hitler's desire to kill off Jewry in Europe.

There has been much debate since about the passive acceptance of the German people to this sickening policy. Yet it is clear that the Germans had suffered a degree of brainwashing by Hitler. Thrilled at the emergence of a strong state in which their personal fortunes had improved tremendously, most

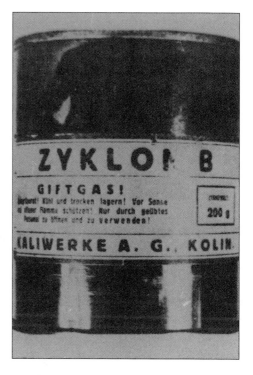

Above: **Zyklon-B was the gas used to kill thousands in Auschwitz after they were herded into fake shower rooms.**

Germans accepted the arrival of concentration camps as necessary to suppress revolutionaries and to house the mentally deranged. There was confusion in the minds of many people who felt being anti-Hitler was tantamount to being anti-German.

As the activities against those targeted minorities like Jews, gypsies, the mentally or physically handicapped and homosexuals increased, the brutalised Germans were already well-practised in turning a blind eye. The punishment for showing any kindness to Jews was severe. Victims of an expert Nazi propaganda machine, native Germans believed they themselves were at risk from a resurgent Jewish force.

■ NO FREE SPEECH ■

If lively discussion of the Jewish question and the extreme measures taken by the regime had been permitted, perhaps a group of people

◆ EYE WITNESS ◆

Peter Strachan, in the 147th Brigade Company of the Royal Army Signals Corps, was an army driver in Europe.

❝ I got a message to pick up a civilian. He never spoke, just gave me directions. As we neared the place, I saw this white stuff on the ground. I thought, has it been snowing? We drove in some massive gates. There were steel ovens on the left hand side. I thought they were bakers ovens.

The air fill filled with this awful smell. Only later did I realise I was in Belsen and these were the ovens used to kill its inmates. The white stuff I saw on the way in was the residue of the quicklime they had put in mass graves. We had to wear gas masks because of the threat of diphtheria and other diseases. I didn't go in any of the huts. I could see the people inside were covered in lice and sores. Quite a lot were still alive but many of them could not be made right. I reckon my brain stopped working while I was there. ❞

opposed to exterminations would have found expression. But free speech was impossible. A Berlin butcher who whispered to a customer that Hitler had started the war was sentenced to death and dispatched to a concentration camp. Germany was, after all, a militarised state which would brook no opposition.

People were subject to the same tools of terror as the so-called 'enemies' of the people. The German underground could operate with only the same degree of effectiveness and in much the same sphere as those resistance movements set up in occupied countries. Veterans of the Eastern front were no longer shocked by extermination and were even convinced of its necessity.

After the war, American interrogators discovered a broad sense of guilt about the fate of the Jews among everyday Germans. But generally people feared revenge, blocked out

KRISTALLNACHT

German citizens chuckled and cheered when Jewish businesses were smashed and businessmen were beaten during a night of horror in November 1938.

Organised by propaganda chief Goebbels, a wave of anti-Semitic attacks took place across Germany apparently in reprisal for the killing of a German diplomat in Paris by a young Jew. On account of the amount of plate glass shattered it was dubbed the Kristallnacht, or Crystal Night.

More than 7,000 Jewish shops were looted and scores of synagogues were set ablaze. An unknown number of Jews died with many more suffering appalling injuries at the hands of thugs employed by the Nazis. Yet as the terror unfolded, middle-class passers-by stopped to applaud the actions of the bully boys and even held up their babies to see the violence administered to Jews.

In order to prevent a recovery by the Jewish faction, the government plotted to confiscate insurance cash paid out following the Kristallnacht and return it.

unsavoury information and put the blame squarely on the shoulders of the Führer.

Abroad, governments had long known about the threat to the Jewish population. There was, however, an unwillingness to believe that systematic murder of a race was taking place. Allied leaders were unwilling to use the facts as they knew them in

Below: **One of the devices which was used to boil human remains down to soap by the Nazis.**

the propaganda war against the Axis powers. The stories of extermination seemed too terrible to be true. Surely no modern nation could be that vile and cruel? Horror stories about Germans had been circulated during World War I which had later been shown to be false.

Torn by political considerations, the British government even went as far as restricting Jewish immigration into Palestine, a vital escape route, to pacify the Arab populations of the Middle East. By 1942 the Swiss

authorities also closed their borders, barring the way to freedom for scores of Jews in Vichy France. Despite its reported independence from Germany, the anti-semitic measures common to the rest of the Reich were also instituted there.

There was enormous sympathy for the plight of the Jews in Britain, reflected in pontifications by the politicians who urged that Britain house more than seven million dispossessed Jews at the end of the conflict. The fact that, given the savage Nazi actions against them, far

By August 1942 news of the mass killings in the Reich reached the free world on a daily basis

fewer Jews than that would remain alive at the end of the war appeared to have escaped them.

Britain's Foreign Office first began hearing about the use of gas chambers in February 1942. A Swedish doctor returned from a visit to the Third Reich confirming that asylums were being cleared by the use of poison. Further reports leaked out of Germany to the same effect. By August 1942 news of the mass killings reached the free world on a daily basis.

■ RIGA MASSACRE ■ ■

On 19 August the Foreign Office in London received via the Belgian Embassy an eyewitness account of a massacre that had taken place outside Riga in Latvia.

'The order was given for the Jews to undress completely. There followed a scene impossible to describe; men and women weeping, falling on their knees, beseeching the German executioners to desist. But all in vain.

'These unfortunate people, among them young children, were lined up at the edge of the trench and machine-gunned. The execution over, the trench was searched to ensure that there was no one alive among the victims. One of the Latvian officers present was unable to stand it and went suddenly mad.'

■ AUSCHWITZ ■

Now some concentration camps had turned into extermination camps, the largest of which was Auschwitz, with its annexe camp of Birkenau. The rate of killings here far exceeded that in other camps of Treblinka, Sobibor, Lvov, Kaunas, Minsk, Vilnius, Riga and Belzec. It was into here that vast numbers of people snatched from their homes in occupied territories disappeared, never to be seen again.

Train loads of deportees arrived to be gassed immediately. On 2 Septem-

> **Everything of value was stripped from them, including gold fillings from the teeth**

ber 1942, 957 Jewish men, women and children arrived from Paris in the early hours of the morning and 918 were gassed before sunset. The same story with victims taken from the length and breadth of Europe was repeated daily on an ever-increasing scale for almost uninterruptedly for three years.

Following the removal of the bodies from the crematoria, everything of value was stripped from them, including the gold fillings from the teeth, and was shipped to the Reichsbank in Berlin where it was paid into an SS account opened in the bogus name of 'Max Heiliger'.

Right: The gas chamber, with its door on the right, and the crematorium at Mauthausen concentration camp where thousands died.

Soap was made of the fats drained from the bodies processed in the enormous crematoria, fertilizer concocted from human bones while hair was kept for stuffing mattresses or for making cloth.

In addition to gassing, people were also shot, usually with a bullet to the back of the neck, received fatal injections or were shot and thrown on a fire while still alive.

When the trainloads of people arrived at Auschwitz, their fate was decided at the flick of an eye. Blinking at the sudden daylight after hours or days penned up in an insanitary boxcar, the fittest that emerged were filed in one direction to work the rest of their useful days as slaves to the Reich. Included in this work was the everyday policing of the camp and the gruesome task of carrying and disposing of bodies. This was carried out by a group called Sonderkommando who enjoyed certain privileges including better rations and quarters. Yet every four months the Sonderkom-

mando were liquidated on the basis that they knew too much of how Auschwitz worked.

Those herded into shacks and sent out to work began their day at 3am when there was a cruel roll call. Each had to stand for four hours in the cold and dark while camp's sadistic criminal 'officials' and then the SS guards counted and re-counted their

◆ EYE WITNESS ◆

Commandant Rudolf Hoess, a veteran of concentration camps, investigated the most efficient way in which to carry out his grim task.

❝ After the war in his affidavit to a war crimes trial, he explained: 'I was ordered to establish extermination facilities at Auschwitz in June 1941. At that time there were already three other extermination camps in the Government General: Belzec, Treblinka and Wolzek.

I visited Treblinka to find out how they carried out their extermination. The Camp Commandant told me that he had liquidated 80,000 in the course of one half year. He was principally concerned with liquidating all the Jews from the Warsaw ghetto. He used monoxide gas and I did not think that his methods were very efficient.

So at Auschwitz I used Zyklon-B which was a crystallized prussic acid dropped into the death chamber. It took from three to fifteen minutes to kill the people in the chamber, according to climatic conditions.

We knew when the people were dead because their screaming stopped. We usually waited about half an hour before we opened the doors and removed the bodies. ❞

◆ EYE WITNESS ◆

For her 13th birthday, Anne Frank received a diary in which she recorded the silly and sentimental, the childish and the charming aspects of her life. And it was no ordinary life. For Anne was the daughter of Jews living in occupied Holland in 1942. Soon the charade of wearing yellow stars to indicate their Jewishness, segregation and harassment was not enough for the Germans. They began transporting Jews to far off concentration camps.

'Rather than risk the unknown, Anne went into hiding with her parents and her sister Margot. Within days they were joined by the Van Daans, who had a 15-year-old son called Peter, and then a dentist called Dussel. Dutch friends kept the hideaway near the centre of Amsterdam a secret. But the Germans finally discovered the secret rooms shut off at the back of her father's former business and her cat-and-mouse game with the Germans was abruptly over.

On 4 August 1944 Anne was sent to Bergen-Belsen concentration camp where she died of typhus in March 1945, three months before her 16th birthday. Her diary was discovered after the family's arrest by a cleaner and given to her Dutch friends. They were able to hand it back to her father Otto Frank when he returned at the end of the war. In her last entry into the diary, made on Tuesday 1 August 1944, Anne echoes many other teenagers with her thoughts and her dreams.

'I never utter my real feelings about anything and that's how I've acquired the reputation of being boy-crazy, a flirt, know-all, reader of love stories. The cheerful Anne laughs about it, gives cheeky answers, shrugs her shoulders indifferently, behaves as if she doesn't care, but, oh dearie me, the quiet Anne's reactions are just the opposite. If I'm to be quite honest, then I must admit that it does hurt me, that I try terribly hard to change myself but that I'm always fighting against a more powerful enemy.'

Below: **Nazi crematoria were built to cope with vast numbers of bodies. Those at Auschwitz worked ceaselessly to cope with the victims.**

numbers. Absurdly, anyone who died in the night was equally required to attend the roll call. It was up to two inmates to support the naked corpse until it was finally collected by wheelbarrow for disposal. Given the physical degeneration in their condition during a long journey with little water and no food, many failed to endure the working life for long.

> ## *On the walls of the camps were posters which read 'Cleanliness brings freedom'*

The rest who arrived by train went another direction, to their doom. This group were informed by loudspeaker that they were going for a shower and delousing before being reunited with their loved ones. Curiously, the camp staff appeared to revel in a charade which never once gave away the fact that people were about to be killed. Every effort was made to convince people of the legitimacy of the 'delousing' including posters which read 'Cleanliness brings freedom'.

■ CHILD KILLINGS ■

This was probably because any signs of panic or dissension from the victims would have seriously disrupted the production-line efficiency of the operation, including the orderly collection of clothes and valuables. Children were always exterminated because they were of little value to the Reich. Their mothers frequently faced the same fate on the basis that loving mums who knew their children had been killed made poor workers.

In a long wooden hut they were forced to strip, their heads were shaved and then they were marched into giant shower rooms. But instead of water, these humiliated, boney figures were gassed to death.

Rudolph Hoess explained the finer points: 'Still another improvement we made over Treblinka was that at Treblinka the victims almost always knew that they were to be exterminated while at Auschwitz camp we

The gas chambers at Auschwitz regularly slaughtered between 6,000 and 12,000 a day

endeavoured to fool the victims into thinking that they were to go through a delousing process.

'We were required to carry out these exterminations in secrecy but... the foul and nauseating stench from the continuous burning of bodies permeated the entire area and all of the people living in the surrounding communities knew that exterminations were going on at Auschwitz.'

Although the gas chambers at Auschwitz housed 2,000 people at a time and they regularly slaughtered between 6,000 and 12,000 people a

day, the camp was unable to cope with the demand it was put under during 1944 when the killings were at their peak. By now Jews in the Yugoslavian states, Greece, Hungary, Rumania and France were deluging into the east. As German successes dwindled in the field, the hierarchy became more focused on its stated aim of killing Jews in which they were achieving greater success. Thanks to the personal attentions of Adolf Eichmann, trains ferrying the victims to Auschwitz and other death camps were given priority above those carrying troops needed for national defence. Until the bitter end, the authorities refused to liberate the inmates of Auschwitz, choosing instead to kill them or march those who were still

Above: Hitler's elite, the Waffen-SS, burgeoned during the war and was responsible for scores of killings.

Below: Emaciated corpses piled up at Buchenwald. The sight shocked and sickened the liberating Allied soldiers.

able-bodied to further camps deeper inside the Reich.

■ WAFFEN SS ■

In charge of the extermination programme for the most part were members of the Gestapo or the rapidly expanding Waffen SS. At the start of the war, this elite band numbered just three divisions. By its end, there were 35 containing more than half a million men. They were pitched by Hitler as a tough state police force against the army and as a reward for their efforts they were promised powers and increased status after the end of hostilities.

The power and prestige of the Waffen SS units didn't appeal to

Germans alone. Many foreigners were enlisted into its ranks and happily carried out the most gruesome and grotesque of its chores. Of the 900,000 men who passed

---

The most feared of the 900,000 men in the Waffen SS were the Ukrainians

---

through the Waffen SS, less than half were Reich Germans. A further 300,000 were racial Germans from outside the boundaries of the Reich, 50,000 were from other Germanic races while 150,000 were foreigners. The most feared of the SS guards were the Ukrainians.

■ FREE AT LAST ■

Their master, SS Reichsführer Heinrich Himmler, urged them to show no restraint. He told them in October 1943: 'One basic principle must be the absolute rule for the SS men; we must be honest, decent, loyal and comradely to members of our own blood and nobody else. What happens to a Russian and a Czech does not interest me in the slightest. What the nations can offer in the way of good blood of our type we will take, if necessary, by kidnapping their children and raising them here with us.'

Such was their enthusiasm that up to 90 per cent of incoming prisoners went immediately to their deaths, depriving the Reich of the slave labour it needed to replenish its armaments and food supplies. This became a source of some dissatisfaction among the Nazi hierarchy.

Battle-hardened soldiers who arrived to liberate Auschwitz and other extermination camps were sickened at what they found. Those who remained alive were little more than skin and bone, their enormous sunken eyes glazed, their heads

Below: **Freedom for the children of Auschwitz. This picture was taken just hours after the camp was liberated.**

Still, he certainly made it to Argentina and felt so secure in his new home that he used his real name to apply for an Argentinian passport in 1956. He also won permits to visit Germany and Switzerland. An extradition bid failed in 1959 on a technicality, by which time Mengele was concerned in a pharmaceutical company in Buenos Aires.

■ DEATH IN BRAZIL ■

He left Argentina for Paraguay in 1960, apparently to work on a cattle cloning project for which he was eminently qualified, thanks to his time at Auschwitz. From there he travelled to Brazil where it is almost certain that he drowned in 1979. His death was cloaked in secrecy for six years. In the early Eighties, Dr Simon

> **It is almost certain that Dr Josef Mengele drowned in an accident in Brazil in 1979**

Wiesenthal had drawn up a list of 10 prominent Nazis whom he wished to see brought to justice. At the time he said: 'If I could get all ten, it would be an achievement. But if I could get only Josef Mengele, I think my soul would be at peace.'

Wiesenthal, among thousands who yearned to see Mengele brought into a courtroom to face his crimes, was cheated by the apparent fluke death of the 'Angel of Death'.

In addition to his forays into medical experiments, Mengele was also guilty of vicious beatings. Afterwards, he would meticulously clean the blood from his hands using perfumed soap.

His research into the incidence of twins was not the end of the

ALDERNEY

Alongside the names of Dachau and Belsen in the annals of horror ranks Alderney, one of the Channel Islands which became the site of three harsh work camps for slave labour and a fourth, fully fledged concentration camp called Sylt.

All four camps, in particular Sylt, became living hell for hundreds of prisoners, particularly Russians, who were sent there to be literally worked to death for the Third Reich.

In charge was the Todt Organisation, tasked with building the defences for Hitler's Fortress Europe. Food was short, the working days long and the beatings meted out by the Germans in control were cruel beyond belief.

One Russian recalled how a fellow countryman died in one of the work camps. 'In Alderney camp, I saw a Russian beaten for half an hour until he bled to death. Willi, a cook, did it. The Russian had taken some potato peelings.'

One Todt officer beat at least one Russian prisoner to death for picking up discarded cabbage leaves.

Officially, the death toll on Alderney is 530 although the real figure is thought to be much higher. Alderney stands out not only because it is on British soil but because the atrocities associated with the Third Reich are normally thought to have been committed by the SS while in this case it was the Todt Organisation building the Atlantic Wall which was responsible. The British government has decreed that records linked to the events on the Channel Islands will be kept under wraps until 2045, probably to save the face of islanders who collaborated.

grotesque activities which took place in the name of medical advances at Auschwitz and other camps throughout the Reich.

Bacterial cultures were grown in live humans afflicting them with the ravages of terrible disease no matter what the pain and suffering that went with it. 'Volunteers' were injected with all manner of vile germs to see what effect they would have.

Surgical operations were carried out by SS doctors without anaesthetics in their crazed attempts to establish the precise effects.

A 'cause celebre' of the manic medic was to sterilise women from the 'sub-human' races around Europe to prevent them procreating further. One technique was to subject each woman to an X-ray for minutes on end to wither the reproductive organs. Poisonous injections were

also administered into the womb, their effects being carefully monitored as the 'guinea pig' female writhed in agony.

In one of the most callous experiments, Jewish people were lined up to be shot so German scientists could assess how many bodies a bullet

Right: **Tests at high-altitude on pyjama-clad prisoners revealed new information to German scientists about the effects of decompression on human beings.**

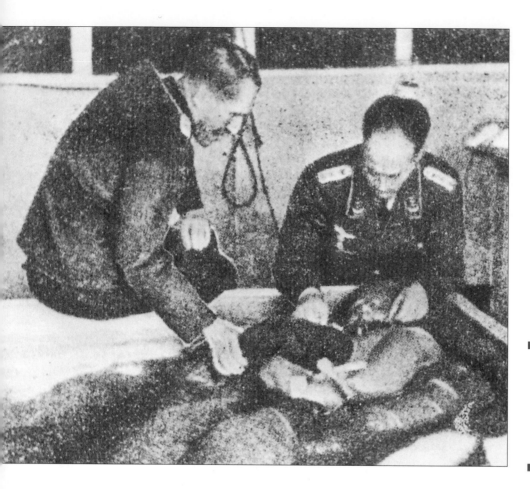

Left: Dr Sigmund Rascher used inmates at Dachau concentration camp for immersion experiments like these, deep in chilling ice water.

In the past, the government has claimed the bones belonged to victims of the Allied bombing raids. Marks on them suggest otherwise but all attempts to analyse the bones have been blocked.

At the head of Japan's grotesque probes beyond the bounds of medical science was Lt-General Shiro Ishii. He oversaw experiments in which prisoners were infected with bubonic

Lt-Gen Ishii oversaw experiments in which prisoners were infected with bubonic plague

could travel through before finally coming to rest.

News of the medical research carried out by the Nazis caused worldwide distress and distaste when details emerged following the war. Yet that stark fact didn't stop medics making full use of the research material gathered by the Nazis amid such appalling anguish and pain.

For more than 40 years British university lecturers showed X-rays taken by the Nazis of their mad work to students. The remains of death camp victims have also been used for teaching purposes.

■ TEACHING AIDS ■

One Cambridge University doctor defended the controversial use of such heartbreaking material in the years following the war by saying: 'It was excellent teaching material. It was used here for over 30 years and served a valuable purpose. There was

obviously a degree of revulsion felt but at least the suffering of those involved was of benefit.'

The X-ray film was in use as recently as 1987. Continued observation of the findings of SS doctors has caused outrage among holocaust survivors who have urged doctors to now give the remains in question a decent burial.

Medical experiments also took place in Japan, an issue which has for years been a source of embarrassment and denials by the government.

Circulating today in Japan are severed skulls and thigh bones. The skull bones contain drill holes, some of them square, indicating brain surgery has taken place.

The bones were discovered in 1989 buried in the grounds of an army medical college where medical experiments are thought to have been carried out following the outbreak of the Sino-Japanese War in 1931.

plague and other fatal diseases and then disembowelled to see the effects on their inner organs. It was his practice to perform autopsies while the 'patients' were still alive. Ultimately, his aim was to perfect a biological weapon which would win Japan's war.

■ COLD EXPERIMENTS ■

Another of his quests was to find a cure for frostbite. Prisoners had their hands dipped in iced water and were then forced outside into freezing winter weather until the hand was thoroughly affected.

The most notorious venue was Unit 731 in occupied China where some 3,000 were killed.

After the war, staff used on the trials admitted the knowledge they gained during these experiments was used after the war. Some felt they had been cheated out of due credit for their endeavours.

A Japanese professor who spoke to these scientists after the war reported: '[They] felt they were victims because they felt they had spent a golden time in fruitful research but the work at 731 would not be recognised by ordinary scientists.' He found only one man who expressed any guilt about what had happened.

He used predominantly Chinese, Korean and Russian guinea pigs but some British and Americans are also thought to have been involved.

Below: **The 'Anatomy Institute of the Academy of Medical Sciences' in Danzig received this human skin.**

SMOKING

Vegetarian, teetotaller and non-smoker, Hitler was keen to use his propaganda machine to spread the word about clean living and good health. When links between smoking a lung cancer were detected by German scientists in the Twenties, he became one of the first anti-smoking campaigners in the world.

Magazines and newspapers contained warnings about the dangers of smoking. Women were forbidden to buy cigarettes in cafes, smoking was restricted among soldiers and banned in scores of public places. It was illegal to use tobacco in advertising to advocate manly qualities and those who abstained were awarded shining qualities of good Aryan citizens.

Despite his iron grip on the propaganda system, his move to cut smoking failed. The number of smokers rose in Fascist Germany in much the same way as it did in other European countries. The shortcomings of preventative medicine in a totalitarian regime where everyone is subject to the message has cast doubt among some doctors on its value in democratic states today.

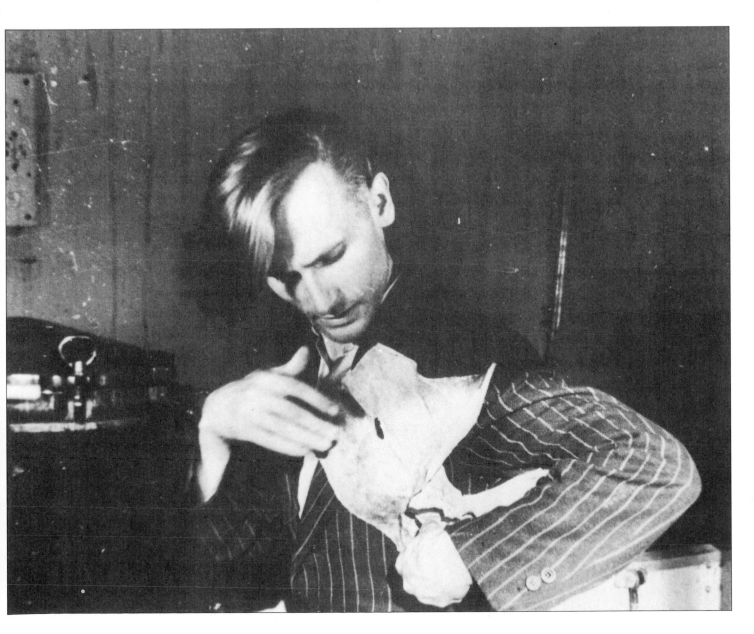

ATROCITIES

Code-named Operation Escape 200, it was better known as The Great Escape. Allied captives, predominantly Royal Air Force officers, planned to spring 200 men from Stalag Luft III, a German prison camp near Sagan, Silesia, now in Polish territory. It was an adventure, a game of chance and a golden opportunity to outwit the enemy.

But the men who slaved to pull off the most memorable prison breakout ever were to be sorely disappointed. On the night of the escape, 24 March 1944, a conspiracy of events allowed just 76 men to flee the barbed wire and watchtowers of the Stalag. And of those, only three made it to freedom, two Norwegians and a Dutchman.

Worst of all, 50 RAF servicemen chosen at random were shot by the Gestapo as a reprisal for the daring plot, to satisfy Hitler's fury. The Nazis committed an atrocity which the men of the Royal Air Force would never forgive and forget.

Stalag Luft III was built in 1941 on the orders of Hermann Göring, head of the Luftwaffe, to house the increasing numbers of Allied airmen shot down in raids over Germany.

It was a far cry from the concentration camps for which Hitler and his henchmen became famous. Although 12 men were forced to share a room, some days around the clock, they were allowed to play games like rugby and football and enjoyed reasonable rations. The prisoners of war totalling 5,000 were even allowed to build their own theatre where they staged productions twice weekly.

It was an indication of the sneaking regard in which Göring held the courageous airmen – as was the treatment dished out to them if they escaped. Until 1944, when the tide of war had turned against Germany, British airmen had to endure only a verbal lashing and a spell in solitary

Left: **By 1944, Waffen-SS troops were battle-hardened desperate men.**
Right: **Stalag Luft III, the camp from which RAF officers planned a daring breakout.**

confinement if they were recaptured. They were treated to applause and cheers when they emerged to rejoin their comrades.

▪ ESCAPE COMMITTEE ▪

Stalag Luft III was constructed on sand. It wasn't long before enterprising airmen housed in the officers' compound desperate to escape to Britain and resume the battle against Hitler had dug a maze of different tunnels from inside the complex. The escape committee run by Senior British Officer, Wing Commander Harry 'Wings' Day, a veteran of the Great War was active if something of a shambles.

Only when South African Roger Bushell, an experienced escapee, took charge did the plans for The Great Escape take shape. He believed the best way to harry the Germans was to have scores of their internees turned loose at one time. To do it, he hit upon the idea of having three tunnels only for escaping purposes, nicknamed Tom, Dick and Harry. Work started in the summer of 1943 but was dramatically halted when the existence of Tom was discovered in October. It wasn't until January 1944 that work resumed. This time the

intention was to complete Harry as quickly as possible.

Its entrance in Hut 104 was disguised beneath a heating stove. Digging with usually nothing more than empty tins, a team of two men squeezed into a tiny shaft scooping away the sandy earth and propping up the extending tunnel with wooden supports taken from the prison bunk beds. Engineers among the prisoners designed and made a trolley running on wooden rails large enough to

The entrance to the tunnel in Hut 104 was disguised beneath a heating stove

carry a man on which the diggers and their sand were eventually ferried. At first the operation was lit by fat-burning lamps. Later however, a supply of electricity was filched from the camp itself by means of some stolen cable. There was also an air pump made of a kit bag and piping constructed of old food tins which provided fresh oxygen to the tunnel while digging was in progress.

Above: RAF men held in Stalag Luft III enjoyed many privileges, thanks to the esteem of Göring.

Beyond the designing and digging, there were teams of prisoners involved in scattering the dug-out sand. One technique was to fill two sausage-like containers with sand to wear down each trouser leg, releasing it slowly during a trudge around the campsite. The sand bags were the ingenious idea of another escape organiser, Captain Peter Fanshawe, taken prisoner during the Norwegian

There were teams of prisoners involved in scattering dug-out sand during exercise

campaign. Nicknamed 'Hornblower' by his comrades, he was dispatched to another camp shortly before the breakout and so, to his immense disappointment, was unable to take part. Following liberation, he was later put in command of the sloop

Amethyst during the Korean War and died shortly before the commemoration of the 50th anniversary of the Great Escape in 1994, aged 82.

Those who made friends with camp guards elicited further tools and even cameras for forging the documents that would be needed outside the camp. Yet another group set to work making service suits look like civilians' garb using dye concocted of boot polish or ink.

■ 200 TO ESCAPE ■

More than 500 officers worked frantically on the project – although not everyone in the camp chose to get involved. Many thought the end of the war was imminent and considered that it would be foolhardy to risk lives at this belated stage. They had a point. The notion that the men were escaping to freedom was quite wrong. They were escaping from the camp into German territory from where it would be a long and dangerous haul home.

Nevertheless, when the 330 ft tunnel was completed by 14 March there was no shortage of volunteers to go through it. Bushell selected the first 25 himself. The rest were drawn out of a hat. Astonishingly, guards noticed nothing as the 200 men converged silently on hut 104 before dusk when the doors were locked. Three men went down the tunnel to complete the last two feet of digging. With horror, when they finally pierced the crust of snowy, frozen ground above them, they discovered the tunnel fell 30ft short of the forest which would give them essential cover. It was in clear sight of the watchtowers and their guards. Quickly, the determined bunch devised a rope alarm system, in which a man in the forest would signal the all-clear to the next in line to escape by giving two tugs.

Below ground, things were not going well. The electric lights rigged up to aid the men in the tunnel cut out due to an air raid on Berlin. The troops of men sweeping through on the trolley caused landfalls which had

Disaster struck. A German soldier happened on the tunnel exit and raised the alarm

to be repaired. In the end, it was decided only 80 men would escape that night before the tunnel had to be sealed. Then disaster struck. A German soldier accidentally happened on the tunnel exit and raised the alarm.

Those in the tunnel had to beat a hasty retreat, gorging their rations and burning their papers and money before being discovered. Seventy-six

men who had made it to freedom had to scatter at speed. While they were mostly British, the number included some Canadians, Australians, New Zealanders, Poles, Czechs and Norwegians as well as one Lithuanian and one Greek. Although there was help and support given by Americans in the construction of the tunnels, all were moved to other camps before the date of the escape.

In the national alert that followed, most of the escapees were picked up almost immediately. With appalling weather conditions, anyone who remained on the loose soon suffered the effects of exposure. Only three made it to freedom, including Norwegian Jens Muller. He described being on the run in the Third Reich as 'just as exciting as the film [The Great Escape] but not in that wild cowboy fashion.'

Fifty officers were chosen by the local Gestapo for execution. With the

exception of Bushell, the selection appears to have been made randomly. Bushell, the barrister and bon viveur, had been warned that if he broke out again he was a prime target for the Gestapo who were irritated by his escape artistry. His sadly ill-advised response was merely to say: 'I am not going to be caught.'

■ SHOT IN THE BACK ■

In groups of twos and threes, they were driven into a forest and shot in the back of the head after being invited to leave the car they were travelling in for a 'pinkelpause' or toilet break. Their bodies were cremated and the ashes taken back as an example to the men left in Stalag Luft III. There, news of the merciless killings was greeted with disbelief.

A poster went up in the camp stating: 'The escape from prison camps is no longer a sport!' It went on: 'Urgent warning is given against making future escapes! In plain English, stay in the camp where you will be safe! Breaking out of it is now

Above: Equipment needed by tunnel builders who burrowed their way through sandy soil beneath barbed wire fences. *Left:* A trolley used to move sand then men sits in the entrance of Harry, the escape tunnel.

a damned dangerous act. The chances of preserving your life are almost nil! All... guards have been given the strictest orders to shoot on sight all suspected persons.'

Below: **A diagram of the escape tunnel and its route out of the Stalag Luft III prison camp.**

■ SENSELESS MURDER

For many, it merely hardened the resolve to escape. Of the survivors of The Great Escape, at least two tunneled out of the next prison camp they were sent to and as punishment for that spent a soul-destroying five months in solitary confinement until the end of the war.

The feat of the men was immortalised on film in 'The Great Escape' made in 1963 with stars James Garner, Steve McQueen, Richard Attenborough, Donald Pleasance and James Coburn. A warm if glorified account of the breakout, it differed from fact because there were no Americans in the escape itself.

The feat of the men was immortalised in the film 'The Great Escape'

However, throughout the Second World War there was no shortage of senseless killings like these which offended against all the common laws of humanity.

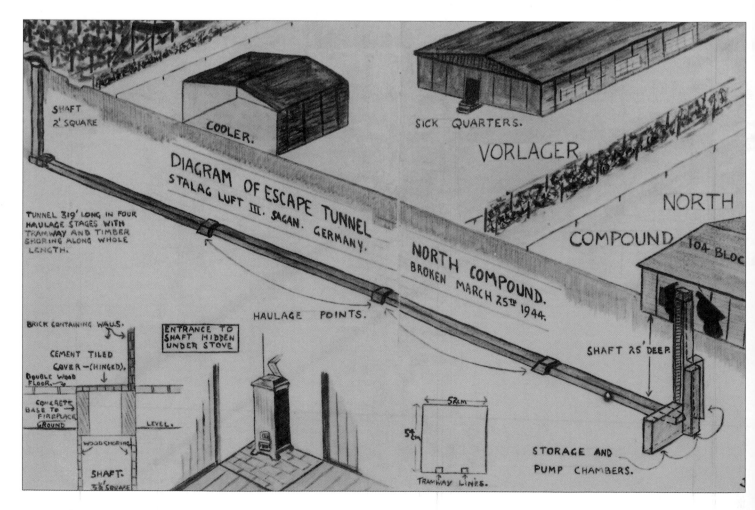

DIAGRAM OF ESCAPE TUNNEL
STALAG LUFT III. SAGAN. GERMANY.

NORTH COMPOUND.
BROKEN MARCH 25TH 1944.

SHAFT 2' SQUARE

COOLER.

SICK QUARTERS.

VORLAGER

NORTH COMPOUND 104 BLOC

TUNNEL 319' LONG IN FOUR HAULAGE STAGES WITH TRAMWAY AND TIMBER SHORING ALONG WHOLE LENGTH.

HAULAGE POINTS.

SHAFT 25' DEEP.

BRICK CONTAINING WALLS.

ENTRANCE TO SHAFT HIDDEN UNDER STOVE

CEMENT TILED COVER (HINGED).
DOUBLE WOOD FLOOR.

CONCRETE BASE TO FIREPLACE
GROUND

LEVEL.

WOODSHORING

SHAFT. 3½' SQUARE

52cm

52cm

TRAMWAY LINES.

STORAGE AND PUMP CHAMBERS.

British servicemen once again bore the brunt in an appalling slaughter which took place as the Germans powered into Europe during the spring of 1940. After an unexpected period of calm following the declaration of war, British troops sent to France to bolster defences suddenly found themselves embroiled in a fast-moving conflict. Their only hope of escape was to reach Dunkirk from where a massive evacuation would take them to England.

It was those soldiers prepared to sacrifice their own chance of escaping to mount a rearguard action who were caught up in the bloodshed.

■ DUNKIRK ■

Men of the 2nd Royal Warwicks dug in at Wormhoudt, 12 miles south-east of Dunkirk, to confound the enemy. Little did they realise that they would encounter the 2nd Battalion of the crack SS-Liebstandarte, Hitler's favoured troops.

The British soldiers put up a brave resistance, claiming clutches of casualties including the commanding

British soldiers have testified that prisoners were shot in cold blood by the Germans

officer of the army group in opposition, Schutzeck. Many German soldiers were already stoked up to fury by the continuing backlash from the British troops. When word of their commander's head injuries spread, the SS men became inflamed. In place of the injured commander came Wilhelm Mohnke.

British soldiers have since testified that prisoners of war, including those who were injured, were shot in cold-

blood by the Germans as they advanced on the retreating enemy.

By 28 May, much of the organised resistance by the British had been knocked out, with only pockets of

Below: A poignant photographic memorial to 25 of the men shot after 'The Great Escape'. All these men were taken in twos and threes to a forest and shot in the back of the head.

```
26. Langford, P.W.
27. Leigh, T.B.
28. Long, J.L.
29. Mc Garr, C.A.
30. Mc Gill, G.E.
31. Marcinkus, R.
32. Milford, H.J.
33. Mondschein, J.T.
34. Pawluk, K.
35. Picard, H.A.
36. Pohe, P.P.
37. Scheidhauer, B.W.
38. Skantzikas, S.
39. Swain, C.D.
40. Stevens, R.
41. Stewart, R.C.
42. Stower, J.G.
43. Street, D.O.
44. Tobolski, P.
45. Valenta, E.
46. Walenn, G.W.
47. Wernham, J.C.
48. Wiley, G.W.
49. Williams, J.E.
50. Williams, J.F.
```

ARMY JAIL

Army jails, named 'glasshouses' because the first military prison at Aldershot had a glass roof, were notoriously barbaric.

They were the destination of those evading military service by faking illness, men who overstayed their leave or were guilty of behaviour which was otherwise interpreted as 'malingering'. During the war a string of jails was established across Britain and across the world in the wake of the British advance.

During the week, inmates had to get up at 6am for a day of strenuous physical activity, deprived of all comforts including razors, knives, forks and plates and performing every task 'at the double'. Talking was often banned for hours on end, as was smoking. At weekends, men were often locked up for hours at a time. There were frequent accusations of beatings from sadistic prison guards although this was denied by the army.

Punishments for misdemeanours inside the jail included three days on bread and water and the withdrawal of bedding so that men were forced to sleep on bed springs.

men remaining to stem the tide of Germans. At Wormhoudt a posse of prisoners about 50-strong had been taken, not only from the 2nd Warwicks but also the Cheshires and the Royal Artillery.

Ominously, they were forced to hand over their dog-tags, personal papers and other identification before being marched through the town to the Germans' Battalion Battle Headquarters. As they trudged on, they spotted with horror the bodies of British soldiers by three burnt-out trucks. The corpses themselves were smouldering. One man saw 20 men lined up and shot by the Germans beside a town's building.

Left: Wilhelm Mohnke, the war crimes suspect, meets with his commanding officer Sepp Dietrich.

Mohnke confronted the officer in charge of the British men and told him 'take no prisoners'

A further 50 prisoners including men from the 8th Battalion of the Worcestershire Regiment and the 20th Anti-Tank Regiment joined their ranks at the HQ where Wilhelm Mohnke was now in charge. It is now believed that a raging Mohnke left the HQ, confronted the officer in charge of the British men and told him: 'Take no prisoners'.

The meaning of the order filtered through to a few of the British men, who were scarcely able to comprehend what grim fate awaited them.

Now a new guard of higher ranking SS men marched with them over fields and in double time. The panting prisoners who fell by the wayside were beaten or bayonetted. Their destination was a wooden barn with a straw roof, about the size of a garage, mucky and airless.

Herded into the barn, four men found their way out through a back door and escaped. Still, there remained about 100 men inside under the eagle eye of the SS men gathered around the main entrance. As one British captain complained about the deplorable conditions the men were forced to endure, there came a taste of what was to come. The irate guard, weary of the Britisher's complaint, suddenly hurled a grenade into the crowd of men.

■ IN COLD BLOOD ■

Two men took their cue and tried to escape in the mayhem. One of them, the vocal captain, was shot dead soon afterwards as he tried to hide in a pond. A private with him was injured and left for dead.

Back at the barn, more grenades were thrown, killing and maiming the men as they exploded. The carnage stopped as suddenly as it had begun when the senior SS men decided on a different approach. They demanded five volunteers to step outside. After a brief hesitation, five brave men stepped forward.

They were marched outside, forced to turn their backs to a five-strong firing squad and shot in cold blood. A further five men marched off to meet the same grisly end. Just as the firing squad pulled the triggers, they turned around to look their executioners square in the eye.

Now the men in the barn were not only frightened but belligerent as well.

Right: US troops advance towards Malmedy, Belgium where 30 vehicles were ambushed and 140 men massacred.

As rain deluged down, the SS men stepped inside the barn and began shooting their prisoners by the score. Those who survived were pinned beneath the bodies of their dead comrades. Some died holding photographs of their loved ones, others reciting the Lord's Prayer. Bodies were piled high around the walls of the flimsy shack in which about 90 people had died. Survivors amounted to perhaps 20, some of whom were so badly wounded they would die of their injuries before receiving help.

> **Some died holding photographs of their loved ones; others recited the Lord's Prayer**

The SS men pulled out, content with the success of their operation. There was no help at hand. Some of the men, in groups or separately, tried to escape. They were to a man all picked up by the Germans although one managed to stay on the run for five months. Their luck had changed, however, and they were captured by patrols of the regular German army who treated them decently and accorded them their rights. When the appalling tale of their plight emerged, many German soldiers expressed their disgust.

The injured who were too ill to move were finally rescued by members of an Austrian Red Cross team. One badly wounded man, Richard Parry, recalled the moment of rescue. 'The one thing which stands out is that their handling of me was ever-so gentle. There were six or seven of us taken from the barn wounded but alive, thank God. I remember the great feeling of relief which came over me as I was placed in the ambulance. Inside the vehicle, I fell asleep.'

It wasn't the last wartime massacre to bear the mark of Wilhelm Mohnke. Four years later disarmed members of the Canadian invasion forces at his mercy were to be killed at his command.

On 8 June 1944, the Battle of Normandy was centred around Caen with Canadian forces making repeated attempts to take the city's environs. Striking back was the 2nd Battalion of the 26th Panzer Grenadier Regiment, Mohnke's regiment, who managed to take about 40 prisoners. The prisoners were marched towards the German lines, pushed into a field and then shot by their guards who were brandishing machine guns. Only five escaped by making a run for it.

The same SS group are believed to have murdered six more Canadians who were attending a first aid post. Their bodies were discovered when the area was finally taken by the Allies – they had suffered various wounds to the body and fatal gun shot injuries to the head.

There were other scattered examples of military terrorism in those frenzied days following the invasion in which Mohnke's men are implicated. Then Mohnke himself becomes a leading player in the killing of three more Canadians.

■ WILHELM MOHNKE ■

As Regimental Commander, he stalked out to interrogate the three prisoners who had been captured laying mines and taken to his headquarters at Forme du Bosq. Bellowing and snorting, Mohnke quizzed the men through an interpreter for some 20 minutes. At the end of the interrogation the prisoners were searched and stripped of all their identification.

Abruptly, the questioning ended and the men were marched across a meadow to a bomb crater. As they approached it, they were shot in the back at close range by an SS man – while Mohnke stood and watched.

Left: **Bodies of men, women and children await formal identification before burial after the massacre at Malmedy, Belgium.**

Malmedy on 17 December. Overwhelmed by Germans, a substantial number of Americans surrendered.

After being searched, the men were lined up in eight rows in a nearby field with their hands held above their heads. There were some 120 men in the field when two armoured vehicles pulled out of the German columns to take aim at the unarmed prisoners. A pistol shot claimed the first victim. Then the machine guns on the vehicles burst into life, killing many before they could even raise their voices in protest.

The bodies collapsed in a heap, some dead already, others dying and still more feigning death in the hope they would escape. Blood oozed from the bodies on to the frosted ground, soaking those still alive who could feel the life ebb from their comrades.

■ EYES BAYONETTED ■

Their agony was far from finished, however. For when the armoured cars moved on, others passing by opened up with a rattle of gunfire at the human debris in the field.

Men began strolling among the bodies, kicking them over and shooting where they saw signs of life. All the time they were laughing hysterically. In common with the other massacres carried out by Mohnke's SS-Liebstandarte men, the perpetrators of the killings were wild-eyed and cackling as if they had been drinking or taking drugs.

Some victims were battered to death. Others had their eyes bayonetted while they were still breathing.

When the coast was clear, the living rose from the dead. About 20 survived. But fortune was not on their side because they were spotted

Mohnke was not alone in overseeing bloody murder following D-Day. Kurt Meyer, who commanded the 25th Panzer Grenadiers, dispatched his prisoners in much the same manner. His headquarters were in the Abbaye Ardenne, near Caen, where 11 Canadian prisoners were killed on 7 June 1944, seven were murdered on 8 June and two more died on 17 June.

According to witnesses, the Canadians killed on 8 June were fully aware of what was about to happen. From a place of interrogation in a stable, each man was summoned to his death by name. He shook hands with his comrades and bade them farewell before walking up the steps to the garden – where a German guard was waiting to put a bullet in the back of his head.

Others who died at the Abbaye were battered to death or cut down in a hail of bullets.

This was not the end of the story, either. Mohnke handed down an order given by Hitler himself, that

during the Battle of the Bulge – Germany's last ditch effort against the Allies – soldiers were to fight with zeal and commitment and to do what it took to achieve victory.

Taken with regard to Mohnke's men and their unenviable past record, the results were not altogether surprising. There was spasmodic violence in the treatment

Christmas 1944 was scarred by one of the worst German excesses of the war

of prisoners of war, this time from the American forces. Yet the German campaign at Christmas 1944 was scarred by one of the worst excesses of the war.

It occurred when an American convoy of 30 vehicles and about 140 men was ambushed at the town of

staggering to a nearby cafe by the German rear guards. The Germans set the building ablaze – and fired on the Americans as they dashed out to escape the flames.

Amazingly, 43 Americans survived the Malmedy massacre while an estimated 86 perished. And the rampaging Germans continued to shoot US soldiers and Belgian civilians as they tried to break through to Antwerp and the Belgian coast.

Colonel Jochen Peiper was in charge of the unit which had so savagely murdered that day.

After the war a military tribunal heard from German Corporal Ernst Kohler about the scope of the operation. 'We were told to remember the women and children of Germany killed in Allied air attacks and to take no prisoners nor to show mercy to Belgian civilians.'

Peiper was sentenced to hang among others deemed responsible for the bloodshed. The case, however, caused disquiet because there was evidence that confessions were beaten out of some of the SS prisoners by vengeful American officers and men.

■ TRIGGER-HAPPY ■

And a question mark hung over the fairness of the trial in view of the lack of action taken against US soldiers who committed a similar atrocity in shooting unarmed prisoners of war as they made they way up Italy. Indeed, there is ample evidence to suggest that Allied soldiers were criminally trigger-happy following D-day. The spoils of victory apparently stretched to immunity from prosecution. Peiper was finally sentenced to 35 years in jail and was released after 11 years.

Mohnke, the man who linked the massacres of Wormhoudt in 1940 and those of Canadian soldiers in 1944, was also alleged to have handed specific orders requiring a

barbarous response to prisoners down to Peiper before his thrust through Malmedy.

He fell into Russian hands at the end of the war and served 10 years in a Soviet jail. Afterwards, he returned to Germany and lived in Hamburg. He has never been brought to court to face charges on account of the deaths of the Allied prisoners.

Authors Ian Sayer and Douglas Botting compiled a detailed dossier about Mohnke called 'Hitler's Last General'. It outlines the disgraceful

---

The disappearance of 15,000 Poles in Russia remained a mystery for 50 years

---

massacres linked with Mohnke, finding proof against the general in the words of men who were there. They maintain: 'It shows beyond all reasonable doubt that a prima facie case exists against Wilhelm Mohnke on a number of counts; and it urges that the American, Canadian, British and Belgian governments should take action now or prevail upon the West German authorities to pursue the case with the utmost vigour in order that justice might take its proper course before it is too late.'

The disappearance of some 15,000 Polish officers in Russia after the division of their homeland remained a mystery for almost 50 years until secret files revealed the grim truth. The men had been liquidated on Stalin's order by his secret police, the NKVD. Their unmarked resting place was Katyn Wood.

R*ight:* Jochen Peiper photographed in 1943. He was to serve 11 years in prison for his part in the Malmedy massacre.

Each man was killed by a single shot in the nape of the neck. It took from 3 April to 13 May to transport the men from three different camps and complete the grisly task.

■ KATYN WOOD ■

Their bodies fell into sandy pits alongside those of their companions. It wasn't until 1943 that the mass graves were uncovered by German soldiers. The shocking story appeared to have all the hallmarks of a German propaganda coup. Instantly, Stalin's regime counterclaimed that Nazis were responsible.

In 1990 the truth was revealed when a box containing NKVD files was handed by the Russians to Poland. It detailed the actions of the violent men who ran the secret police, the forerunner of the KGB,

and revealed they themselves had fallen victim to Stalin's ruthlessness and were later killed. While the shroud of mystery had at last been lifted, nothing could erase the grief of the families whose young men were killed so meaninglessly.

■ LIDICE ■

Atrocities in wartime were not confined to fighting men. Civilians in the occupied territories saw many unspeakable horrors, like the ill-fated residents of Lidice. The village outside Prague may have had its fair share of those keen to see the Nazis thrown out of their land and a return to independence. Every village in

Below: At a war crimes trial in 1946, a Malmedy survivor identifies the man who fired the first shot of the massacre.

Chester Wilmot reported the words of an anonymous Frenchman on the BBC in April 1945 which revealed another German atrocity carried out against slave labourers travelling by train away from the Allies.

❝ On Sunday evening the train stopped in the yard at Celle while the engine filled up with water and coal. Our carriages were left standing between an ammunition train and a petrol train and we hadn't been there long when some Allied bombers came over. We heard them coming and we tried to get out of the train, but as we jumped down on to the tracks the SS guard opened fire on us with machine guns. Then the bombs began to fall and they hit the train. The ammunition and petrol began to explode. Many must have been killed. But those who survived tried to get away from the fire and explosions. Some of us reached shelter but most of the rest were shot down by the SS guards. After it was all over, there were only 200 left out of the 4,500 and we 200 were rounded up by the SS and herded into a stable – a filthy stable, and there we lay on straw that barely covered the manure underneath. Many of us were wounded or burnt but they left us there for four days without medical attention, food or water. We were rescued only when the British came. ❞

Czechoslavakia, taken by Hitler by force in 1938, had the same. It was no more of a thorn in the side of the German rulers than any other.

Yet on 10 June 1942 it was surrounded by German security police prepared to carry out a massacre. All

Lidice was surrounded by German security police prepared to carry out a massacre

the men and boys of Lidice and a neighbouring village Lezaky, amounting to 199, were shot dead. Their wives were shipped off to Ravensbruck conentration camp and 90 children were dispatched to other camps around the Reich. The entire village was then burned to the ground. Its name was even erased from German maps. In addition, there were the usual round-ups in reprisal, bring-

and were parachuted onto their home territory from an RAF plane.

After tossing a bomb in Heydrich's car on 27 May, they sought sanctuary in a church but were eventually killed following a gun battle. The name of Lidice was found in the papers of a third Free Czech agent, unrelated to the pair who carried out the killing. The razing of Lidice was nothing more than a crude kick-back

by the Germans to repay the death of one of their own.

■ ORADOUR ■

One of the best remembered civilian slaughters of the war took place at Oradour-sur-Glane, near Limoges, in south-west France. One summer's afternoon in June 1944 the streets of this quiet village ran red with the blood of its inhabitants.

The atrocity was carried out as a reprisal for the assassination of Reinhard Heydrich

ing the total dead to some 2,000. The village of Lidice was paying dearly for the death of one German. Reinhard Heydrich, one of the arch exponents of the Final Solution, died on 4 June from injuries he received when his car was blown up.

■ BUTCHER ■

Heydrich, the Governor of Bohemia, was a particularly loathsome Nazi who had well earned his nickname of 'the Butcher of Moravia'. From the velocity of the revenge thought up by Himmler, one might have thought the killers were from Lidice or were in hiding there.

In fact, the assassins were two members of the Free Czech movement, Joseph Gabcik and Jan Kubis, native Czechs who joined the French Foreign Legion and the 1st Czech Brigade in Britain. They had trained for their mission in Britain, were in the pay of the British army

Right: Weeping Polish wives and mothers flock to identify the bodies of their loved ones cut down in Katyn Wood by Stalin's secret police.

◆ EYE WITNESS ◆

Stanislaw Mikolajczyk, successor to Sikorski as leader of the Polish government in exile, recalled how a Soviet bureaucrat explained the Katyn Wood massacre. It happened following rumours that the Polish officers would join the Red Army.

❝ Senior commanders were aware of such talk but had nothing specific to go on. The staff officer was sent to get Stalin's clarification. The staff officer saw Stalin and briefly explained the problem. Stalin listened patiently. When the staff officer finished, Stalin supplied him with a written order. Such orders were common, often requested by subordinates as a matter of self-protection. In this case, said the informant, Josef Stalin took a sheet of his personal stationery and wrote only one dreadful word on it: 'Liquidate'. The staff officer returned the one-word order to his superiors but they were uncertain what it meant. Did Stalin mean to liquidate the camps (housing the officers) or to liquidate the men? He might have meant that the men should be released, sent to other prisons or to work in the Gulag system. He might also have meant that the men should be shot or otherwise eliminated. No one knew for sure what the order meant but no one wanted to risk Stalin's ire by asking him to clarify it. To delay a decision was also risky and could invite retribution. The army took the safe way out and turned the whole matter over to the NKVD. For the NKVD, there was no ambiguity in Stalin's order. It could only mean one thing: that the Poles were to be executed immediately. ❞

Every one of the village's 254 buildings was reduced to rubble as the population looked on aghast. More than 200 men were locked into a barn and cut down in a hail of bullets. Women and children were herded into the church and the doors were locked behind them. Then explosives rained down into the building, all thoughts of its traditional use as a sanctuary forgotten by the bloodthirsty killers.

If the 450 women and children were not dead from suffocation through the choking smoke, they

Below: **It is thought that NKVD men murdered these Polish officers at Katyn Wood rather than query an ambiguous order from Josef Stalin.**

were killed by grenades thrown through the blasted windows. To ensure the massacre was done thoroughly, however, the doors were finally opened and bullets from a machine gun were pumped inside. Anyone who tried to run or was too sick or old to leave their home was mercilessly shot.

Today Oradour looks exactly the same as it did at the moment when the murdering German troops pulled out. Although the smell of fear, death and spent explosives has long since faded, the walls of the wrecked church are still scorched and the doctor's car remains in the street in the same spot it was when he was pulled from its seat and taken away for execution. Visitors come to pay homage to those 642 innocent people who died and wonder at the barbarity of those responsible.

Indeed, the reason behind this most brutal of repressions has perplexed and intrigued observers of

Above: **The funeral of Reinhard Heydrich. His death led to the razing of the Czech village of Lidice.**

Today Oradour looks exactly the same as it did when the murdering German troops left

subsequent generations. For years it was believed the action was carried out as a reprisal following the deaths of three German soldiers at the hands of the French resistance.

However, another explanation has come to light which better explains the severity of the massacre.

A truck allegedly containing plundered loot intended to line the pockets of three SS commanders was attacked by the resistance on its way to being hidden in the Loire valley. Only

one German soldier who fled with his clothes aflame escaped the ambush. And the return of fire killed five out of six of the French attackers. The remaining member of the Maquis could hardly believe his eyes when he cautiously probed the back of the truck and discovered it packed with gold.

Known only as 'Raoul', the wide-eyed peasant hurriedly buried the boxes of treasure at the roadside before himself fleeing. When the three German officers heard about the ambush and the subsequent loss of their booty, they were furious. Recent intelligence pinpointed Oradour as a centre of the resistance. General Heinz Lammerding and his cohort Major Otto Dickmann decided here would be a good place to start their search for the missing gold. In addition, the third member of their conspiracy Helmut Kampfe had co-

incidentally been taken prisoner by the resistance. His prospects for survival were not good.

Consequently, Lammerding sent troops from the Waffen SS under the command of hardline Nazi Captain Kahn into Oradour to extract from its residents the whereabouts of the gold. When they protessed ignorance, Kahn simply shot them.

■ SHOCKING TALE ■

The shocking tale of what happened at Oradour-sur-Glane only emerged much later when an entrepreneur called Robin Mackess met the mysterious and still unidentified Raoul long after the war during some dubious business transactions. Mackess was unable to prove conclusively the validity of Raoul's story when he was arrested for customs irregularities and jailed for 21 months. But in his book 'Oradour – Massacre and Aftermath' he outlines his amazing theories for the appalling events that took place.

DEATH RAILWAY

Defenders of the Philippines were cornered and cut off by the Japanese. But it wasn't until the men were sick, starving and virtually without ammunition that the combined forces of US and Filipinos surrendered to the triumphant Japanese forces. If they had thought the release from daily nerve-bending bombardment was to be a blissful one, however, the prisoners were sorely mistaken.

mmediately, the captured forces of 12,000 Americans and 63,000 Filipinos were compelled to embark on a 60-mile trek to a prison camp. Heat, hunger, thirst and barbaric treatment from the Japanese guard soon won the gruelling expedition a new title, that of 'Death March'.

Up to 10,000 died as they made their way along the jungle track, victims who were already dangerously weak from the deprivations of fighting on the island peninsula for so long.

Afterwards, men told how they were pushed past cool streams and plentiful wells even though they were parched. Sadistic guards would club men who stumbled. Little or no food was handed out to men who became faint with desperate hunger. Many who fell by the wayside were summarily shot.

US Air Corps pilot William Dyess was among the prisoners. His account of the march, published in 1944, gave an insight into the sufferings endured.

■ STARVATION ■

'I heard a cry, followed by thudding blows at one side of the paddy. An American soldier so tortured by thirst that he could not sleep had asked a Jap guard for water. The Jap fell on him with his fists then slugged him into insensibility with a rifle butt...

'...Troop-laden trucks sped past us. A grimacing Jap leaned far out, holding his rifle by the barrel. As the truck roared by he knocked an American soldier senseless with the gun's stock. From now on we kept out of reach if we could...'

Following a day without food, the prisoners came to a camp where they found bubbling cauldrons of rice and hot sausages.

'They ordered us out of the patio and lined us up in a field across the road. As we left, grinning Japs held up steaming ladles of sausages and rice. The officer followed us to the field then began stamping up and down, spouting denunciations and abuse. When he calmed enough to be understood we heard this:

'When you came here you were told you would eat and be let to sleep. Now that is changed'

'"When you came here you were told you would eat and be let to sleep. Now that is changed. We have found pistols concealed among three American officers. In punishment for these offences you will not be given food. You will march to Orani [five miles to the north] before you sleep."

■ MENTAL TORTURE ■

'The accusation was a lie. If a pistol had been found, the owner would have been shot, beaten to death or beheaded on the spot. Besides, we knew that the searchers hadn't overlooked even a toothbrush, to say nothing of a pistol. The Japs simply were adding mental torture to the physical.'

Not all the men on the march received the same treatment. Some arrived in poor physical shape at the other end following their exertions but were nevertheless unaware that brutalities had taken place en route.

Left and below: **Two scenes from 'The Death March' from Bataan which claimed the lives of 10,000 men.**

Above: **Mean Japanese guards staged a picture of a lavish prison camp Christmas dinner before removing the food from the hungry men.**

Some men even rode in trucks. For those still able to summon up the energy, there was ample opportunity for escape. Yet the death toll was a shocking one.

■ CAMP O'DONNELL ■

Those that did arrive at the destination – Camp O'Donnell – had further nightmares to counter. Four out of ten men inside the primitive camp died of disease, starvation or cruel treatment during the first three months of their stay.

There is evidence that the Death March won its inglorious name thanks to the actions of a few barbaric guards, that the orders from Lt General Homma, now in charge of the Philippines, were to treat the prisoners humanely, to supply food, water and medicines along the way.

Yet the cruelty and viciousness of the guards were symptomatic of the treatment dished out to US, Australian, Canadian, British, New Zealand and Dutch prisoners of war all over the Japanese empire.

The range of obscene abuses which were time and again revealed to prisoners stemmed from their culture which viewed fighting men who surrendered as dishonourable. For them, truly brave men would die in battle rather than lay down their arms to the enemy. Consequently, few Japanese soldiers were ever taken prisoner and those that were often tried to commit suicide.

Japan was a signatory of the Hague Convention of 1907 which decreed that prisoners of war must be treated humanely. Alas, the convention went on to rule that prisoners should be treated similarly to the men in the army of the state which

The Japanese were brutal even to their own men, and prisoners got even worse treatment

held them. The military regime in Japan was brutal even to its own men. Captains frequently lashed out at sergeants who in turn would bash rank and file soldiers. There was to be little respite for the unfortunate men who fell into the clutches of the forces of the Rising Sun.

Red Cross officials were hindered and hampered in their attempts to observe what was happening in the Japanese-run prisoner of war camps. Despite enormous efforts, they were blocked by a deluge of red tape. When Red Cross officials did gain entry to camps, they were closely

One Red Cross delegate was executed after being charged with conspiracy against the Japanese

chaperoned, their access to prisoners severely restricted and their questions stonewalled. One Red Cross delegate was himself executed after being charged with conspiracy against the Japanese government. Few, if any, parcels of aid were received by the men in the camps.

Below: **Though General Homma, the victor in the Philippines, was thought 'too soft' by Japanese High Command, he was still condemned by a war crimes trial.**

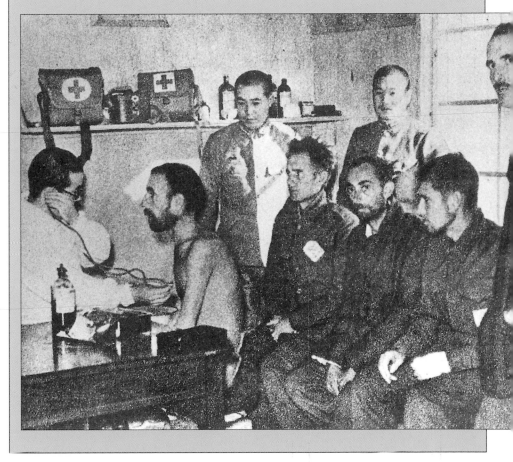

◆ EYE WITNESS ◆

Ken Gray, of the Australian 8th Division, was one of the few to survive an epidemic of cholera when he was a 22-year-old Japanese prisoner of war in the Far East.

❝ I finished up in a camp called Sonquari. The number of deaths that occurred in that camp during the height of the cholera far outweighed deaths that occurred in others. There were no medical supplies. On one day alone 38 men died.

I saw a doctor on one occasion weep over the body of a dead Allied soldier, saying he could have saved the man with a sixpenny packet of Epsom Salts.

One of my mates was about the first to die from cholera. Within 36 hours he had gone from a man weighing perhaps 10 stones to five stones. The normal body fluids ran out of him from the bowels and the mouth. His body just shrivelled up. Unless cholera is arrested in three to four hours, that is the end.

I was delirious for seven days. Apparently I was given a saline solution in a home-made injection kit which saved me.

The survivors were not strong men, they were lucky men. Those far more robust than I went down like ninepins. I feel the public today cannot possibly comprehend how shocking conditions were. ❞

■ TORTURE ■

The worst treatment was meted out to Allied airmen who were kept blindfolded and bound until they were tortured, usually until they died.

It has left the names of Japanese prisons including Rangoon Central Gaol in Burma, Changi and Selerang Barracks in Singapore, Padang on Sumatra, Kuching in Borneo, Karenko in Formosa and Mukden in Manchuria haunting the annals of wartime horror. Perhaps the most appalling memories among survivors are those evoked by the building of the Burma-Siam railway.

Above: Changi jail, 'home' for thousands of British and Australian servicemen following the fall of Singapore.

Japan was looking for a means of transporting supplies to its posts in southern Burma other than the sea route which was subject to attack by the Allies. Only when this route was complete could the Japanese consider extending their imperial tentacles into India.

On 14 May 1942 a 3,000 strong force left the confines of Changi prison to begin work on the massive project. Before the main building force left Changi, however, the camp commander Major General Fukuye insisted that all prisoners sign the following statement. It read: 'I, the

Japan was looking for a means of transporting supplies to its posts in southern Burma

undersigned, hereby solemnly swear on my honour that I will not under any circumstances attempt escape.'

British troops under the authority of Lt Colonel E. B. Holmes and Australians under Lt Colonel 'Black-jack' Galleghan flatly refused to make the undertaking.

Outraged, Fukuye ordered the men from Changi into Selarang Barracks, cut their meagre rations to a third and allowed the 15,000 men to get water from just two taps. It meant endless hours of queuing in the heat of the day. The overcrowded conditions were a sure indicator that disease epidemics would follow.

The Japanese commander was finally convinced to make his request for prisoners to sign an outright order. Leaders of the prisoners decided this meant the men could sign the document but were not obliged by it.

There was little to inspire the men to escape. Deep in Japanese territory, they could not rely on local assistance nor, with their Western appearance, could they disappear into a crowd. The penalty for escape bids was death.

Four men who had slipped away from an island working party were brought to Changi in order that senior Allied commanders could witness the executions. Two of the men were British, two Australians. The older of the two Australians pleaded for the life of his young accomplice, maintaining he had only been obeying orders. It was to no avail.

■ FIRING SQUAD ■

All four came before a firing squad manned by Sikhs who had joined the Japanese. Their aim was awry and round upon round had to be let off before the bullets found their targets. The courageous older Australian, Corporal R. Breavington – who had refused to be blindfolded – finally bellowed: 'For God's sake, shoot me through the head and kill me.' It was a deeply scarring experience for those forced to watch.

Four more Australians who later attempted to escape from Burma were killed in the same grotesque way. The brigadier who witnessed their executions wrote in his diary: 'They spoke cheerio and good luck messages to one another and never showed any sign of fear. A truly courageous end.'

The courageous Australian bellowed: 'For God's sake shoot me through the head'

The nightmare of those sent to build the railway began almost immediately. Travelling to the site was deeply unpleasant. For example, the men who first left Changi were crammed into the hold of two rusty tubs for 12 days during which time the only food given to them was rice. Dysentery was rife and rats had the monopoly on the floor space and the health of the men plummeted.

■ SLAVE LABOUR ■

Still, when they arrived they were put to work as slaves of the Nippon empire. The Japanese, eager to complete the ambitious task and armed with strict schedules and quotas, brought in more and more prisoners to speed up the rate of progress. Suddenly, life in the harsh prison camps seemed positively bearable set against the appalling conditions which faced men in the camps along the railway. Each new batch of men was horrified at the sight of those who had been working there for weeks or months before.

Malaria, dysentery, infestations, biting bugs and all manner of other jungle afflictions plagued the working men. Eventually, when monsoon rains had turned camps into mires, the dreaded cholera spread, shrinking men's bodies through painful dehydration.

As their clothing deteriorated, men were reduced to wearing only under-pants or home-made loin cloths, battered hats and often no footwear at all. At night there were few mosquito nets available, exposing the men to all the dangers of the tropics. Often, they had little more than a blanket or rice sack with which to cover themselves.

As previously, the lack of proper nutrition brought its own miseries for the men who had to battle with problems brought about by vitamin and calorie deficiencies. Every day, the toil made huge demands on the

Below: **Two bridges built over the River Kwai with the sweat and blood of Allied prisoners of war.**

◆ THE JAPANESE IN BURMA

he Japanese invasion of Burma egan in mid-December 1941 in he south of the country. General da's Southern Army seized the egion's airfields and began ombing Rangoon. On 20 January 942, the main ground assault began from the direction of Raheng. The Allies struggled to hold back the tide but on 8 March Rangoon fell. The British and Empire forces, reinforced by Chinese troops, then carried out a fighting withdrawal to India.

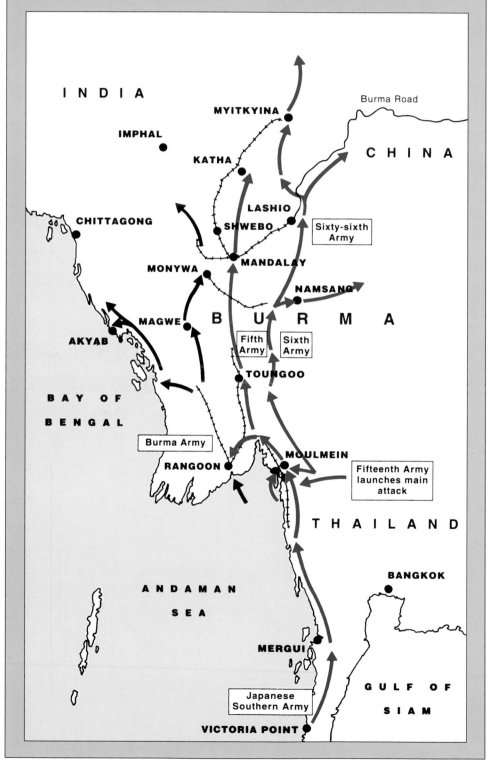

men's bodies which grew ever more emaciated and unfit for work.

Work began at both ends of the railway and the parties were to join up in the middle. It entailed clearing vast tracts of jungle, felling giant trees and constructing cuttings. The tools they had were primitive and all the clearance of rocks and stones had to be done by hand. Men worked by day and night, when their labours were lit by bamboo fires. Even the elephants brought in to assist in the heavy work lost their health.

There were stories of extreme mental torture as well as physical hardship. Sometimes the guards threw rocks and boulders at the men working below. Others forced individual prisoners to push mighty

Men worked by day and night in the light of bamboo fires; even the elephants fell ill

rocks up a steep gradient. It would take every ounce of the victim's strength to stop the rock from crushing him and others below. Those who perished by plunging down the forested ravines or being crushed by rock falls were considered by their comrades to be the lucky ones.

In total, more than 60,000 Allied prisoners were used on the project alongside 270,000 forced labourers from China, Malaya, Thailand, Burma and India. These conscripted civilians enjoyed even fewer comforts than the prisoners with no medical facilities at hand and less concept of hygiene and discipline.

It was undoubtedly the commitment and enterprise of the medical men which saved many Allied lives. One such hero was Lt Colonel

Right: Printed leaflet dropped by B-29s on 28 August 1945 into POW camps in Japan, Taiwan, Sumatra and Malaya. The drop killed three and seriously injured two.

Edward 'Weary' Dunlop. His dedication to the survival of his fellow men never wavered nor did his courage in the face of the tyrannical Japanese. The plucky Australian wrote in his secret diary: 'I pledged myself to face them unflinchingly.'

■ WHIRLING SWORD ■

Dunlop was in Java before he and his men were moved to work on the railway. During his time in captivity he leapt between a Japanese soldier charging with a bayonet and one of his crippled patients; stood almost unblinking while an enraged Japanese commander whirled a sword around his head; defied Japanese orders to force patients into work and carried one of his men like a baby across to a sadistic commander, pronouncing: 'This man can't walk, Nippon.'

He kept a radio set, an offence punishable by death in Japanese eyes.

> *Dunlop was chained to a tree trunk; four men fixed their bayonets and prepared to charge*

In the absence of the necessary evidence, an officer screamed at him: 'We know all about you and your set. You will be executed but first you will talk.'

When he refused to co-operate, Dunlop was chained to a tree trunk and four men with bayonets fixed prepared with the customary screeches and yells to charge.

'Have you a message for relatives? I will convey,' barked the officer.

'Conveyed by a thug like you? No, thanks,' said Dunlop. Only after several hours was he cut loose.

Dunlop devised a system to treat men dying of cholera. The steam from water boiled in petrol cans was funnelled through a lorry feed pipe and mixed with rock salt. The saline solution was then stored, filtered through cotton wool, fed into bamboo pipes and into a syringe. It helped to save countless Australian lives.

Afterwards, Dunlop, who died in 1993, said: 'I can say that the Australians outworked and outsuffered any nationality on that accursed river [Kwai]. I hardly ever saw a man refuse to go out in another's place or a man's spirit break until the time came to turn his face to the wall.'

Work was for the most part completed by September 1943 when the two ends met near Three Pagodas

---

レンゴウグンホリョヘ
ALLIED PRISONERS

The JAPANESE Government has surrendered. You will be evacuated by ALLIED NATIONS forces as soon as possible.

Until that time your present supplies will be augmented by air-drop of U.S. food, clothing and medicines. The first drop of these items will arrive within one (1) or two (2) hours.

Clothing will be dropped in standard packs for units of 50 or 500 men. Bundle markings, contents and allowances per man are as follows:

BUNDLE MARKINGS				BUNDLE MARKINGS			
50 MAN PACK	500 MAN PACK	CONTENTS	ALLOWANCES PER MAN	50 MAN PACK	500 MAN PACK	CONTENTS	ALLOWANCES PER MAN
A	3	Drawers	2	B	10	Laces, shoe	1
A	1-2	Undershirt	2	A	11	Kit, sewing	1
B	22	Socks (pr)	2	C	31	Soap, toilet	1
A	4-6	Shirt	1	C	4-6	Razor	1
A	7-9	Trousers	1	C	4-6	Blades, razor	10
C	23-30	Jacket, field	1	C	10	Brush, tooth	1
A	10	Belt, web, waist	1	B	31	Paste, tooth	1
A	11	Capt, H.B.T.	1	C	10	Comb	1
B	12-21	Shoes (pr)	1	B	32	Shaving cream	1
A	1-2	Handkerchiefs	3	C	12-21	Powder (insecticide)	1
C	32-34	Towel	1				

There will be instructions with the food and medicine for their use and distribution.

C A U T I O N

DO NOT OVEREAT OR OVERMEDICATE   FOLLOW DIRECTIONS

INSTRUCTIONS FOR FEEDING 100 MEN

To feed 100 men for the first three (3) days, the following blocks (individual bundles dropped) will be assembled:

3 Blocks No. 1
(Each Contains)

2 Cases, Soup, Can
1 Cases Fruit Juice
1 Case Accessory Pack

3 Blocks No. 2
(Each Contains)

3 Cases "C" Rations
1 Case Hosp Supplies
2 Cases Fruit

1 Block No. 5
(Each Contains)

1 Case Soup, Dehd
1 Case Veg Puree
1 Case Bouillon
1 Case Hosp Supplies
1 Case Vitamin Tablets

1 Block No. 7
(Each Contains)

1 Case Nescafe
1 Sack Sugar
1 Case Milk
1 Case Cocoa

1 Block No. 3
(Each Contains)

1 Case Candy
1 Case Gum
1 Case Cigarettes
1 Case Matches

1 Block No. 10
(Each Contains)

3 Cases Fruit
2 Cases Juice

Above: In the Japanese prisoner of war camps, men had to queue in the heat of the sun to collect their meagre rations. This is the officers' mess at Kanburi.

Pass. The railway was peppered with graves of men who died as they worked. An estimated 12,000 British, American, Australian and Dutch men died. In addition, 70,000 of the Asian labourers perished.

■ DIET OF RATS ■

Life had not improved much in the camps during this period. Officers were tortured in order that the Japanese might elicit military information. Hospitals were periodically cleared so that the ailing patients could join work parties. Food was reduced to snails, rats and snakes as the tide of war turned against Japan and supplies were sunk at sea.

Scores of prisoners were shot, stabbed or died from exhaustion during the forced marches

In Borneo there were a series of forced marches inflicted on the captive Allies as the liberating forces closed in. This claimed the lives of scores of prisoners who were shot, stabbed or died from exhaustion en route. Prisoners installed after just such a march at the Ranau camp were subsequently massacred in August 1945 before the arrival of Australian forces. Only six Australians who escaped on the march or from Ranau itself survived.

It wasn't only captured troops who suffered at the hands of the Japanese. There were an assortment of Dutch women who had been residents of the invaded Dutch East Indies, Australian nurses and British women snared in Singapore and an assortment of Western children and other refugees. They, too, were victims of forced marches, food shortages and disease.

The Japanese showed their disregard for the fairer sex when 22 nurses were washed up on an island beach after their boat was sunk off Singapore. All the surviving ship's crew were bayonetted and the nurses were herded into the sea where a machine gun was turned on them. Just one survived.

In 1994, Prince Mikasa, brother of the Emperor Hirohito and a cavalry officer in China in 1943 and 1944 admitted Japanese responsibility for war crimes. Besides talking of atrocities committed on the battlefield, he also spoke of an incident in 1931. That year a team of investigators from the League of Nations led by

◆ **EYE WITNESS** ◆

English-born Dickson Smith, who emigrated to Western Australia, recalls some of the horrors of being a captive of the Japanese.

❛ The main thing about the tropics is the insects and small animal life. There are barking lizards, croaking bull frogs, red ants, black ants, flying ants, dragonflies measuring four inches across the wings, wasps, hornets and cockroaches. in addition there are mosquitoes, some big and black, others white, and bugs which latch onto your skin. I kept wondering what my family was doing at home. Each month of the war seemed like an eternity. News from the outside world was sadly lacking and we felt totally isolated. I came to realise it was probably the most eventful period of my life, an adventure without pleasure filled with new and unimagined horrors and the terrible uncertainty of when it would all end. ❜

the Earl of Lytton had visited Japan to analyse who was to blame for the start of the Sino-Japanese conflict. There was apparently an attempt to poison them. The Prince claimed that 'fruit laced with cholera germs' had been administered to the high-ranking officials in their food although none of them died.

The bitterness felt towards Japanese camp guards by those who came home is still very much in evidence on four continents, even today.

> *The bitterness felt towards Japanese camp guards is still very much in evidence, even today*

Left: **When they were released, PoWs were shadows of their former selves. Years of deprivation took their toll on previously strong, healthy men.**

JUSTICE AT NUREMBERG

World War I was billed as the 'war to end all wars'. It wasn't. And warfare came of age when the World War II broke out just 21 years after the end of the Great War. It was politically more complex and shocking than its predecessor, its effects far more wide-ranging and its aftermath wholly different.

For the victors there was the dilemma of how to lay the foundation for tomorrow's world and build a lasting peace. More immediately, in their custody were some of the architects of Hitler's Third Reich. What would be their fate now?

Some believed that with Hitler, Himmler and Goebbels dead (all three committed suicide) the arch villains were already dispatched. There were a series of other trials taking place simultaneously in Germany dealing with those at the dirty coal face of the concentration camps. Their obscene activities amounted to murder of the worst degree for which suitable charges and penalties already existed.

Many felt the high-profile men held, including diplomats and banking chiefs, could essentially be absolved. There was at least a

Left: The Palace of Justice at Nuremberg housed the most momentous trial of the century. *Below:* Tojo, the Japanese Prime Minister, was brought to justice in 1948.

question mark over whether or not these men truly had blood on their hands. In addition, it would be wrong to punish a military man – soldier, sailor or airman – for doing his job during times of war.

Others thought the only good Nazi was a dead one and that those held by the Allies should be shot, the sooner the better. With so many lives lost and families in mourning, it was wrong to allow these types to posture and pedal their propaganda ever again.

■ TRIALS OF NAZIS ■

Yet there was a different school of thought, equally enthusiastic about wiping the slate clean, which won the day. The captured Nazi leaders should face a trial and answer for their crimes. The Americans particularly among the Allies felt the application of the rule of law was fair and correct and would define once and for all who was guilty by association. Here was the opportunity of laying the blame for the disaster that befell Europe in the early Forties on the heads of those responsible and freeing the German people as a whole of guilt. The trials held at the end of

World War I were nominal, inconclusive affairs which barely reflected the carnage that had gone before. This time it was going to be different.

Once the British, French and Russian allies had been persuaded, there were a host of difficulties to unravel which would make the difference. Firstly, no statute books held charges which befitted the appalling crimes carried out in the name of Nazism. There was the clear danger that if the prosecutions were bodged, the world's best-known killers could end up getting away with murder.

The legal brains of the victorious countries got to work in creating charges which reflected the crimes which had taken place, identifying and closing possible loopholes at the same time as creating a scrupulously even playing field, fair to all sides. All this had to be done swiftly. Everyone

> **There were four main charges at Nuremberg, including Crimes Against Humanity**

was keen to get the business of retribution out of the way in order to look ahead.

Afterwards, there were accusations that the charges had been worded to fit the crimes and so offended the principle of justice. Yet as early as November 1945 the groundwork was laid for the most sensational trial of the century, Nuremberg, an astonishing feat by any standard.

There were to be four main charges which broadly covered a variety of individual acts. They were Crimes Against Peace, which covered the planning and waging of aggressive war; War Crimes, including the execution of prisoners of war; Crimes

Left: The judges at the Nuremberg trials (*left to right*) Britain's Mr Justice (Norman) Birkett and Lord Justice Lawrence, US Attorney General Francis Biddle and Judge John J. Parker.

Against Humanity, dealing with the the genocide of Jews and other minorities; and finally the Common Plan or Conspiracy.

The final charge was defined as follows: 'All the defendants, with divers other persons, during a period of years preceding 8 May 1945, participated as leaders, organisers, instigators or accomplices in the formulation or execution of a common plan or conspiracy to commit, or which involved the commission of, Crimes Against the Peace, War Crimes and Crimes Against Humanity... and are individually responsible for their own acts and for all acts committed by any persons in the execution of such plan or conspiracy.'

An important precedent was being created, that acts of war were the responsibilty of the individual not just the state.

Each of the four countries on the winning side had their realms of responsibility. The Americans sought prosecutions on the conspiracy count in addition to probing the criminal organisations like the SS. The British proceeded with the charge of Crimes Against the Peace. The Russians and

The trials created the precedent that acts of war were the individual's responsibility

the French dealt with the remaining two charges for Eastern and Western powers respectively.

Due to the complexity of the conflict, it remained an irony that Russia was prosecuting Germany for war crimes when it was also involved in waging aggressive wars against Poland and Finland.

■ WHY NUREMBERG? ■

The army of occupation in Germany was almost rivalled in size by that of lawyers, interpreters, researchers, clerks, prison guards, journalists and other observers linked to the Nuremberg Trial. Hearing the case were two judges from each of the main Allied countries, any four of whom would sit together at one time.

From America came Francis Biddle and John Parker, the British judges were Sir Geoffrey Lawrence and Norman Birkett. Professor Henri Donnedieu de Vabres and Robert Falco represented France while Russia sent Major-General I. Nikitchenko and Lieutenant-Colonel A. F. Volchkov. Prosecuting was

◆ EYE WITNESS ◆

Seaghan Maynes was a journalist working for Reuters who attended the Nuremberg trials. In 'Eyewitness at Nuremberg', a book by Hillary Gaskin, he recalls his impressions.

'The trial to me was a showpiece. It wasn't a juridical process; it was a revenge trial. This is my opinion and I think it was shared by a lot of other correspondents. It doesn't say that they shouldn't have been held because the purpose was to show crime followed by punishment, as an example to the other. But the legal process was very suspect. They made a charge to fit a crime after the crime had been committed. In that atmosphere, as distinct from now, I can see good reasons for having the trial because public opinion all over the world had been convinced that an example must be made. But take the case against Schacht. If Germany had occupied Britain, would our Minister of Transport, or somebody, be on trial for his life? Should Ribbentrop, the German foreign minister, have been executed? He was a diplomat; he didn't take part in any killing. I had niggling doubts about these things at the time. "What did he do to deserve death? After all his country was at war." In hindsight, I can say that the winner calls the shots and fixes the charges and the vanquished haven't as much of a chance as they should have. I wouldn't have missed it but I wouldn't want to see it again.'

◆ EYE WITNESS ◆

Following the armistice, John Gorman, VC, a 22-year-old captain in the Irish Guards, was put in charge of a German prison camp housing 500 men suspected of war crimes.

The camp was at Sieburg, near the Dutch border. The majority of men were Germans but there were some French, Belgian and Dutch collaborators who had been denounced in their local communities. They were accused of various crimes including slaughter and other atrocities.

I had six officers to help me. We were superimposed on a structure which already existed with an administrator, who was not thought to be a criminal, and his team of warders.

Our job was to run the prison as humanely as possible and to produce these people for trial before the war crimes commissions. We did what we could and organised football matches, sport and encouraged them to help in the prison garden.

I was given a platoon of Belgian soldiers to help me who had previously been members of the resistance. They didn't like the inmates at all. I was away for a weekend in Brussels when I received a frantic telephone call from the officer in charge. The Belgians had decided they couldn't stand the prisoners having the freedom to look out of the window. Every time one of them had the temerity to show his face, the Belgians tried to shoot him.

I rushed back, thinking I would find a pile of corpses. Fortunately, the Belgians were bad shots. All we had was a badly pock-marked wall. They didn't hit any of them.

As for the British officers there, we prided ourselves on our discipline. We ran the prison on orthodox lines. We certainly didn't want them to say we were doing to them what they had been doing to others.

For their part, the prisoners were very servile and obsequious. They would have kissed our boots if they thought it would do them any good. The bully, when bullied, becomes a coward. They were not nice people.

It was very difficult finding enough to eat. Everybody was hungry. The Dutch had been eating their bulbs, the seedcorn of their future, to keep themselves alive.

We had to order the German authorities in the local town to produce food for the prison. The inmates had diet of soup, rice and occasionally meat.

One man died while I was there. He was terribly thin and a doctor told us he was severely undernourished. That gave the idea that something was amiss.

I used to patrol the prison at all times of day and night. Early one morning I happened on the German prison administrator leaving the kitchen with a large suitcase. When I ordered him to open it, I found it was fulll of meat. He was stealing meat from the prison kitchens to sell on the black market and had made a fortune. It was most underhand when you consider that the majority of the prisoners were his fellow countrymen. He went straight into a spare cell. 🙶

Justice Robert Jackson from the United States, Sir Hartley Shawcross from Britain, Francois de Menthon of France and General Roman Rudenko of Russia.

The location of the trial was not a random choice. Few could forget the impressive and sinister rallies held by Hitler and his Nazi followers at

Nuremberg before and after the outbreak of hostilities. And it was there in in 1935 that a special session of the Reichstag unanimously approved the Nuremberg Laws, depriving Jews of German citizenship and associated rights.

■ PALACE OF JUSTICE ■

The session went on to agree further anti-Jewish legislation which prevented marriages between Germans and Jews and forbade the employment of German servants by Jews. Nuremberg represented the fiery heartland of the Nazi doctrine and it would be here that the evil light would be extinguished.

Symbolically, the notorious city, in the American zone of occupation, was by now in ruins, the victim of the saturation bombing so potently used by the Royal Air Force in the last few years of the conflict.

The courtroom of its Palace Of Justice was now to house the momentous – and frequently monotonous – proceedings that were designed to

Right: **US soldiers mounted a heavy-weight guard outside the Palace of Justice during the trial.**

Above: **Flamboyant Göring refused to be cowed. Here he is quizzed by journalists shortly after being captured.**

turn the page on one of the worst periods of Europe's history.

In the dock were 20 by-now infamous characters from Hitler's hierarchy. Hermann Wilhelm Göring had been a long time cohort of Hitler and was best known as Commander in Chief of the German air force. In addition, he was a general in the feared SS and the Reich Hunting and Forest Master.

Next to him sat the enigmatic Rudolf Hess, a co-author of 'Mein Kampf', the book by Hitler explaining his dubious philosophies. A question mark remained over his sanity following his mysterious flight to Britain in 1941, apparently to seek

a peace settlement with King George VI. He had been held by the British since then, latterly in an asylum.

Joachim von Ribbentrop was next in the line-up. A Nazi party member since 1932, he rose quickly to become Hitler's adviser on foreign affairs. His devotion was rewarded with the post

It was no coincidence that the trials were held at Nuremberg, the site of the great Nazi rallies

of ambassador to London between 1936 and 1938 and finally with the plum job of foreign minister.

World War I spy Alfred Rosenberg took part in the abortive 1923 putsch

when Hitler tried to seize power in Germany. The anti-semitic Reich Minister for the Occupied Eastern Territories wrote 'Mythos des 20 Jahrhunderts', a tome reflecting the Fatherland's distasteful philosophies under Hitler.

Lawyer Hans Frank had been Bavarian Minister of Justice and was in 1939 made Governor General of occupied Poland. Ernst Kaltenbrunner, born in Austria, coupled his own legal talents with those of commanding key SS units. Wilhelm Frick was also legally trained and strongly associated with the SS. When the war ended, he was Reich Protector.

Former schoolmaster Julius Streicher was a well-known anti-Semite who had been editor of the Fascist newspaper Der Sturmer and honorary leader of the thuggish SA force.

Wilhelm Keitel was a Field Marshal and held the title Chief of Oberkommando der Wehrmacht. His loyalty to Hitler was never in question.

Dr Walther Funk, paymaster of the Reich machine in his post as President of the Reichsbank, sat beside another economist Hjalmar Schacht, latterly out of favour with the Führer.

leading light in the propaganda machine. Tried in his absence was Martin Bormann, Hitler's personal secretary who went missing in the chaos of the Reich's last days. Only in 1973 was it established that, despite various post-war sightings of him, he had probably committed suicide in May 1945.

'In the prisoners' dock sit twenty broken men... their personal capacity for evil is forever past. Merely as individuals their fate is of little consequence to the world. What makes this inquest significant is that these prisoners represent sinister influences that will lurk in the world long after their bodies have returned to dust.

Ex-teacher Julius Streicher had been editor of the anti-semitic newspaper Der Sturmer

The second row of defendants began with Karl Dönitz, the U-boat supremo who had become Commander in Chief of the Kriegsmarine and, on Hitler's death, Chancellor to the ruins of Germany.

Beside Dönitz sat longtime Hitler Youth leader Baldur von Schirach, who wrote songs and verses which inspired the country's youth to lay down their lives without question.

Fritz Sauckel was an eminent Reich Defence Commissioner assigned to the organisation of slave labour who sat in the shadow of charismatic Albert Speer, the man responsible for arming Germany's forces.

Diplomat Franz von Papen was seated beside Alfred Jodl, Chief of Staff in the High Command of the Wehrmacht, who in turn was next to Constantin von Neurath, an eminent member of the Reichstag and SS General.

▶ MARTIN BORMANN ■

Dr Arthur Seyss-Inquart was an SS general, Reich minister without portfolio and President of the German Academy. Erich Raeder, the former Commander in Chief of the German navy, was next to him and beside him sat Hans Fritzsche, a

The defendants were charged with all or a combination of the charges. The trial opened on 12 November 1945. Making the opening speech was Justice Robert Jackson, the American attorney:

'The privilege of opening the first trial in history for crimes against the peace of the world imposes a grave responsiblity. The wrongs which we seek to condemn and punish have been so calculated, so malignant and so devastating, that civilisation cannot tolerate their being ignored because it cannot survive their being repeated.

'That four great nations, flushed with victory and stung with injury, stay the hand of vengeance and voluntarily submit their captive enemies to the judgement of the law is one of the most significant tributes that power ever has paid to reason...

Above: **Top Nazis on trial** *(front row, left to right)* **Göring, Hess, Ribbentrop, Keitel, Rosenberg.** *Back row (left to right):* **Dönitz, Raeder, Shirach, Sauckel, Jodl.**

Martin Bormann went missing at the end of the war but was tried in absentia

We will show them to be living symbols of racial hatreds, of terrorism and violence and of the arrogance and cruelty of power.'

It was for the prosecution to prove that the primarily frail, vacant and occasionally quivering men lined up in the dock should be held responsible

Jackson's examination of Göring drew crowds into the courtroom expecting to see this swaggering man scythed to pieces. In fact, gloating Göring turned the tables and batted off questioning from the American prosecutor with ease. Jackson, hindered in no small part by inaccurate translations of evidence against

Guilty of racial hatreds, terrorism, violence and the arrogance and cruelty of power

Above: Lt Thomas F. Lambert, Jr presents the case for the US prosecution against the absent Martin Bormann, who was sentenced to death but never caught.

for the calamities of wartime Europe. One of the first problems facing the prosecution was that posed by Hitler's one-time deputy, Rudolf Hess.

Hess was showing the signs of a disturbed character – and had been since his escapade to Britain back in 1941. Was it right for a man in this state to stand trial? The decision to press charges against him came in December 1945 when he admitted that he faked amnesia to fool British interrogators and Hess chose to conduct his own defence. Many privately felt that he was nevertheless a man devoid of many of his senses.

■ HERMANN GÖRING ■

For different reasons Hermann Göring caused the Allied prosecutors a major headache, too. Göring was a somewhat glamorous and charismatic figure, the last commander of

Right: Hermann Göring conducted his own defence at Nuremberg and made mincemeat of US prosecutor Jackson.

the Richthofen Fighter Squadron of World War I known for his unscrupulous and amoral behaviour. He relished the luxuries of life including good wines and flashy cars and had acquired a magnificent collection of art during his tenure, pilfered from the cultural capitals of Europe. Even in the courtroom, he could not contain his lustful gaze which appraised young women on the staff. More than that, he was witty, razor sharp and intelligent as Justice Jackson discovered to his cost.

Göring, had to appeal to the court to control the defendant and finally retired flustered and frustrated. It was left to the cool-headed Briton Sir David Maxwell-Fyfe who was assisting with prosecution to compromise the German.

Despite his straitened circumstances, Göring was always ready with a quip for the interpreters, an insult for witnesses or a putdown for his fellow defendants as they tried to wriggle out of some damning evidence as it was presented against them. He

PATTON

US General George Patton won his reputation for revelling in warfare after making comments like: 'Compared to war, all other forms of human endeavour shrink to insignificance. God, how I love it.' He also wrote to his wife: 'Peace is going to be hell on me.'

remained a dominating force roundly unapologetic for his beliefs.

For the most part, the other defendants sat listening raptly to the evidence, occasionally aloof but for the most part displaying little or no emotion. Hess would read from a book of fairy tales by the Brothers' Grimm. Those with sufficient English occasionally corrected or aided the interpreters. Others simply sank into a murky silence. Stripped of their braid and regalia, they were grey-faced men who knew they faced a bleak future.

The prosecution relied heavily on documentary evidence – and there was plenty of it

Kaltenbrunner suffered a stroke early in the proceedings but recovered sufficiently to appear in the dock again later on. Streicher suffered a heart attack in January 1946 but later returned to the stand.

Finally, tension gave way to tedium as each day passed. The

Right: The Japanese war crimes trial went on for three years after the end of the war and lacked the drama of Nuremberg.

prosecutors relied heavily on documentary evidence – and there was plenty of it. With characteristic Germanic efficiency, the Nazi regime had noted many of its activities down for its own future reference. Even in the grimmest of the concentration camps details of the exterminations were put into writing. The worst of the massacres were often filmed and now provided excellent evidence. Although there were many German witnesses to the Holocaust, it was felt their testimony could be unreliable because they might try either to ingratiate themselves with the victors or else to settle old scores with the defendants in the dock.

■ DEATH SENTENCE ■

The trial ended on the last day of August 1946 and the International Military Tribunal, as it was also known, began delivering its judgement a month later.

A dozen of the men on trial were sentenced to death. Hess received a life sentence, six more were also jailed and three were acquitted.

On 16 October 1946 the gallows were prepared in the prison gymnasium at Nuremberg. In a final

flourish, Göring cheated the executioner by taking a cyanide pill smuggled in to him, perhaps by his Swedish wife Karin.

Julius Streicher screeched 'Heil Hitler' before the trap door opened beneath him

First to the rope at 1.11am was Hitler's Foreign Minister Ribbentrop. As the black hood was placed over his head, he called out: 'I wish peace to the world'.

Next to the gallows was Field Marshal Wilhelm Keitel. His final words were: 'More than two million German soldiers went to their death for their fatherland. I follow now my sons – all for Germany.'

Filing up the steps after him were Kaltenbrunner, Rosenbrug, Frank (a recent convert to Roman Catholicism), Frick, Streicher (who screeched 'Heil Hitler' before the trap door opened beneath him), Sauckel, Jodl and Seyss-Inquart. Martin Bormann was sentenced to death in absentia.

Funk and Raeder were jailed for life, Doenitz for 10 years, Speer for 20 years, Neurath for 15 years and Schirach for 20 years. Fritzsche, Schacht and von Papen were acquitted.

It was far from the end of the story. The Subsequent Proceedings dealt with a further 182 Nazis from the doctors who set up experiments in the concentration camps to industrialists, government ministers, military men and SS officials.

Twenty-six were sentenced to death while the rest received various prison sentences, forfeited property or were acquitted. The last of the Subsequent Proceedings ended in October 1948.

When Japanese Emperor Hirohito came before General Douglas MacArthur on the surrender of Japan in September 1945, he told him: 'I come to you to offer myself to the judgement of the powers you represent as the one who bears sole responsibility for every political and military decision made and action taken by my people in the conduct of the war.'

Yet despite his frankness, he was not charged as a war criminal. It wasn't until December 1948 that General Tojo, one of Japan's prime ministers during the war, was hanged along with six others. He had tried but failed to kill himself even though a Japanese doctor refused to treat his wounds.

■ ATROCITIES ■

The accused were convicted of 'crimes against peace and responsibility for atrocities'. The sentence was carried out by the American Army at Sugamo Prison in Tokyo. A further 16 men were jailed for life their roles in the war.

Among those executed for war crimes was Lt General Homma, the Japanese commander victorious in

◆ EYE WITNESS ◆

Hugh Trebble, a clerk with the Royal Air Force, was taken prisoner by the Japanese on Java after fleeing Singapore.

I was taken prisoner at the beginning of March. We were rounded up in Dutch Air Force hangars at Tasek Malaja and dispersed all over the island. I was sent to Surabaya, the principle port on the north coast to help repair bomb damage – by scraping burnt sugar coating the jetties into the sea. We dug air raid shelters – which was against the Geneva Convention – and then began planting castor oil plants.

A party of about 30 was taken to a walled garden. Our guard was a Korean, built like a barn door. He was a Christian. He produced an English bible, selected me to read it and I started with verse one, chapter one of Genesis. While the others worked I sat beside him reading the bible, interpreting what I could for him.

Soon after we were lined up in a playing field with a manned Japanese machine gun post in each corner while they decided whether to shoot us or not.

The Japanese were very ready with their fists and their rifle butts.

I contracted malaria and eventually dysentery in two forms. I was finally sent for treatment at a hospital staffed by Dutch medics. After I recovered I was sent by boat to Singapore then on to Sumatra to build a railway. We managed to wreck three full-sized steam locomotives in the process!

We had to work 16 hours a day, seven days a week. We had a bowl of rice in the morning and a bowl of rice at night and it was all we had to live on. At our base camp we used to bury about 16 men a day.

The Japanese were utterly ruthless and they were all the same. It was impossible to find anything good about them. The only mitigating circumstances were that they treated their own troops in the same way they treated us.

One of the native soldiers pushed a Japanese guard while he was being beaten with a rifle butt. He was tied up with wire, put in a bamboo cage with no roof and kept there for days. Every time a guard went past he would poke his rifle butt in to give him a thump. Eventually, the bloke died. There was nothing we could do about it. We would squirm every day when we had to file past him – but that kind of treatment was commonplace.

When we were building the railway, we were beaten with rails and spanners. The thing to do was to stay concious. If you fell over and blacked out you were beaten and could get badly injured. One of the guards was so short he would make you stand in a monsoon drain in order to beat you.

When I was released in 1945 I was 6 stones 7lb instead of my usual 12 and a half stones. I was blown up like a balloon and as yellow as a guinea fowl.

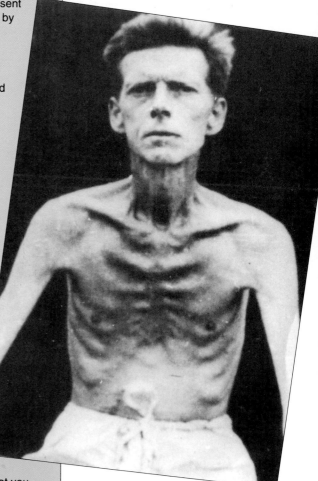

Above: **A PoW of the Japanese displays the classic signs of malnutrition.**

the Philippines who was removed by his overlords for being too soft. He ordered his men to treat the Filipinos as friends and refused to distribute propaganda criticising US rule. It was General MacArthur, whose forces had been routed in the Philippines, who ordered the trial of Homma.

The trial of Lt Gen Homma was ordered by US General Douglas MacArthur

Below: In the dock, those accused of carrying out war crimes on behalf of Japan listen intently to proceedings.

HITLER'S BODY

After Hitler shot himself in his Berlin bunker alongside his wife Eva Braun who had taken poison, his body was taken out and burned by the few remaining faithful in his entourage.

Yet Russian dictator Stalin was convinced that his arch enemy had somehow cheated death by using a double and staging the suicide. When the bodies were recovered by a Russian soldier in the rubble outside the bunker, it seems Stalin's crack troops from Smersh, a trusted security team, took over. The charred bodies of Hitler and Braun underwent not one but two post mortems as Stalin quested to know for certain whether they were the genuine articles.

After that, the fate of the bodies and their final resting place is subject to controversy. Some ex-Russian soldiers have claimed that Hitler and Braun, together with the Goebbels family, are buried at Magdeburg in a garage. A few historians are convinced the body is buried in the grounds of a Moscow prison. Others believe it to have been destroyed following Stalin's death.

Even if it was turned to dust, at least a few remnants remain. In 1993 a Russian journalist claimed she had held some of the the skull of Hitler in her hand after she discovered parts of it in the Moscow state archives. The two sections were believed to have been discovered in Berlin following the removal of the bodies. It is also thought that Hitler's jaw bone and that of Eva Braun are kept in Moscow where they were taken for identification purposes.

HITLER

He was the world's most loathed and feared dictator yet German Führer Adolf Hitler's origins were, to put it kindly, unremarkable.

His book'*Mein Kampf* portrayed a rough and even deprived childhood. Not so. He was the son of a minor civil servant, the family was comfortably off, and Adolf was no more emotionally neglected and deprived than the next child.

Born in 1889 in Braunau, a small town on the Austrian and Bavarian border, Adolf was the sole surviving child of Alois Hitler and Klara Polzl. The two were second cousins and needed special dispensation from the church to wed. Alois was 23 years older than his wife and was marrying for the third time. By all accounts, he was a cold and stern man like many patriarchs of the age.

At school, the young Hitler showed little application and was fired with enthusiasm by one teacher only, a fervent German nationalist called Dr Leopold Potsch.

Hitler resolved to become an artist, apparently oblivious to his glaring lack of talent. His chosen career caused friction between himself and his father, who hoped the young Adolf would be a civil servant. It appears Hitler thought little of his father, who died in 1903, although he remained fond of his gentle mother. He even took steps to conceal the chequered background of Alois, who was born illegitmately of peasant stock.

Curiously, there is believed to have been Jewish blood in the family, which is perhaps why Hitler chose to hide his roots. For after he was twice turned down for the Academy of Fine Arts in Vienna he looked for something or someone to blame for his failure. He focused on the Jewish people.

When World War I broke out, Hitler joined the army and served with distinction in the trenches, winning two decorations for bravery. Yet he failed to rise above the rank of corporal despite his dedication to Germany. His brooding hatred of authority made superior officers uncomfortable.

Germany's failure to win the war and its political floundering following the conflict left Hitler with a profound desire to renew the badly battered national pride and make Germany great again.

He got the taste for politics when he attended regular meetings of the German Workers' Party in Munich from 1919 and discovered a talent for public speaking.

By 1921 membership had swelled, it had changed its name to the National Socialist German Workers' Party, or Nazi Party, and Hitler was its leader.

An attempted rebellion led by Hitler in 1923 against the Bavarian authorities landed him in jail. From his cell he wrote *Mein Kampf*, setting out the theories on which his thrust for power would be based. Central themes were the detested Treaty of Versailles, which ended World War I, and the reviled Jewish race.

Germany was still a democracy and Hitler's party failed to make much of a mark in the 1928 elections. Yet thanks to the support of an industrialist and newspaper owner, Hitler managed to spread his message effectively throughout the country.

This message was music to the ears of many of Germany's six million unemployed. His popularity grew until, in 1932, the Nazi party won more than a third of the votes cast in the election. The following year President Paul von Hindenburg was struggling to contain the burgeoning power of the Nazis and invited Hitler to become Chancellor in the hope it would satisfy his lust for power.

At last Hitler had the chance to seize total domination with a programme of intimidation and aggression. Then, a year later, on the death of President Hindenburg, Hitler assumed the post of Führer – leader. Fair and free elections were not held again in Germany in his lifetime. He set about making his dearest ambitions a reality. Communism and socialism were ruthlessly quashed, Jews were hounded and unemployment was slashed. Further, he sought to give the esteemed German race a new empire of which they could be proud.

armoured divisions and eight motorised divisions sweep across the country. The Polish air force is shot out of the sky. Poland appeals to France and Britain to intervene.
Saturday 2: Poland remains under

fire – with Luftwaffe jets raiding the capital, Warsaw, killing at least 21 people. The National Service Act is passed in Britain. Hitler remains confident the Western powers will not act against him.

A furnace in the grounds of the German Embassy in London is lit to incinerate and destroy scores of papers and documents.
Sunday 3: Britain issues Germany with a 9am ultimatum. Unless Hitler

gives firm assurances within two hours that he will withdraw troops from Poland, Britain will be at war with Germany. When the 11am deadline passes without word, Britain goes to war. Hot on her heels, Commonwealth countries including India, Australia and New Zealand, also declare war on Germany. Eire declares itself neutral.

Speaking from 10 Downing Street, Prime Minister Neville Chamberlain broadcasts the grim news. 'This country is now at war with Germany,' he tells the House of Commons when it meets at noon. His voice wavered as he added: 'For no one has it been a sadder day than for me. Everything I work for, everything I hoped for, everything I believed through my public life has crashed in ruins.

'I trust I may live to see the day when Hitlerism has been destroyed so as to restore the liberty of Europe.'

Soon afterwards Winston Churchill made a stirring contribu-

tion. 'Outside the storms of war may blow and the land may be lashed with the fury of its gale, but in our own hearts this Sunday morning there is peace. Our hands may be active but in our consciences are at rest. . . We are fighting to save the world from the pestilence of Nazi tyranny and in defence of all that is most sacred to man.'

France delivers a similar ultimatum to Germany due to expire the following day. But it fails to await the outcome of its message to Berlin. By 5pm France is at war with the Third Reich.

In a joint Anglo-French declaration, both governments stated they would avoid bombing civilians and added there was no intention of using poison gas or germ warfare. Japan assures Britain of her neutrality in the war.

King George VI makes a personal broadcast to the nation. 'The task will be hard. There may be dark days ahead, and the war can no longer be confined to the battlefield. But we

can only do the right as we see the right, and reverently commit our cause to God.

'If one and all we keep resolutely faithful to it, ready for whatever service or sacrifice it may demand, then, with God's help, we shall prevail.'

The Royal Air Force drops six million propaganda leaflets on northern Germany.

Monday 4: A War Cabinet is brought together with Winston Churchill as First Lord of the Admiralty and Anthony Eden as Dominions Secretary. Both men had been in the political wilderness, following outspoken attacks on the British policy of appeasement towards Hitler. Although Labour and Liberal politicians refuse to join the war team they pledge full support for Chamberlain's government.

British passenger ship SS Athenia, out of Glasgow, is sunk by a German U-boat. There are 112 fatalities, 28 of them American. It causes considerable anti-German feeling in the USA, causing the Germans to insist that the sinking was staged by Churchill in order to create tension between the two countries.

The RAF makes early strikes against ships at Wilhelmshaven in the North Sea entrance to the Kiel Canal, although with only limited success.

Tuesday 5: French troops fire their first shots of the campaign, engaging the Germans on the Western front and crossing into the Saarland. German troops continue to make

---

Polish lancers on horseback confront well-equipped German Panzers on the Bzura

---

huge gains in Poland, crossing the key Vistula river. The USA declares its neutrality, embargoing arms shipments to those countries at war.

Wednesday 6: General Jan Smuts persuades his South African cabinet to declare war on Germany.

The Polish government leaves Warsaw as the invaders threaten the city boundaries.

Thursday 7: German troops are sent in reply to French forays into Third Reich territory.

Identity cards are introduced into Britain through the National Registration Bill.

Saturday 9: Polish lancers on horseback confront well-equipped German Panzers on the Bzura river. German troops march on into Warsaw.

Sunday 10: Canada declares war on Germany.

Tuesday 12: The armed forces' entertainment organisation ENSA is formed.

An Anglo-French Supreme War Council convenes under Chamberlain and French premier Daladier. Convoys are planned for merchant shipping in an attempt to combat the threat from U-boats.

Saturday 16: Petrol rationing begins in Britain.

Sunday 17: Russia invades Poland from the east by prior arrangement with Germany.

Monday 18: Britain's aircraft carrier HMS Courageous is sunk by a U-boat torpedo. Although there are 687 survivors of the sinking, more than 500 sailors are lost.

Tuesday 19: Chamberlain declares that the war will not end until Hitlerism is defeated and destroyed. Privately, he believes that it will take three years to win.

The first war casualty list is published in Britain.

Wednesday 20: Chamberlain claims that at least six U-boats have been sunk by the Allies in the first few weeks of action.

Friday 22: Germany and Russia agree on the partition of Poland. The Soviets lay claim to 76,000 square miles in the east of the country, while Germany earmarks most of the west.

Saturday 23: Famous Austrian psychoanalyst Sigmund Freud dies.

Wednesday 27: Warsaw falls. In a war budget, Chancellor Sir John Simon raises income tax to seven

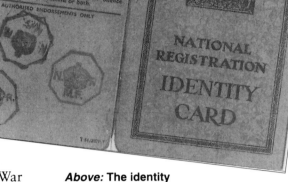

Above: The identity card issued to all in a flurry of bureaucracy by the British government.

shillings and six pence (thirty-seven and a half pence) in the pound, the highest rate ever levied.

September 29: Poland surrenders. An estimated 60,000 Poles were killed, 200,000 injured and a further 700,000 taken prisoner.

September 30: Polish government-in-exile bases itself in France.

◆ EYE WITNESS ◆

E. Rickman was a schoolboy when the war broke out and served with the Home Guard as London was bombed.

❛ I was a cyclist messenger for the Home Guard in Raynes Park, south west London, at the start of the war. When the air-raid sirens went it was my job to go around to arouse the members of the Home Guard and have them report for duty.

Just as I came back from doing that I reached off my brand-new £6 Raleigh bike to open the double gates of the detached house which was the Home Guard headquarters when a bomb dropped. I knew nothing more until I came around inside the building, lying on a settle in the hallway.

The sergeant told me a shell had landed in the road just three feet away from me. I was blown 35 feet onto the front steps. My bike was a write-off. I had not got a scratch or a bruise. ❜

Above: Actor Douglas Fairbanks was mourned by millions.

■ OCTOBER ■

Sunday 1: British men aged between 20 and 22 become eligible for conscription into the armed forces.

Thursday 5: Hitler enters the Polish capital, Warsaw, in triumph.

Friday 6: Hitler makes peace proposals to Britain and France. He assures neighbours Belgium and Holland of his friendship, too.

Sunday 8: RAF reconnaissance plane shoots down a German flying-boat in the North Sea.

Monday 9: The Prices of Food Bill is introduced to control profiteering. Chamberlain announces a committee of ministers to take charge of the British economy.

Wednesday 11: The British Expeditionary Force in France now numbers 158,000 men who, together with 25,000 vehicles, have been shipped across the Channel in just five weeks to help defend France.

Saturday 14: More than 800 men die when the battleship Royal Oak is torpedoed at her home base of Scapa Flow. Only 396 crew members survive the surprise attack. No one had believed a U-boat could penetrate the defences of the harbour or that a torpedo would pierce the outer defences of the ship.

Monday 16: German bombers attack the Firth of Forth and the naval base at Rosyth. Three British ships are damaged while four enemy bombers are brought down.

Tuesday 17: French troops pushed back in the Saar.

Thursday 19: The Turkish government signs a mutual assistance pact with France and Britain.

Saturday 21: The Luftwaffe attacks North Atlantic convoys.

Saturday 28: Nazis insist all Jews in the Third Reich should wear a yellow Star of David.

Monday 30: The British government produces a White Paper outlining the horrific treatment meted out to Jews in Nazi concentration camps. It declares: 'The treatment is reminiscent of the darkest ages in the history of man.'

■ NOVEMBER ■

Monday 6: First major air battle on the Western front takes place.

Wednesday 8: Hitler survives an assassination attempt in Munich, where he was celebrating the anniversary of his bid for power – the Munich Putsch – staged in 1923. Seven people are killed and more than 60 are injured when a bomb hidden near the platform from which the Führer was speaking exploded. Hitler himself had already finished his speech and left. The Nazi newspaper, the Volkischer Beobachter, claims British agents were responsible for the outrage.

Monday 13: First German bombs hit British soil when the Shetland Islands come under enemy fire.

Two German supply ships are scuttled after being cornered by the Royal Navy.

Saturday 18: Eighty people are killed when the Dutch ship Simon Bolivar hits a new type of magnetic mine laid in the North Sea. Other neutral ships are sunk by the same method. Minesweepers endeavour to clear the shipping routes of the hazards but their efforts are hampered by the mines running adrift.

Three IRA bombs explode in London's Piccadilly Circus.

Wednesday 22: German aircraft sow parachute-retarded mines in the Thames Estuary.

Thursday 23: RAF fighter aircraft shoot down seven German planes over France.

Thursday 30: The Soviet Union invades neighbouring Finland after the tiny independent country refused Stalin's demands to hand over some land. Heavy fighting is reported along Finland's defensive Mannerheim line.

■ DECEMBER ■

Saturday 2: South African Defence Force bombers force the German liner Watussi to be scuttled.

Wednesday 6: Britain pledges arms for Finland.

Tuesday 12: Hollywood film star Douglas Fairbanks dies in his sleep of a heart attack, aged 56.

Wednesday 13: The Battle of the River Plate. 'Pocket battleship' Admiral Graf Spee, which has been picking off merchant ships in the South Atlantic and Indian Ocean, is attacked by British cruisers Exeter, Ajax and Achilles. After a day-long battle, the Graf Spee limps into Montevideo harbour with 36 dead, 60 injured and widespread damage.

Thursday 14: The League of Nations expels Russia

Above: The life of Canadian soldiers in Britain appeared tranquil to those back home.
Left: Australian troops were the subject of curiosity when they marched through a British village.

for its hostile actions against Finland.

Friday 15: Uruguayan authorities order the Graf Spee out of the safety of its harbour before full repairs can be carried out.

Sunday 17: Hitler orders the Graf Spee be scuttled rather than fall into British hands. Captain Hans Langsdorff takes the 10,000-ton warship out of Montevideo harbour where she is blown up and sunk. Three days later Langsdorff kills himself.

Tuesday 19: First Canadian troops arrive on British soil.

Friday 22: Women working in munitions factories demand the same pay as men.

Tuesday 26: The first squadron of Australian airmen arrives in Britain.

Sunday 31: Determined Finns see off another Russian division.

1940

After the 'phoney' war ended, Britain was bombarded by Hitler's Luftwaffe, and city after city fell foul of the Blitz. Yet despite deprivation and desperation, the island stood firm while other European countries succumbed. Hitler's planned invasion was called off.

■ JANUARY ■

Monday 1: Conscription in Britain is extended to include all able-bodied men aged between 20 and 27.

Friday 5: Secretary of State for War Leslie Hore-Belisha resigns and is replaced by Oliver Stanley.

Monday 8: Butter, sugar and bacon rationed in Britain.

Tuesday 9: More than 150 people are feared dead after a Union Castle passenger liner hits a mine off the south east coast of Britain.

German bombers claim three merchant ships in the North Sea.

Monday 15: The British government comes under pressure to review its blackout policies after it is revealed that nearly twice as many people have been killed on the roads than by enemy action.

Tuesday 16: British submarines Seahorse, Undine and Starfish are sunk after operating in enemy waters.

Wednesday 17: A cold snap hits Europe with the River Thames freezing over in London for the first time in more than 50 years.

Sunday 21: War at sea intensifies as 81 crew are lost when the Grenville is sunk.

US golfer Jack Nicklaus is born.

Monday 22: British destroyer Exmouth is sunk by U-boat off Wick, Scotland, with the loss of all hands.

Friday 26: Nazi leaders warn Germans that listening to a foreign radio station is a serious offence, carrying the death penalty.

■ FEBRUARY ■

Thursday 1: Frustrated by its lack of progress, the Red Army launches another offensive against the Finns in the disputed region of Karelia.

Thursday 7: Two convicted IRA men are hanged in Birmingham.

Saturday 10: In Czechoslovakia, Jews are ordered to shut down their shops and cease any business involvements.

Hitler orders all German U-boat commanders to consider neutral shipping as fair game

Tuesday 13: Soviet Red Army troops make gains at last in their invasion of Finland.

Friday 16: The Royal Navy destroyer HMS Cossack sails into a Norwegian fjord and its sailors free 300 British prisoners from the German tanker Altmark. All the men had been taken when their ships were sunk by the Admiral Graf Spee. Britain protests to Norway about its apparent protection of the prison ship.

Saturday 17: Norway registers a protest with the British government about its flouting of neutrality.

Monday 19: Destroyer Daring is torpedoed, with 157 casualties.

Tuesday 20: Hitler orders all German U-boat commanders to consider neutral shipping as fair game. Norway, Sweden and Denmark register their anger at the ruling.

Friday 23: The crews of HMS Exeter and HMS Ajax are cheered through

Above: The passions depicted in the romantic melodrama *Gone with the Wind* still shine out 50 years later.
Far left: Vapour trails over St Paul's.

the streets of London when they return home after their successful battle against Admiral Graf Spee.

Thursday 29: Newcomer Vivien Leigh wins an Academy Award for her performance as Scarlett O'Hara in the hit film Gone with the Wind. The award for Best Actor goes to Robert Donat for his performance in Goodbye Mr Chips.

■ MARCH ■

Saturday 2: British India liner Domala bombed in the English Channel with the loss of 100 lives.

Thursday 7: Prestige liner the Queen Elizabeth completes a secret dash from Britain across the Atlantic to wait out the war in the safety of American waters.

Wednesday 13: After a bloody conflict claiming hundreds of thousands of lives, the Russian war with Finland is concluded with a peace treaty. Russian troops were continually outmanoeuvred by their enemy. Only sheer force of numbers settled the war in Stalin's favour. The embarrassing rout has made Stalin look silly in the eyes of the world.

Saturday 16: A mission by American envoy Sumner Welles intended to prepare the ground for peace talks in Europe fails, with both Britain and Germany unequivocal in their refusals to negotiate.

Scapa Flow naval base is bombed by Luftwaffe. The action claims the life of the first British civilian killed in an air raid.

Tuesday 19: RAF seek revenge for the Scapa Flow raid by bombing a German air base.

Wednesday 20: Paul Daladier resigns as premier of France to be succeeded by Paul Reynaud.

Monday 25: The new two-seater Mosquito bomber aircraft makes its maiden flight.

Wednesday 27: Under the orders of SS chief Himmler, the foundations for the concentration camp at Auschwitz are laid.

Below: **Winston Churchill (centre) in 1940 with British and French senior military officers. From left to right, Ironside, Georges, Gamelin and Gort.**

CHURCHILL

Looking back, it seems Winston Churchill, Britain's best-remembered statesman, was born to be in politics.

Churchill's father before him was a respected Conservative Member of Parliament and he was descended from an established and powerful family. Yet 'Winnie' had a sad childhood, in which he was noted only for his academic shortcomings. It appeared for much of his life that he would shine more at soldiering and writing than ever he could in the see-saw world of politics.

He was born in 1874, the son of Lord Randolph Churchill and New Yorker Jennie Jerome. He had little to do with his father, who despaired of his underachievement in the classroom. The young Churchill adored his beautiful mother but she in turn made her business elsewhere than the nursery. In her absence, there was a nanny, Mrs Everest, nicknamed 'Womany' by her charge, with whom she forged a deep and lasting bond.

He was rebellious and uncontrollable, and it wasn't until he discovered a love of English literature that Churchill put his mind to work at Harrow public school. He went on to the Royal Military College at Sandhurst, excelling in the subject of soldiering.

Flirting first with journalism, Churchill seized the opportunity to see some action on India's troubled North West Frontier in 1898. There followed a spell in the Sudan before he choose a life of politics. His first bid to enter Parliament was unsuccessful and he returned as a reporter to Africa to cover the Boer War.

Aged 26, Churchill won a seat in the House of Commons in 1901, representing Oldham for the Conservatives. Just three years later, frustrated by the confines of the Tory party, he became a Liberal. His change of colours happily coincided with a Liberal election victory. Now he was in the Cabinet, enjoying a taste of power until he unexpectedly lost his seat at the subsequent election.

While he was campaigning for a by-election he met Clementine Ogilvy Hozier, who was to become his loyal wife.

During World War I his reputation became stained with the debacle at Gallipoli. As First Lord of the Admiralty, Churchill was convinced the assault against the Turks would be a sparkling success. It turned into a bloody failure for which he carried the can. Churchill saw out the next few years as a soldier in France until he was recalled to the Cabinet in 1917.

Between the wars, Churchill fared best as a writer. He faded from the political scene after his brutish treatment of the workers during the 1926 General Strike. From the back benches he continually warned about the threat posed by Germany but few heeded his words.

Then, in 1939, as war was declared, Prime Minister Chamberlain capitalised on Churchill's experience and made him First Lord of the Admiralty once more.

Churchill's spirited commitment to Britain's role in the war won hearts and minds. By May 1940 he was head of a coalition government charged with bringing Britain through its darkest hour. And win through he did although his performance was by no means exemplary and his support was far from universal.

Many of the military disasters which plagued Britain during the opening years of the war could be laid at Churchill's door, notably the British rout in Norway in 1940 which cost Chamberlain his job.

Yet Churchill had one abiding point in his favour – he was committed beyond question to the defeat of Hitler. He refused to entertain ideas of a negotiated peace even when Britain appeared to be on the brink of defeat. His energy and enthusiasm for the obliteration of Nazism were inexhaustible. Such was his fervour he even overcame a loathing of Communism in general and Stalin in particular to bring about the downfall of Hitler.

Nevertheless, Labour was elected at his expense in the 1945 elections and he was compelled to lead the opposition until the Tory victory in 1951. Churchill stayed in politics until the end of his life. When he died on 24 January 1965, the nation recognised his colossal contribution with the honour of a state funeral.

Thursday 28: Dutch fliers shoot down a British bomber near Rotterdam in error, with the loss of one life.

■ APRIL ■

Tuesday 2: Scapa Flow comes under attack from Germans again, who also target North Sea convoys.

Mussolini orders a general mobilisation, involving all Italians aged 14 years plus.

Dutch troops placed on full alert along the German border.

Wednesday 3: In a Cabinet reshuffle, Churchill is given the task of directing the war effort.

Friday 5: RAF strikes at German ships in the Kiel Canal.

Monday 8: British submarines torpedo three German ships.

Germany invades Denmark and Norway. Denmark is overrun with only nominal resistance.

Tuesday 9: Germans take control of Norwegian capital, Oslo, with the arrival of airborne troops in order to ensure the Third Reich can maintain

Above: **German soldiers feel the chill on their march into Norway.**

The German cruiser Blücher *is hit and sunk with loss of 1,000 crewmen*

---

vital supply lines from Scandinavia. Norwegian forces are driven back but still put up fierce resistance as they retreat. Major Vidkun Quisling, who gave his name to World War II traitors, sets up a national government in the occupied capital. He appeals for fighting to end, while Norway's King Haakon asks every Norwegian to take up arms.

Wednesday 10: Battle of Narvik.

Thursday 11: German cruiser Blücher is hit and sunk with the loss of 1,000 crewmen. Royal Navy

submarine Spearfish leaves the 'pocket battleship' Lützow with extensive damage.

Saturday 13: Second Battle of Narvik. The Allies emerge victorious, with the loss of eight German destroyers and a U-boat.

Sunday 14: Royal Navy submarine Tarpon falls victim to a minesweeper.

Monday 15: Allies land in Norway. Quisling's short-lived government resigns in favour of an 'Administrative Council'.

British unemployment figures fall to 973,000, the lowest jobless total since 1920.

Tuesday 16: British forces land in the Faeroe Islands.

Wednesday 17: Stavanger, the Norwegian port now in German hands, is raided for a second time by the RAF.

Thursday 18: British submarine Sterlet is sunk by German aircraft off the Norwegian coast.

Friday 19: The Swiss government orders a general mobilisation, in fear of an attack from Nazi Germany.

Monday 22: When the Allied Supreme War Council meets in Paris, Poland and Norway are represented.

Wednesday 24: British troops forced

to pull out of Trondheim after clashes with German forces.

Thursday 25: Allied forces driven out of Lillehammer, central Norway.

■ MAY ■

Wednesday 1: Trondheim is evacuated by the Allies. Norwegians surrender at Lillehammer.

German bomber carrying magnetic mines crashes in Clacton, Essex. Four Germans and two people on the ground are killed, and a further 156 are injured.

Women in Britain are given the green light to work in munitions factories by the Amalgamated Engineering Union.

Postage rates in Britain more than double, increasing from a penny to twopence halfpenny.

Thursday 2: Britain begins to evacuate its troops from Norway.

Sunday 5: Norwegian government-in-exile sets up in London.

Monday 6: American author John Steinbeck wins the Pulitzer Prize for his novel The Grapes of Wrath.

Wednesday 8: A Parliamentary

Right: Women at work on presses producing shells. It was in May 1940 that the Amalgamated Engineering Union gave the go-ahead for women in Britain to work in munitions factories.

motion rapping Chamberlain for the military failures in Norway fails by 81 votes. However, more than 40 government MPs join the opposition in condemning his leadership and a further 60 abstain.

Thursday 9: British upper age limit for conscription raised to 36.

Friday 10: Germany invades Holland, Belgium and Luxembourg with the by-now familiar tactics of 'Blitzkreig', or lightning war.

Chamberlain resigns. Churchill is prime minister, forming a coalition cabinet with Labour leader Clement Attlee as his deputy. 'I have nothing to offer but blood, toil, tears and sweat,' Churchill tells Parliament.

Sunday 12: The German armed forces continues their sweep through the Low Countries.

The Luftwaffe begins a bombing campaign in northern France.

In Britain, Germans are interned.

Rommel wins a key tank battle in northern France, spreading fear among French forces

---

Monday 13: The Dutch royal family flees to London as Dutch troops pull back in the face of the German invasion of Holland.

Tuesday 14: German army units under Field-Marshal von Runstedt cross River Meuse and the rugged landscape of the Ardennes to enter northern France.

Germans capture key port of Rotterdam. Meanwhile, the Dutch

government arrives in London.

British boat owners are required to register with the government.

Local Defence Volunteers – soon to be known as the Home Guard – created to protect Britain in the event of parachute attack or seaborne invasion. In the space of a week, 250,000 men enlist.

Wednesday 15: Dutch surrender as the German forces roll into Belgium.

Rommel wins a key tank battle in northern France, spreading fear and confusion among French forces.

Britain's weekly butter ration per person is halved to four ounces.

Thursday 16: Belgian government quits Brussels for London.

Friday 17: Germany continues to make gains in Belgium and north eastern France.

General De Gaulle counter attacks at Montcornet.

The RAF strikes at Bremen and Hamburg, vital German fuel depots.

Sunday 19: General John Gort, commander in chief of the British Expeditionary Force in France, orders a withdrawal of his men to the English Channel.

Monday 20: Invading Germans force a wedge between retreating French and British troops.

Tuesday 21: Bombs fall on English Channel ports while the RAF hits refineries in occupied Rotterdam. Hard-pressed British troops in northern France mount a counter-attack at the town of Arras.

Wednesday 22: The Emergency Powers Act passed in Britain, bringing businesses under state control and bringing a new brand of authority over the working population.

Thursday 23: British troops in fierce fighting as they are backed up to the coast of northern France.

In Britain Sir Oswald Mosley, leader of the British fascists, and his cohorts are arrested.

Saturday 25: Survivors of the British Expeditionary Force are surrounded on the French coast. Advancing German units are just 20 miles behind them. The Royal Navy succeeds in snatching nearly 28,000 men to safety.

Sunday 26: Evacuation of British, French and Belgian troops – code-named 'Operation Dynamo' – begins from Dunkirk. An official fleet is joined by a flotilla of small boats eager to aid the war effort and ready to brave enemy fire. Privately, officials estimate only 45,000 men will be saved. Within a week 338,226 men are taken back to Britain. There are 289 tanks, 64,000 vehicles and 2,500 guns left behind in France.

Tuesday 28: King Leopold III of Belgium surrenders.

Wednesday 29: Narvik, in Norway, is won from Germany.

Thursday 30: Italian dictator Mussolini makes his decision to enter the war known to Hitler.

The Luftwaffe bombs Paris, killing 45 people and injuring hundreds more

■ JUNE ■

Saturday 1: British troops on the run again in Norway.

In case of invasion, British road signposts are taken down.

Monday 3: Last ships leave Dunkirk under cover of darkness.

The Luftwaffe bombs Paris, killing 45 people and injuring hundreds more.

A night curfew is placed on all aliens and stateless people living in the United Kingdom.

Tuesday 4: Germans seize Dunkirk, taking 40,000 French prisoners.

French planes bomb Munich and Frankfurt in the reply to the German sorties against Paris.

Thursday 6: Germans penetrate French defences along the River Somme, with the defenders suffering heavy losses.

Right: **Although thousands escaped, there were scores of Britons left dead in the ruins of Dunkirk.**

◆ EYE WITNESS ◆

As a conscientious objector, Ron Tansley of Nottingham, England, refused to fight. After joining the Friends Ambulance Unit as a volunteer in 1940, at the age of 23, he nevertheless found himself in the thick of the action.

'I was a pacifist but I realised that I couldn't just stand by. I had to do something if it was only humanitarian work. Some of my greatest friends were in the forces and I certainly had no animosity towards those who did join up.

The factory where I was working began making aeroplanes so I left.

I came before two government tribunals, both very sympathetic, which decided my reasons for not fighting were genuine. I then joined the Friends Ambulance Unit. I was in various hospitals up and down the country working on the wards, from operating theatres to casualty, treating Blitz victims in London and Liverpool.

After two years training I was sent to Birmingham to study German culture and language. In the autumn of 1944 I was sent to Ostend. About 40 of us went in sections of ten. Mostly our orders came from the Red Cross. From there we went to Antwerp, which was receiving 100 German rockets a day at the time.

We were attached to a fire station. Whenever there was an alarm, we followed the fire engines. Once we arrived at a bombed cinema where hundreds of British soldiers had been killed.

As the front line pushed forward to the Rhine, it was our job to bring people back from their homes to the safety of a large hospital so the tanks could go straight through. We kept putting more and more people inside this three-storey building and tried to feed and care for them as best we could. Then typhoid broke out. We had to wrap the dead bodies in paper or what linen we could find. There were no coffins. Several hundred people died.

While I was there a German lit a bonfire in the grounds. I was walking past with a German helper when suddenly there was an explosion from the bonfire. A piece of shrapnel just went straight through the middle of the man next to me and killed him.

Eventually, I was sent to Hamburg. On the way some Germans tried to give themselves up to us but we wouldn't accept prisoners. I have never seen anything like the sight of that city. There was utter destruction for miles and miles. I wondered why the women and children had to suffer so much.

Apart from medical work we also traced lost relatives and worked with refugees, including a German Quaker who was put in a concentration camp because he refused to fight. I helped put him in touch with a contact in England.

We got great admiration from the soldiers because we were there when we didn't have to be. I don't think I heard any adverse remarks except in the military hospital I worked at in England.'

Friday 7: Allied troops pushed back again. French aircraft bomb the German capital, Berlin.

Saturday 8: Norway falls.

Monday 10: Italy enters the war, declaring its opposition to Britain and France. The New York Times reports the move with derision. 'With the courage of a jackal at the heels of a bolder beast of prey, Mussolini has now left his ambush. His motives in taking Italy into the war are as clear as day. He wants to share in the spoils which he believes will fall to Hitler and he has chosen to enter the war when he thinks he can accomplish this at the least cost to himself.'

Italy enters the war, declaring its opposition to Britain and France

Tuesday 11: Air raids begin on Malta while the RAF bomb the Italian city of Turin and petrol dumps in Italy's African colonies.

The RAF strikes German shipping in the Norwegian port of Trondheim.

Wednesday 12: Italian submarine sinks British cruiser Calypso off the island of Crete.

Friday 14: Victorious Germans enter Paris while Rommel captures the key northern port of Le Havre. The French government moves to Bordeaux in the south west.

Right: Germany's top brass, including von Ribbentrop and Rudolf Hess, joined Hitler in witnessing the humiliating peace deal made with France.

Saturday 15: The Soviet army occupies Lithuania.

Sunday 16: British submarine Grampus sunk by Italians off Sicily, the second British submarine loss in four days.

Monday 17: French leader Marshal Pétain orders his army to stop fighting as he seeks 'honourable' peace terms with Germany.

The liner Lancastria, carrying 3,000 British troops, is bombed at St Nazaire in northwestern France.

Tuesday 18: De Gaulle appeals to the French living in Britain to join him. 'Whatever happens, the flame of the French resistance must not go out and it will not go out.'

Saturday 22: French representatives sign an armistice at Compiègne, forced to use the same train carriage in which the Germans capitulated 1918. Hitler presided over the humiliation of France, half of which will now be occupied by Germany.

Italy bombs the British stronghold of Alexandria, Egypt.

Sunday 23: De Gaulle announces the launch of a French National Committee based in London which will continue to fight against Hitler.

French representatives sign an armistice at Compiègne

Monday 24: France led by Marshal Pétain signs a peace accord with Italy near Rome.

Tuesday 25: A ceasefire in France takes effect from the early hours.

London hears air raid sirens in the early hours for the first time.

Friday 28: Churchill recognises Charles de Gaulle as the leader of the 'Free French', now forming into a volunteer legion.

LINES OF DEFENCE

During World War II, Europe was crossed with lines of defence, none of which would stand the test of a sustained offensive.

THE CURZON LINE:
The line that divided Poland following its defeat by German and Russian forces in 1939. It had been drawn by Lord Curzon after World War I and allowed the Russians to claim they were only taking back what was rightfully theirs.

THE MAGINOT LINE:
French defensive line built between the wars which was easily overrun by Germany in 1940.

THE SIEGFRIED LINE:
Also known as the West Wall, Germany's border defensive line penetrated by Allied troops in 1944.

THE MANNERHEIM LINE:
The line between Lake Lagoda and the Gulf of Finland beyond the Russo-Finnish border; the main line of fortification for the Finns which was finally overwhelmed by superior numbers of Russians.

THE GUSTAV LINE:
Germany's line across Italy which ran through Cassino and encompassed some fearsome natural defensive positions. It held the Allied troops at bay for five months in 1944.

German aircraft bomb Jersey.

Saturday 29: Swiss artist Paul Klee dies. He had been a professor at Düsseldorf until expelled by the Nazis in 1933.

Sunday 30: Germans occupy the island of Guernsey.

■ JULY ■

Monday 1: Marshal Henri Pétain moves the French government to Vichy, where it operates as a satellite to the powerful Germans. The established Third Republic is dissolved and the familiar cries of 'Liberty, equality, fraternity' are to be replaced by the Germanic 'Work, family, fatherland'.

Jersey is occupied by the Germans. British forces had already pulled out after deciding that the defence of the Channel Islands would be too problematic. The British evacuated

many islanders, crops and cattle though some people chose to remain.

British milk increases to fourpence (two new pence) a pint.

Right: **Marshal Pétain, though leader of the new France, was a German puppet.**

Right: Leon Trotsky, born Lev Davidovitch Bronstein, and his wife in exile in Mexico shortly before Trotsky's death at the hands of a vicious Stalinist agent. Trotsky had been defeated by Stalin in the power struggle that followed Lenin's death.

The government asks women to conserve wood by wearing flat heels.

Tuesday 2: Hitler begins work on plans to invade Britain.

Wednesday 3: Royal Navy attacks a French naval squadron in Algeria to keep it out of German hands. It happens after a French commander ignores a British ultimatum to sail his ships to Britain or America. The bombardment from the British kills 1,000 French sailors.

Friday 5: Romania throws itself behind Hitler and the Axis powers.

Destroyer Whirlwind sunk by a U-boat off Land's End.

Saturday 6: British submarine Shark scuttled off Stavanger after sustaining damage in German attacks.

Tuesday 9: Royal Navy chases Italian ships back into port after skirmishes at Cape Spartivento.

RAF begins night bombing operations over Germany.

Tea rationing introduced in Britain. Everyone is allowed two ounces a week.

Wednesday 10: Battle of Britain gets underway with Luftwaffe attacks on English Channel convoys and a blitz on the Welsh docks. Luftwaffe chief Hermann Göring hopes to lure the RAF into dog-fights over the English Channel to deplete its waning strength still further.

In Britain the British Union of Fascists is barred.

Saturday 13: Italians launch an attack on the British from Ethiopia.

Sunday 14: Bastille Day in France is declared a 'day of meditation'. The Free French, led by de Gaulle, lay wreaths at the London Cenotaph.

Tuesday 16: Japanese government resigns under pressure from the powerful army.

Wednesday 17: Britain closes the Burma Road, a supply route for the Chinese army, following fierce demands from the Japanese.

Friday 19: Hitler, speaking at the Reichstag, appeals to the Allies to listen to reason and halt the war.

Saturday 20: British destroyer HMS Brazen is sunk off Dover.

Battle of Britain gets underway with Luftwaffe attacks on English Channel convoys

Casualty list reveals 336 Britons were killed last month, 476 injured.

Sunday 21: Czechs join the host of exiled governments in London.

Tuesday 23: In a third War Budget, Chancellor Sir Kingsley Wood raises income tax to eight shillings and sixpence (forty-two and a half pence) in the pound. A 33 per cent purchase tax on luxury items is also introduced to help cover the costs of war, estimated at £3,470,000 for the coming year.

Wednesday 24: Four hundred French sailors die when a neutral liner shipping them back to France is torpedoed by the Germans.

Thursday 25: In Germany the use of forced labour from occupied territories is announced.

British-held Gibraltar is evacuated of women and children.

Monday 29: Dover harbour attacked.

British Air Ministry accuses Germany of using Red Cross planes for reconnaissance.

■ AUGUST ■

Thursday 1: Russian foreign minister Molotov speaks out against Britain and America while declaring his country still neutral.

Friday 2: Italy gathers troops on the border of Libya, and Italian colony, and British-held Egypt.

A French military court condemns de Gaulle to death in his absence.

Meanwhile, the Vichy government continues to harry former leading lights of the Third Republic, including ex-prime minister Paul Daladier and former army commander General Maurice Gamelin, who have been arrested and charged with 'causing the defeat of France'.

Sunday 4: Italy invades British Somaliland from Ethiopia

Monday 5: Residents of the Third Reich will now need to carry an Ahnenpass, or Certificate of Ancestry, to prove they and their family have been kept racially pure during the past 150 years.

Thursday 8: Rates of pay for British servicemen increase by sixpence (two and a half pence) a day. The weekly rate for a private now stands at seventeen shillings and sixpence (eighty-seven and a half pence).

Friday 9: British government states its intention to withdraw its troops from Shanghai and north China.

Below: **Dulcie Street, Manchester, became one of hundreds of residential and commercial roads wrecked in the Blitz.**

THE GEORGE CROSS

World War II saw the institution of the George Cross. Its creation was announced by King George VI on 23 September 1940 with the words: 'Many and glorious are the deeds of gallantry done during these perilous but famous days. In order that they should be worthily and promptly recognised I have decided to create at once a new mark of honour for men and women of all walks of life.'

The George Cross (left) is Britain's highest bravery award that may be received by a civilian. Among the first to receive one was Thomas Alderson, an Air Raid Precautions detachment leader on the home front, for bravery during enemy attacks on Bridlington in Yorkshire. Bomb disposal experts Squadron Leader John Dowland, Leonard Harrison and Major Cyril Martin also received awards. The George Medal (right) is the country's second-highest decoration for bravery awardable to civilians.

Saturday 10: HMS Transylvania is sunk off Northern Ireland after being hit by a torpedo.

Sunday 11: Britain's coastal ports come under bombardment from 400 Luftwaffe planes. British claim 65 hits for the loss of 26 RAF aircraft.

Monday 12: Wasting food is now against the law as Britain fears for future food supplies.

Tuesday 13: Christened 'Eagle Day' by the Germans, who believed they would have won dominance of the British skies by now, it has been

dominated by dog-fights across southern England. Once again, it seems British fliers inflict great losses on the attackers while sustaining far fewer casualties.

Thursday 15: Another day of bombardment this time from 1,000 Luftwaffe planes. Airfields and radio installations remain the prime targets of the German bombers.

Friday 16: Sixth day of aerial harassment of southern England by German air force.

Saturday 17: British warships attack ports in Italian-held Libya

The Duke of Windsor, the former King Edward VIII, who abdicated so he could marry American divorcée Wallis Simpson, is sworn in as governor of the Bahamas.

Sunday 18: Still more swoops by the Luftwaffe over southern England. The RAF suffers less than a quarter of the losses of the Luftwaffe.

Monday 19: Italian troops move into Berbera, the capital of British Somaliland. Evacuated troops head for Aden.

'Never in the field of human conflict was so much owed by so many to so few'

Tuesday 20: In Parliament, Churchill pays tribute to the courage of the men of the RAF. 'Never in the field of human conflict was so much owed by so many to so few.'

Wednesday 21: Exiled Bolshevik Leon Trotsky dies after assassin Ramon Mercader, a one-time confidant, plunges an ice-pick into his skull. Trotsky was working from his base in Mexico towards establishing international socialism. His killer was almost certainly working for

Above: **German soldiers gather at a port in northern France in preparation for 'Operation Sealion', the invasion of Britain. Hitler was forced to postpone the operation, and in the end it never came.**

Trotsky's old enemy, Stalin.

Saturday 24: London Blitz begins with an all-night bombing raid.

Sunday 25: RAF takes revenge for London strikes with a night raid on Berlin, dropping not only bombs but also propaganda leaflets. All aircraft involved were reported to have returned safely to base.

Monday 26: Luftwaffe planes shed bombs on County Wexford, killing three Irish girls. The Eire government makes a protest to Hitler.

Tuesday 27: Air raids continue over southern England, London, and now the Midlands. In total, 21 towns and cities are hit.

Wednesday 28: The Vichy government abandons laws in France which protect Jews.

Thursday 29: Germany says sorry to Eire over the Wexford bombing.

■ SEPTEMBER ■

Sunday 1: British destroyer Ivanhoe sinks off the Dutch coast after running into a mine.

Tuesday 3: Britain barters leases on two naval bases with the USA in exhange for 50 destroyers.

Hitler sets a date for 'Operation Sealion', the invasion of Britain. It is to be 21 September.

Wednesday 4: A furious Hitler promises Britain will suffer for the air raids it carried out against Berlin.

Thursday 5: In the casualty figures for August, it is revealed 1,075 civilians were killed in enemy action, while 1,261 were seriously injured.

A Royal Navy submarine sinks the troop ship Marion, with the reported loss of 4,000 German fighting men.

Saturday 7: German air attacks on Britain are increased. Night raids on sites by the River Thames claim 306 lives but Britain declares it has suffered only about a third of the aircraft losses inflicted on Germany.

Sunday 8: More bombardments under cover of darkness, this time killing 286 civilians and injuring 1,400.

Monday 9: London under attack from 350 Luftwaffe planes causing devastation in the East End.

Italians bomb Tel Aviv, killing 111.

Tuesday 10: Buckingham Palace damaged in another night of heavy German bombing.

Wednesday 11: A daylight air raid on London kills more than 100 people while the Channel port of Dover comes in for heavy bombing.

Thursday 12: Germany claims the RAF are dropping destructive Colorado beetles over its potato crops.

Buckingham Palace damaged in another night of heavy German bombing

Friday 13: Italy moves troops across the border from Libya into Egypt.

Sunday 15: Largest air raid to date launched against London. Meanwhile the RAF targets invasion forces gathering in French and Belgian ports. BBC assertions that 185 Luftwaffe planes were shot down over London in a day are later disproved. The actual figure was 56.

British units strike at advancing Italians in Egypt and claim to have inflicted severe losses.

Monday 16: London landmarks including Bond Street, Piccadilly and Park Lane, are struck in night raid.

Tuesday 17: With his attempt to cripple Britain through air raids apparently failing, Hitler postpones his invasions plans. 'Operation Sealion' is postponed short term.

In the Commons, Churchill announces that, in the first half of September, 2,000 civilians have died under enemy fire. The number of fatalities in the armed services in the same period is just 250.

Thursday 19: London and Brighton bombed. Minister of Labour Ernest Bevin announces that more than 51,000 have registered as conscientious objectors.

Sunday 22: The Japanese land in French Indochina.

Evacuee ship City of Benares, whose passengers include 99 children bound for Canada, is sunk by a U-boat torpedo. Only 46 survive while more than 300 are drowned.

Left: It was a relief to the government when Buckingham Palace was bombed, showing war hit rich and poor alike.

Monday 23: De Gaulle and a force of Free French are taken to Dakar, Senegal, by the Royal Navy.

Tuesday 24: London suffers 18th successive night raid. Southampton and Brighton also bombed.

The king introduces the George Cross and George Medal 'for valour and outstanding gallantry'.

Civilian casualties during September amounted to nearly 7,000 dead and 10,000 injured

Wednesday 25: Norwegian King Haakon is deposed by the German invaders. Vidkun Quisling's government is installed.

Friday 27: Japan signs a ten-year pact with Germany and Italy cementing ties between the three. German foreign minister Ribbentrop declares: 'The pact is a military alliance between the three mightiest states of the world, comprising over 250 million people.'

More daylight raids on Britain.

Monday 30: British civilian casualties in September amounted to nearly 7,000 dead and 10,600 injured.

■ OCTOBER ■

Tuesday 1: A British island off China is occupied by the Japanese.

Finland signs a treaty of alliance with Germany.

Thursday 3: Chamberlain resigns Conservative Party leadership through ill-health.

Friday 4: Hitler and Mussolini meet at the picturesque Brenner Pass for a three-hour summit.

Monday 7: In further anti-semitic measures, Pétain repeals a long-standing law which gives Algerian Jews French citizenship.

German troops go into Romania on the pretext of helping maintain law and order.

Tuesday 8: Churchill tells Parliament the Burma Road is to be reopened.

Wednesday 9: The Conservative Party unanimously elects Winston Churchill as party leader.

The musician and future Beatle John Lennon is born.

Dutch puppet government declares that Jews and half-Jews can no longer work in the public domain.

Saturday 12: Hitler further postpones 'Operation Sealion', the planned German invasion of Britain, until spring 1941. Meanwhile, night raids continue over London.

Tuesday 15: Sixty-four people die when a bomb blasts through the roof of Balham tube station where scores of people take nightly shelter from the air raids.

Royal Navy submarine Rainbow is sunk by Italian submarine Toti.

Monday 21: Churchill, in a radio broadcast, makes an emotive appeal

Below: **Carnage after a bomb falls through Balham tube station, which was being used as a night shelter.**

to the wavering French. 'Frenchmen, rearm your spirits before it is too late.'

Tuesday 22: Sir Stafford Cripps, British Ambassador, tries to entice Russia back to the Allies with a tempting co-operation plan.

Wednesday 23: Hitler meets Francisco Franco, Spanish fascist dictator, to discuss Spain's possible entry into the war. Last year Hitler turned down Franco's overtures to join the Axis powers. Now he is keen to enlist Spanish help. Franco remains cool. Hitler also tries to persuade Pétain to join Germany against Britain but fails.

Football legend Pele is born in Brazil, with the name Edson Arantes do Nascimento.

Britain's Fleet Air Arm bombs the Italian fleet at Taranto with spectacular success

---

Saturday 26: London suffers longest air raid yet, with widespread damage and many casualties.

Monday 28: Italians enter Greece from Albania. Churchill promises aid to the Greeks.

Tuesday 29: British troops bound for Crete to bolster Greek defences.

Thursday 31: British forces occupy a Cretan town while Italians make gains on the mainland.

Naples is bombed by the RAF for the first time.

British civilian casualty figures covering October reveal 6,334 dead and 8,695 injured.

◼ NOVEMBER ◼

Friday 1: Turkey announces its neutrality in the conflict between Italy and its old enemy, Greece.

Britain mines the Bay of Biscay.

Sunday 3: Greeks score a significant victory against the Italian invaders.

Tuesday 5: Franklin D. Roosevelt is elected for the third time as American president. The Democrat, the first American to return to presidential office for a third time, triumphed over his Republican rival by a majority of five million votes.

Saturday 9: Neville Chamberlain, the former British prime minister, dies of cancer, aged 71.

Above: Franklin D. Roosevelt became a record breaker when he was returned to office for a third consecutive term.

Trades unions and employers organisations are made illegal in Vichy France.

Monday 11: Britain's Fleet Air Arm bombs the Italian fleet at Taranto with spectacular success. Three battleships, two cruisers and two other vessels are crippled. As a reprisal, Italy mounts its only air raid against Britain.

In America the Jeep is put through its paces by the army for the first time.

Tuesday 12: Soviet foreign minister Vyacheslav Molotov visits Berlin for talks with Hitler.

Wednesday 13: Fantasia, Walt Disney's cartoon set to classical music opens in New York.

Thursday 14: In Coventry, 554 civilians die in ten-hour bombing raid by the Luftwaffe, in which 400 tons of bombs rain down on the city.

Friday 15: In the Polish capital, Warsaw, 350,000 Jews are confined to a ghetto.

Saturday 16: The RAF makes its most devastating attack yet on Hamburg, dropping 2,000 bombs.

Tuesday 19: Greek rout of Italian invaders continues.

Wednesday 20: Hungary aligns itself with the Axis powers.

Saturday 23: Romania signs up with Germany and her allies, too.

Wednesday 27: Romanian extremists, known as the 'Iron Guard', begin a killing campaign, claiming more than 60 victims.

STALIN

The man who brought wholesale misery and death to his people set out in life hoping to be a priest. But he was expelled from theological college when his Marxist sympathies became known.

Born in Georgia in 1879, Joseph Vissarionovich Dzhugashvili was a sickly child who survived the privations of a peasant upbringing to enter the theological college in Tblisi in 1894. But he had little time for the ritual of the Orthodox Church. Instead he was fired by the new socialist ideals brewing in Tsarist Russia. His growing involvement with this underground movement led to his expulsion from the college in 1899.

He became a Bolshevik in 1903 when the militant movement was led by Lenin. Before the 1917 Russian Revolution, he was repeatedly imprisoned and exiled for his radical views. In 1913 he was editor of the Bolshevik newspaper *Pravda* before another spell in Siberia.

There was little glory for Stalin, as he was now known, in the Russian Revolution or the years immediately following. Instead of fighting for the cause, he was battling on his own behalf, climbing up the rungs of power in the party. Then, as general secretary of the Communist Party, Stalin was waiting in the wings for absolute power on the death of Lenin in 1924. He strove to eliminate all his rivals and enemies, a pattern to which he was faithful throughout his leadership.

By 1929 he was undisputed leader of the Soviet Union. His simplistic way ahead was through five-year plans, which brutally enforced collectivised industry and agriculture on his people, making them poorer than ever before.

Peasants who objected were summarily shot or sent to labour camps where they would often perish in appalling conditions. An estimated ten million Russian peasants died while Stalin tried to modernise his country.

The terror he inflicted on his people knew no bounds. When he suspected a plot to oust him in the armed forces, he sought a terrible revenge, killing countless officers and men. And there were further purges, not only in the army but also among academics, teachers, politicians, judges and just about anyone who might conceivably disagree with him.

Privately, he was deeply unhappy. Two marriages failed and one of his sons committed suicide. His insecurities continued to fester, mirroring the liquidation of possible opposition.

Given this background, it is astonishing that Stalin managed to inspire such dedicated patriotism in his people after Hitler's attack. Yet still they rallied to his call. The mounting body count which had sparked the Russian Revolution during World War I failed to do anything other than unite the Soviet subjects.

Following the war Stalin's iron grip on the Soviet Union tightened still further. He orchestrated an empire and menaced non-Communist countries in the free world. Some say he became eaten up with suspicion to the point of being deranged. After his sudden death in 1953, his savage policies were denounced by his successors.

Royal Navy and Italian ships clash off Sardinian coast with both sides sustaining damage.

Friday 29: Initial plans for invasion of Russia are drawn up in Berlin.

Saturday 30: Civilian casualty figures reveal that 4,588 people were killed and more than 6,200 injured in the German attacks on Britain's major cities. Now Birmingham, Southampton, Sheffield, Manchester, Glasgow, Coventry, Dover, Liverpool and Brighton have all suffered appalling bomb damage as Luftwaffe chief Reichsmarschall Hermann Göring changes his tactics and aims to obliterate British industry.

■ DECEMBER ■

Sunday 1: Joseph Kennedy resigns as US ambassador to Britain. He is in opposition to what he believes is escalating American involvement in the conflict.

Monday 2: Franco is wooed away from Hitler with a British aid package. In return Franco declares he will stay neutral in the war.

Tuesday 3: Hungry Britons are promised extra rations of 4oz of sugar and 2oz of tea for Christmas.

Wednesday 4: Victorious Greeks begin to make headway in Albania against shamed Italians.

Friday 6: Italian chief of staff Marshal Pietro Badoglio is sacked following

Below: An early Jeep, the four-wheel drive 'general purpose' vehicle which revolutionised military transport during World War II.

the breaches of defences in Albania.

Monday 9: First British campaign in Africa gets underway when General Sir Archibald Wavell orders a surprise offensive against the Italians in the Western Desert. 'Operation Compass' is a success with 1,000 prisoners being taken.

Thursday 12: British troops capture 30,000 Italian prisoners in Egypt.

Friday 13: German forces move into Romania from neighbouring Hungary.

Sunday 15: Vice-Premier Laval is arrested when his plot to replace Pétain and align France more fully with Germany is revealed.

Tuesday 17: Hitler orders the release of Pierre Laval.

A German spy is hanged at Pentonville Prison, London, and a Winchester housewife is sentenced to death for working for the enemy.

Saturday 21: US novelist F. Scott Fitzgerald, author of The Great Gatsby, dies aged 44.

'Operation Compass' is a success with 1,000 prisoners being taken

An 18-year-old girl from Lancashire, who was kept in by her father who locked up her clothes was arrested in London after she escaped out of a bedroom window and caught a train to London without paying the fare. Elsie Fisher, who made her bid for freedom after finding some old clothes, refused to go home.

Sunday 22: Anthony Eden becomes Foreign Secretary and Lord Halifax is appointed British ambassador to the United States.

Sunday 29: President Roosevelt tells Americans in a radio broadcast that the United States is 'the arsenal of democracy'. He proclaimed his intention was 'to keep you now, and your children later, out of a last-ditch war for the preservation of American independence'.

Monday 30: A request by miners for bigger beef rations turned down by Britain's Ministry of Food.

Tuesday 31: Civilian casualty figures for the month of December indicate 3,793 British people have been killed by enemy action, with 5,244 more being injured.

Below: Hoses line the streets as firefighters go to work in London following a night bombing raid by aircraft of Hermann Göring's Luftwaffe.

1941

The war escalated in June, when Hitler turned his attentions to Russia, and again in December, when hours of debate about whether or not America should enter the war were abruptly ended at Pearl Harbor. Japan's expansionism made global conflict a reality.

■ JANUARY ■

Thursday 2: Eire is hit by German bombs although no one is hurt.

Friday 3: Australian troops launch a major assault on an Italian stronghold in Libya, taking 5,000 prisoners.

Saturday 4: German actress Marlene Dietrich, the woman who turned down Hitler as a lover, turns her back on her native country and becomes a US citizen.

Sunday 5: The Libyan town of Bardia falls. The Allies capture 25,000 Italian prisoners.

Monday 6: British aviator Amy Johnson is killed, aged 38, when her aircraft plunges into the Thames. Her job had been to ferry newly built aircraft from factories to their bases around Britain.

Wednesday 8: Founder of the Boy Scout movement, Lord Robert Baden-Powell, dies aged 84.

British government suppresses the Communist newspaper, the Daily Worker, which continually snipes against the war effort. Only 11 left-wing MPs voted against the ban. Many have been angered at the stance of the newspaper, particularly its activities following air raids when leaflets were handed out to those who had been blitzed claiming the war was just a plot to make profits for capitalists.

Friday 10: Air attacks begin on Malta by combined German and Italian air forces.

Saturday 11: Cruiser HMS Southampton severely damaged by Luftwaffe as it fights Italian navy in the Sicilian channel.

British and Australian forces capture Tobruk, in Libya, with the loss of just 500 men

Monday 13: Irish writer James Joyce dies in Zurich, Switzerland, aged 59, almost three decades after he last set foot in Ireland.

Tuesday 14: British government announces new controls on shopkeepers and food wholesalers in a bid to curtail the naked profiteering which has hit the market.

Sunday 19: British forces press on into Sudan and Italian-held Eritrea.

Tuesday 21: British and Australian forces capture Tobruk, in Libya, with the loss of just 500 men. The victory was marked by an Anzac hat being run up the flagpole in the absence of a Union Flag.

Below: Australian troops kick up dust on an exercise in the Western Desert.
Inset: The communist newspaper, the *Daily Worker*, barred by the government following its anti-war stance.
Far left: German troops in Athens.

Left: **Lord Robert Baden-Powell was dedicated to the success of the Scouts. He was created a peer in 1929 and died in January, aged 84.**

capital of Italian Somaliland. Back-up troops include regiments from South Africa, the Gold Coast and the King's African Rifles.

Wednesday 26: Mussolini admits to the loss of 1,000 aircraft in addition to the 200,000 troops taken prisoner in the North African campaign. His only hope is the support of Germany.

Friday 28: British civilian casualties this month fall to 789 dead and 1,068 injured.

■ MARCH ■

Saturday 1: Italy pares the rations for its people by 50 per cent to allow food exports to ally Germany.

Bulgaria, already under German occupation, joins the Axis alliance.

Sunday 2: Turkey closes the Dardenelles, linking the Aegean with the Sea of Marmara, to all shipping without permits and Turkish pilots.

Monday 3: German troops proceed through Bulgaria towards Greece and are poised to move into Yugoslavia.

An advance guard of the Afrika Korps arrives in Tripoli under the command of Rommel

---

Tuesday 4: Turkey, by now on full alert, refuses to join Germany's fight.

British troops mount a raid on Norway's Lofoten Island, sinking 11 German ships, destroying a munitions factory and a power station and setting fire to an oil depot. Aided by Norwegians, the British returned with 300 volunteers ready to fight against Germany.

Monday 27: British and Common-wealth troops make gains against the Italians in Eritrea.

Wednesday 29: South African troops invade Italian Somaliland.

Friday 31: RAF makes devastating strikes against key German ports.

■ FEBRUARY ■

Wednesday 5: Official estimates put the daily cost to Britain of the war at a staggering £11 million.

Italians flee the beleaguered town of Benghazi, only to run into a flank of British forces.

Thursday 6: Benghazi is captured by Australian forces.

Saturday 8: Englishman Percy William Olaf de Wet is sentenced to death in Berlin after being convicted of spying for France.

Sunday 9: After Laval turns down an opportunity to re-enter Pétain's cabinet governing Vichy France, Admiral Jean Francois Darlan becomes vice-president.

Monday 10: Iceland is bombed by the Luftwaffe.

The British government vows to close a loophole in call-up regulations which allows young men to avoid conscription by refusing a medical. The only penalty they face at the moment is a £5 fine.

Wednesday 12: First successful trial of penicillin is carried out in Oxford, on a policeman with septicaemia.

Friday 14: With the taking of Kurmak, the British claim the only Italians on Egyptian, Sudanese or Kenyan soil are those held prisoner.

An advance guard of the Afrika Korps lands in Tripoli, Libya, to aid the unsuccessful Italians. They are under the command of Lieutenant-General Erwin Rommel, who was a successful exponent of tank warfare in the West.

Monday 17: Bulgaria and Turkey sign a non-aggression pact.

Saturday 22: Rommel attacks British-held El Agheila.

Sunday 23: A unit of the Free French lands in Eritrea.

Monday 24: Hitler threatens to step up U-boat activities.

Tuesday 25: British Nigerian troops take control of Mogadishu, the

Wednesday 5: Britain breaks off diplomatic ties with Bulgaria.

Monday 10: Hitler invites Yugoslavia to join the Axis powers.

Tuesday 11: British diplomats arrive in Istanbul where a bomb in their luggage explodes, claiming two lives.

America agrees to allow Britain use of its military hardware without charge. The debt will be settled after the war. President Roosevelt likens it to lending a neighbour a hose to put out a fire. Churchill replies: 'Give us the tools and we'll finish the job.'

Monday 17: Minister of Labour Bevin calls for women to operate factories to free more male workers for military service. For many women, it is the first time they have worked outside the family home.

Monday 24: Rommel occupies El Agheila once more for the Germans.

Tuesday 25: Prince Paul of Yugoslavia signs an agreement with Nazi Germany.

Italian navy defeated off Cape Matapan with loss of three cruisers

Thursday 27: A coup overturns the pro-Nazi government in Yugoslavia. Figurehead Prince Paul flees, leaving 17-year-old King Peter as sovereign. Street marches in favour of Britain and Russia and against Hitler are staged even though German troops are massing on the Bulgarian border.

Friday 28: Writer Virginia Woolf dies, aged 59, after apparently throwing herself in the River Ouse, Sussex.

Italian navy defeated off Cape Matapan with the loss of three cruisers. Britain loses two aircraft.

Sunday 30: Rommel mounts counter-offensive in North Africa.

Monday 31: Italy sinks HMS York and HMS Bonaventure off Crete.

British civilian casualties for the month rise again with continued raids on London, Portsmouth, Merseyside, Clydeside, Bristol and Plymouth. This time 4,259 people are killed and 5,557 injured.

Below: **The wreckage of the aircraft in which Rudolf Hess flew from Germany.**

sizeable Royal Navy and Royal Air Force contingents.

French police round up about 1,000 Jews in Paris and hand them over to the Germans.

Thursday 15: 'Operation Brevity', to relieve Tobruk, is launched.

Britain test-flies its first jet aircraft at RAF Cranwell. Frank Whittle is the engineer and designer.

Friday 16: Final batch of British reinforcements arrives in Crete.

RAF raids Cologne.

Italian forces surrender at Amba Alagi in Ethiopia.

Sunday 18: German vessels Bismarck and Prinz Eugen set sail in the Baltic.

Monday 19: Egyptian liner Zamzam is sunk by Germans in the South Atlantic. Among the casualties are 200 US passengers.

Tuesday 20: German paratroopers drop into Crete. Defending, the British, Anzac and Greek forces inflict heavy casualties on the airborne invaders.

Below: **Charismatic Luftwaffe chief Hermann Göring surveys a battle plan with his aides. The unique rank of Reichsmarschall was created for him by Hitler.**

Wednesday 21: America is asked to withdraw its representatives from Paris by the occupying Germans.

Thursday 22: Royal Air Force withdraws from Crete.

Saturday 24: The British battlecruiser HMS Hood is sunk off Greenland, with the loss of 1,300 lives. The Royal Navy vows to 'pursue and destroy' the 45,000-ton battleship Bismarck, responsible for the tragedy.

Crete is bombed by Germans, forcing King George II of Greece to flee to Cairo.

US cult singer Robert Zimmerman, better known as Bob Dylan, is born.

Sunday 25: Bismarck eludes its Royal Navy pursuers as it makes a dash from Greenland, aiming for the safety of a northern French port.

German navy chief Admiral Raeder warns US that its protective action of convoying British merchant ships would soon be considered an act of war by the Germans.

Monday 26: After Bismarck is spotted it is chased by every Royal Navy vessel in the region and is bombed by Swordfish planes from the Ark Royal, suffering severe

damage. The British continue attacking after dark. In the Mediterranean the Royal Navy aircraft carrier Formidable is bombed.

Tuesday 27: The Bismarck is finally sunk off the coast of France by torpedoes from the cruiser Dorsetshire.

Wednesday 28: Roosevelt announces that the American Neutrality Act is to be scrapped.

Thursday 29: More than 200 men are killed when the cruiser Orion comes under attack off Crete.

Pétain imposes new restrictions on Jews in Vichy France, barring them from public office

Friday 30: Pro-Nazi Rashid Ali flees Iraq as his government collapses with the advance of British troops on the capital, Baghdad.

May 31: British evacuate to Egypt from Crete.

Australian women between the ages of 16 and 60 are banned from leaving the country, to conserve womanpower for nursing and associated services.

Peace is made in Iraq.

Civilian casualties for May amount to 5,394 dead and 5,181 injured.

■ JUNE ■

Saturday 1: Clothes rationing is introduced in Britain.

Monday 2: Manchester badly hit by an air raid. Reichsmarschall Göring tells the Luftwaffe: 'There is no unconquerable island.'

Industry of the Ruhr is bombed by Royal Air Force.

Pétain imposes new restrictions on Jews in Vichy France, barring them from public office.

Wednesday 4: Following a devastat-

◆ THE COMING OF THE DESERT FOX

In February 1941, Rommel arrived in North Africa in command of the Deutsches Afrika Korps. Germany's Italian allies were struggling in the desert, and Rommel had been dispatched to stiffen the Axis presence in the region.

He wasted little time in going on the offensive, striking at El Agheila in March, before launching a three-pronged attack across Cyrenaica at the start of April. The Australians in Benghazi retreated, and eventually pulled back into Tobruk, which was then isolated as the tide of Axis forces swept eastwards. On 25 April, the Afrika Korps crossed into Egypt. Yet the Allies were to recover and eventually succeeded in driving Rommel from Africa.

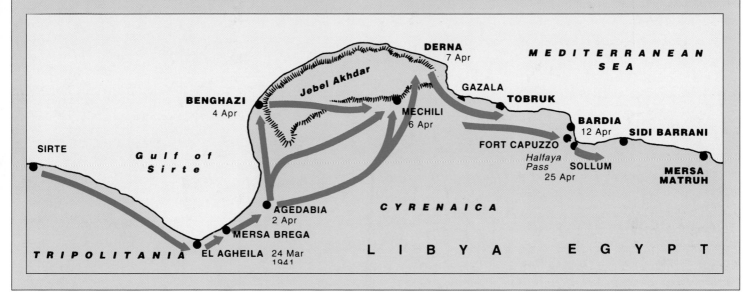

ing air raid on Alexandria the Egyptian cabinet resigns.

Thursday 5: At least 13,000 British prisoners were taken in Crete, the government admits.

Saturday 7: Launch of heavy night air raid on French Atlantic port of Brest by the RAF, in an attempt to destroy the German heavy cruiser, *Prinz Eugen*, which had operated with the battleship *Bismarck* during the latter's one and only cruise the previous month.

Sunday 8: Allied troops backed up by the Free French attack Syria. Colonial power Vichy France is outraged when Britain offers Syria its independence.

RAF launches largest air raid to date using 360 planes.

Thursday 12: RAF bombs Ruhr, Rhineland and a number of German ports in the start of a 20-night bombing campaign.

Hitler tears up the agreement between Berlin and Moscow and launches invasion of Russia

Sunday 15: 'Operation Battleaxe', to relieve Tobruk, is launched.

Monday 16: British jobless figures at an all-time low with just 243,656 registered unemployed.

Last Italians fighting in Ethiopia surrender to the British in disarray.

Tuesday 17: 'Operation Battleaxe' fails, with British forces being beaten back by Rommel's forces.

Thursday 19: Germany and Italy expel American Embassy staff in retaliation for hostility to consuls representing Hitler and Mussolini.

Saturday 21: Empire troops take Damascus, with the defending Vichy

force fleeing in confusion.

Sunday 22: 'Operation Barbarossa' begins. Hitler tears up the non-aggression pact between Berlin and Moscow and launches invasion of Russia. Finnish and Romanian soldiers are with the German army along a 1,300-mile front. Churchill offers Stalin aid.

Tuesday 24: Axis troops advance through Russian territory, inflicting severe damage on the Red Army and Air Force with familiar Blitzkrieg tactics. Lithuania is overrun.

Thursday 26: Finland declares war on Russia.

Sunday 29: Luftwaffe chief Göring wins the internal power struggle in the Nazi hierarchy and is named as Hitler's successor.

■ JULY ■

Tuesday 1: Germans seize the Baltic port of Riga.

Above: **Retreating Russian troops practise a 'scorched earth' policy and destroy everything in their wake.**

Thursday 3: Stalin orders his retreating forces to destroy everything as they fall back.

Friday 4: British Communist Party declares it is no longer in opposition to the war and throws its weight behind the nation's efforts.

Coal rationing gets underway.

Wednesday 9: Russian soldiers are defeated at Minsk.

Thursday 10: Hitler encourages Japan to enter the war. He knows a new front to occupy Allied forces would significantly increase his chances of victory.

Saturday 12: A mutual assistance plan is signed by Britain and Russia in Moscow, restraining both from seeking a separate peace.

Monday 14: A Syrian peace agreement is signed.

Tuesday 15: Empire forces continue their march through the Middle East, entering Beirut.

Saturday 19: George Armstrong is hanged at Wandsworth prison, south-west London, for spying.

Sunday 20: Britain adopts a 'V-for-Victory' motif and urges all resistance groups in occupied countries to join the simple but effective campaign by chalking a 'V' on doors and walls at every opportunity.

Tuesday 22: First German air raid on Moscow. Meanwhile the land-based troops are halted by marshland.

Wednesday 23: A vital convoy breaks through the U-boat blockade and arrives in Malta.

Japanese troops land in Indochina, occupying Saigon and stationing men in Phnom Penh

Thursday 24: All Britons are kicked out of Vichy France.

Monday 28: Japanese troops land in southern Indochina, occupying Saigon and stationing men in Cambodia's capital, Phnom Penh.

Unable to halt their actions, Marshal Pétain has given the blessing of Vichy, France, which controlled the region. The US reacts with total ban on trade with Japan.

Wednesday 30: US authorities seize 17 Japanese fishing boats suspected of spying around the waters of Hawaii.

Poland and Russia, finding themselves on the same side, sign an uneasy pact of friendship.

Thursday 31: With the let-up in raids on London and elsewhere, the civilian casualty figures fall, with 501 dead in July's air raids.

■ AUGUST ■

Friday 1: Roosevelt halts aviation fuel exports to Axis countries.

Tuesday 5: Romanian troops lay siege to the port of Odessa.

Wine drinking in Vichy France restricted to two litres per week.

Thursday 7: National Service is extended by 18 months in America.

Mussolini loses his second son, Bruno, in an air crash.

Friday 8: Russia's Red Air Force srikes at Berlin.

Left: The back of a bridge in Kiev is broken by German bombardment prior to its fall to the Third Reich. In September 1941, German forces succeeded in surrounding the Ukrainian city and forcing its surrender.

Thursday 14: Churchill and Roosevelt sign the Atlantic Charter, setting out the objectives of both nations during wartime and peace. While declaring that neither had territorial gains to make, it says that war-mongering nations had to be disarmed and that, following the conflict, 'all men shall be enabled to live in freedom from fear and want'.

Saturday 16: Britain and the Soviet Union sign an agreement that they will exchange resources.

Wednesday 20: In France 50,000 are held as the German occupiers try to root out railway saboteurs.

Thursday 21: In Paris, 5,000 Jews are rounded up and interned before being deported.

With Germans at the gates of Leningrad, Russian marshal Voroshilov tells the residents to defend the city to the last.

Monday 25: British and Russian troops march into Iran.

Stalin orders the destruction of the huge Lenin-Dnjeproges dam, completed only ten years ago to meet all the power needs of the Ukraine.

Tuesday 26: French Hitlerite Pierre Laval is shot and wounded by young Frenchman Paul Colette.

Canadian troops land on an Arctic island north of Norway in a bid to hamper coal supplies to Germany.

Germany admits to losses of 440,000 on the Russian front – more than in their offensives worldwide before 'Operation Barbarossa' got underway.

Wednesday 27: Iranian government negotiates a ceasefire.

British government commandeers domestic railways, paying compensation to the owners.

■ **SEPTEMBER** ■

Tuesday 2: Fighting between Germans and Russians reported within 30 miles of Leningrad.

Wednesday 3: Gas chamber at Auschwitz brought into use.

U-boat attacks US destroyer Greer off Iceland.

Saturday 6: All Jews in Germany are forced by law to wear a yellow Star of David when they appear in public. Further, they will require special permission from the police before leaving their neighbourhoods.

Thursday 11: King Leopold III of Belgium secretly marries Mary Lilian Baels, the 29-year-old granddaughter of a Flemish fisherman. As a 'commoner', she renounces claims to the title of queen and is to be known as Princess of Rethy.

Friday 12: Snow falls on the Russian front.

Saturday 13: Germans declare their intentions to allow fewer rations to Russian prisoners of war than to POWs of other nationalities.

Monday 15: German siege of Leningrad begins.

German troops come under fire on the Champs Elysees, the heart of German-occupied Paris.

Fighting between Germans and Russians reported within 30 miles of Leningrad

Tuesday 16: Unpopular Shah of Iran abdicates in favour of his son, 21-year-old Mohammed Reza Pahlavi.

Wednesday 17: British and Russian units reach Iranian capital Teheran.

Thursday 18: Russians evacuate Kiev.

Friday 19: Kiev falls to Germany.

Sunday 21: Germans isolate the Crimean peninsula from the USSR.

Wednesday 24: Nine governments-in-exile put their names to the Atlantic Charter.

Friday 26: RAF flies in relief supplies to Leningrad.

Monday 29: Germans kill Jews left behind in Kiev.

Tuesday 30: Newcastle bombed for the second time. Civilian casualties from air raids in September amount to 217.

■ OCTOBER ■

Wednesday 1: An estimated 163,696 Jews are thought to be living within the borders of Germany.

Thursday 2: While Hitler sets his sights on Moscow, the Red Army presses German forces back around Leningrad.

Friday 3: The number of people killed on the road in Britain last year is up 65 per cent on pre-war figures.

Tuesday 7: Stalin allows religion once more in Russia in an effort to unite his beleaguered people.

Thursday 16: Soviet government pulls out of Moscow, although Stalin stays behind.

The Black Sea town of Odessa falls to the Romanians.

The Japanese government falls, to be replaced by hardline militarists.

Friday 17: German U-boat hits USS Kearny off Iceland.

Saturday 18: Germans within 70 miles of Moscow.

Sunday 19: A state of siege is declared in Moscow.

German papers reveal 673,000 Russian prisoners have been taken during October alone.

American ambassador in Japan hears rumour of an approved plan to attack America

---

Wednesday 22: After a German military commander is killed by an assassin, 50 hostages are shot in Nantes, France.

Thursday 23: De Gaulle asks French resistance to bide their time after another 50 French people are killed in reprisal for the death of a German major. The Vichy government blames British agents for the killings.

Thursday 30: In the third U-boat attack on a US warship in a month, destroyer Reuben James is sunk off Iceland with the loss of 70 lives.

Friday 31: British civilian casualty figures for October are 262. Dover is the most severely hit target.

■ NOVEMBER ■

Saturday 1: Crimean capital Simferopol falls to the Germans.

Monday 3: American ambassador in Japan hears rumours of an approved plan to attack America and warns President Roosevelt.

Thursday 6: America gives Russia an interest-free loan amounting to $1,000 million.

German soldiers serving on the Eastern front begin to experience the pains of frostbite.

Friday 7: Churchill declares: 'Britain's resolve is unconquerable.'

Monday 10: Churchill warns that any act of war by Japan against America would be taken as an act of war against Britain.

Thursday 13: German troops in

Below: A tank struggles to stay moving as the bitterly cold Russian winter sets in on the Eastern front. Now frostbite claims more casualties than warfare does.

Russia are crippled as temperatures plunge minus 22 degrees Celsius.

HMS *Ark Royal* is hit by a German U-boat and sinks while being towed back into port.

Tuesday 18: British commandos mount a daring night raid on German headquarters in Libya. 'Operation Crusader', involving the British 8th Army, gets underway to liberate Libya.

Wednesday 19: German raider ship *Kormoran* attacks an Australian navy cruiser off Western Australia. Both are sunk.

An estimated 82,000 Poles have been shot or hanged since German occupation of Poland.

'Operation Crusader', involving the British 8th Army, gets underway to liberate Libya

Sunday 23: A South African brigade is broken during an attack by Rommel near Tobruk.

New Zealand troops occupy Bardia, north east Libya.

Tuesday 25: 8th Army comes under attack from Rommel.

Thursday 27: American Pacific forces on alert.

Sunday 30: Japan's prime minister, General Hideki Tojo, warns he will 'purge' Anglo-American power bases in the Far East.

■ DECEMBER ■

Monday 1: Malaya and Hong Kong on alert in case of Japanese action.

Tuesday 2: The Royal Navy's *Prince of Wales* and *Repulse* sail to bolster defences of Singapore.

Right: Japanese prime minister Hideki Tojo, who was also minister of war.

◆ EYE WITNESS ◆

New Zealander Peter Llewelyn, who served in North Africa, wrote about the plagues of flies which followed the troops there. His account appeared in the official history of New Zealand's involvement in World War II.

‘...And when you shut your eyes – and this is the plain truth – flies tried to open them, mad for the delectable fluid.

We couldn't always be killing them but we had to keep on brushing them away, otherwise even breathing would have been difficult. Our arms ached from the exercise but still they fastened on our food and accompanied it into our mouths and down our throats, scorning death when there was an advantage to be gained. They drowned themselves in our tea and in our soup. They attended us with awful relish on our most intimate occasions. ’

German troops within five miles of the Kremlin.

Friday 5: Hitler abandons for the winter his goal of seizing Moscow.

Saturday 6: With the Japanese fleet already sailing south, Roosevelt makes a last-ditch appeal to Emperor Hirohito for peace.

Britain formally declares war on Finland, Romania and Hungary.

Sunday 7: Pearl Harbor comes under attack from 360 Japanese planes, with the loss of 2,729 lives. Malaya, China, the Philippines, Thailand and Hong Kong are also under attack by the Japanese.

Monday 8: Canada declares war on Japan.

Tuesday 9: Thai capital Bangkok is occupied by Japanese.

Wednesday 10: British Naval Force Z destroyed by Japanese. Prince of Wales and Repulse are sunk, the first major ships in history to be sunk by air power alone. British on the retreat in Malaya.

Siege of Tobruk is finally ended.

Thursday 11: Germany and Italy declare war on America.

Friday 12: Britain's army, navy and air force, aided by Free Norwegian troops, raid a German base in north Norway, sinking eight ships and killing or capturing an entire garrison.

Better equipped against the gruelling winter weather, Russian troops stage a series of attacks against the invading Germans.

Saturday 13: Widespread rumours that enemy parachutists had landed on the west coast of America were officially denied today. The US Army stated the reports had been thoroughly investigated and completely discredited.

Monday 15: Gun battles echo through Hong Kong.

Wednesday 17: Japanese land in North Borneo and are poised to win Malayan peninsula.

Rommel is forced to retreat in North Africa.

Above: The pride of America's fleet lies shrouded in smoke following Japan's surprise attack on Pearl Harbor. Crucially, the US carriers were absent on exercise.
Opposite: Victorious Australians march in Benghazi, Libya.

Friday 19: Hong Kong is occupied by Japan.

Hitler, now in personal charge of his army, orders: 'No withdrawal'.

Monday 22: Philippine Islands invaded by Japanese.

Tuesday 23: Wake Island garrison surrenders to Japanese.

Thursday 25: Hong Kong garrison, just 6,000 strong, surrenders to Japanese when the supply of fresh water is in jeopardy.

Empire forces retake Benghazi.

More than 3,000 residents starve to death in Leningrad.

Friday 26: To cheers and riotous applause, British prime minister Winston Churchill addresses the American Congress.

◆ EYE WITNESS ◆

Gordon Kendall, from Portsmouth, England, served with 4 Commando. In late 1941 he took part in the first British attack since Dunkirk, targeting the Norwegian islands of Lofoten and Vaagsö. Its success was a major morale booster for the dejected Allies.

'Our job was to blow up fish oil tanks which the Germans were using to make nitroglycerine. There were 250 men involved from both 3 and 4 Commando and we made an amphibious assault at dawn on the landing ships *Beatrice* and *Emma*.

Lofoten wasn't so bad because there were only about 40 Germans on the island. We later called it the "coffee-break raid" because the place was full of Norwegians handing round cups of coffee.

Vaagsö was different altogether because there were 400 Germans there and we met some stiff resistance. But the mission was a complete success. We picked up some Quislings, who were pointed out to us by the Norwegian Resistance, and they were taken prisoner to be interrogated. We also took 120 islanders who wanted to fight with the Allies. They just dropped everything and jumped on our ships, even though they had no advance warning. I suppose their hatred of the Germans was so strong.

As a final touch just before leaving a naval demolition team detonated limpet mines on six German merchants.

We knew a lot was resting on this operation because it was the first time Britain had struck back since Dunkirk. In fact, the powers-that-be hadn't told us the whole truth. We were the sprat to catch the mackerel.

The Navy knew that two of the German fleet's biggest warships, *Tirpitz* and *Prinz Eugen*, were lurking in the fjords nearby. It was hoped our attack would lure them out to search for us. Had they followed us they would have found HMS *Rodney*, HMS *Nelson* and HMS *King George V* out there waiting for them. Unfortunately, they stayed put.'

1942

As Japan and Germany struggled to consolidate their gains, the Allies were preparing their fight back. Yet still the British, Americans and Australians were short on success stories. Could they turn the tide of war in their favour?

■ JANUARY ■

Thursday 1: Twenty-six countries sign a declaration of 'United Nations', stating that none will seek a separate peace with any Axis power.

A pit tragedy in Stoke on Trent claims the lives of 57 miners.

Friday 2: Japanese troops take Manila, in the Philippines.

Saturday 3: General Sir Archibald Wavell is made head of Allied forces in the south west Pacific.

Tuesday 6: US forces to be based in Britain, Roosevelt tells Congress.

Sunday 11: Japanese forces invade Dutch East Indies.

Monday 12: Kuala Lumpur, capital of Malaya, falls to the Japanese.

Tuesday 13: Allied conference pledges justice for war criminals at the end of the conflict.

Thursday 15: Japanese invasion of Burma begins.

Saturday 17: US world champion boxer Muhammad Ali is born.

Actress Carol Lombard dies when an airliner crashes in Las Vegas.

Tuesday 20: Nazi hardliner Reinhard Heydrich, nicknamed 'the hangman', announces a 'final solution' to the 'Jewish problem'.

Japanese daylight bombing raids begin on Singapore.

Wednesday 21: Field-Marshal Rommel launches another counter-attack in North Africa.

New Guinea, north of Australia, is bombed by the Japanese.

Friday 23: Australia demands extra reinforcements from Britain and US as Japanese forces edge closer.

Monday 26: US troops arrive in Northern Ireland.

Wednesday 28: Rommel takes control of Benghazi.

■ FEBRUARY ■

Sunday 1: Traitor Quisling forms a pro-German government in Norway.

Monday 9: Japanese forces land on Singapore Island.

Friday 13: Soviet Army presses back into White Russia, in the face of fierce German resistance.

Saturday 14: Fall of Sumatra in Dutch East Indies to Japanese

Sunday 15: Singapore falls with the loss of 9,000 lives. An estimated 80,000 Allied troops are taken prisoner by the Japanese.

Tuesday 17: Japanese invade Bali in Dutch East Indies.

Left: Carole Lombard, wife of Clark Gable, was killed in an air crash, returning from a US Bond-selling tour in the Midwest.
Far left: The Japanese take Bataan.

Above: Japanese soldiers capture Manila, the Philippine capital. It was defended by native soldiers and Americans.

Wednesday 18: In a bid to save precious resources, people are urged to bathe less and use no more than five inches of water. Shared baths are being encouraged.

Thursday 19: Japanese aircraft bomb Darwin, north Australia, killing 240 people and wounding 150 more.

Singapore falls with the loss of 9,000 lives. 80,000 Allied troops are taken prisoner

Friday 20: Fall of the island of Bali to Japanese, cutting a vital air link between Australia and the Dutch East Indies.

Sunday 22: Air Marshal Sir Arthur T. ('Bomber') Harris appointed chief of Bomber Command.

Monday 23: Californian coast comes under fire from Japanese submarine.

Friday 27: Start of the three-day Battle of the Java Sea.

Saturday 28: Allied paras destroy a radar station in northern France.

ROOSEVELT

It was probably the most difficult job in history. When he was president, Franklin Delano Roosevelt had to steer his huge country out of the gruelling international depression.

If that wasn't enough to contend with, along came a war in Europe which threatened to engulf the world. Roosevelt suspected it was an itch he would have to scratch. But at home there were keen isolationists who didn't want any more of America's youth sacrificed on the pyre of freedom and democracy overseas. An isolationist at heart himself, Roosevelt was also a realist.

The prospect of doing business with a triumphant Germany was not a happy one. Moreover, a Third Reich spread across western Europe and eastern Asia would surely soon turn its sights on the New World. Roosevelt took America as close to war with Germany as it could possibly get without committing troops. Then came the Japanese attack on Pearl Harbor and America, the victim, came into the conflict united and determined.

Franklin Roosevelt was born in 1882 in New York, the product of an enlightened father and an all-consuming mother. When he was 18 he went to Harvard University and enjoyed the parties and competitive sports every bit as much as the studies.

His thoughts turned increasingly to politics when his fifth cousin, Theodore Roosevelt, won the presidency in 1901. That interest was compounded when he met and married Eleanor Roosevelt, niece of the president, who shared Franklin's passion for humanitarian causes. Not always a happy marriage, it remained a fruitful partnership to the end.

Anxious that his family links should not act as an automatic ticket, Franklin worked hard when he stood as the Democratic candidate in Duchess County, New York. It paid off and he was successful. And, as if to hammer the point home, he backed Woodrow Wilson above his cousin when it came to the 1912 presidential election.

In 1913, he became Assistant Secretary of the Navy in Wilson's administration, forming a life-long loyalty to the naval service.

Following the Republican victory in the 1920 presidential election, Franklin returned to his legal practice until, the following year, he was struck down by poliomyelitis. Now the active, enthusiastic campaigner was confined to a wheelchair and would remain so until he learned to walk again with the aid of a walking stick and leg braces.

It could have spelled the end of his career. But his wife Eleanor suddenly blossomed to work on behalf of her ailing husband until he could assume his duties once more.

By 1928, Roosevelt was governor of New York State and got a taste for reform. Four years on he won the presidential election. Domestic problems loomed, including large-scale unemployment and a delicate economy. His answer was the New Deal – legislation to aid banks, regulate currency, re-finance farmers and give strength to workers. The improvements were wholesale. His success at home and later as a war leader were sufficient to win him the presidential election a record four times in total.

Roosevelt died in 1945, shortly before his country's victories over Germany and Japan. His wife went on to be US delegate to the United Nations, a cause which her husband worked so hard to achieve, and also chair of the UN Commission on Human Rights.

Cruisers Perth and Houston attack Japanese vessels disembarking troops at Merak. Although both cruisers are lost, they sink a Japanese minesweeper and transport and damage three destroyers.

■ MARCH ■

Sunday 1: Fall of Java, in Dutch East Indies, to Japanese.

Sunday 8: Japanese forces land in New Guinea.

Tuesday 10: British expenditure on the war to date has already exceeded that spent in the entire duration of World War I.

Cruisers **Perth** *and* **Houston** *attack Japanese vessels disembarking troops at Merak*

Saturday 14: American troops arrive in Australia.

Sunday 22: Royal Navy successfully escorts a convoy to the beleaguered island of Malta despite an air and sea onslaught from the Axis powers. However, the supply ships are sunk while in the Maltese harbour.

A Polish newspaper editor is beheaded after being found listening to the BBC.

The BBC begins broadcasting

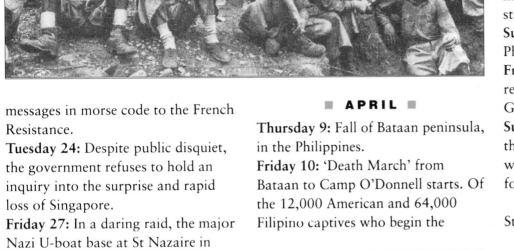

Left: Thousands of British and Australian troops were captured when Singapore fell to Japan.

messages in morse code to the French Resistance.

Tuesday 24: Despite public disquiet, the government refuses to hold an inquiry into the surprise and rapid loss of Singapore.

Friday 27: In a daring raid, the major Nazi U-boat base at St Nazaire in western France is wrecked by British commandos. Travelling aboard the destroyer Campbeltown, the commandos go into action after the ship has rammed open the dock gates. However, many are captured as they try to head off down river on speedy launches.

President and government of the Philippines flee to Australia.

Saturday 28: A large-scale RAF attack is launched against the Baltic port of Lübeck, a centre of industry as part of a round-the-clock strategy against key German-held sites.

Tuesday 31: In Belgium, the death penalty is brought in for those caught forging ration cards, as the food shortage becomes critical.

An Allied convoy defies German attacks and arrives at Murmansk in the USSR.

In the last four months, British civilian casualties have amounted to 189 killed and 149 injured.

Right: The war was brought home to Australians when the Japanese bombed Darwin, in the Northern Territory, setting fire to a US destroyer in the harbour.

■ APRIL ■

Thursday 9: Fall of Bataan peninsula, in the Philippines.

Friday 10: 'Death March' from Bataan to Camp O'Donnell starts. Of the 12,000 American and 64,000 Filipino captives who begin the

In a daring raid, the U-boat base at St Nazaire is wrecked by British commandos

march, 2,330 Americans and 7,500 Filipinos die of exhaustion, dehydration and harsh treatment.

Wednesday 15: Malta receives George Cross from King George VI in recognition of its suffering and its stalwart resistance in the war.

Sunday 19: Japanese capture the Philippine island of Cebu.

Friday 24: Exeter is bombed in reprisal for the air raids on historic German towns.

Sunday 26: Hitler tells the Reichstag that the Russian winter has been the worst in 140 years but voices hope for success in a spring offensive.

US singer and actress Barbra Streisand is born.

■ MAY ■

Saturday 2: HMS Edinburgh is sunk by a German submarine while escorting a Russian convoy.

Monday 4: British troops land in Madagascar, a province of Vichy France. The defending garrison surrenders with little resistance and the Allies gain a big naval and air base for their fight against the Japanese.

Tuesday 5: Naval battle of the Coral Sea commences.

IT'S HIS SEAL ON LIVING HISTORY

Saturday 9: Malta is reinforced with 60 Spitfires from two aircraft carriers. Many are subsequently lost in the bitter air battles over the island.

Monday 11: Three destroyers, Lively, Jackal and Kipling, are sunk in attacks by German planes.

Tuesday 12: A U-boat steals into the entrance of the Mississippi and sinks a US merchant ship.

Wednesday 20: The US Navy recruits its first blacks.

Tuesday 26: Rommel signals the start

Two Czech freedom fighters toss a bomb into the car of Reinhard Heydrich

of the third German counter-offensive in the Western Desert.

Friday 29: Two Czech freedom fighters toss a bomb into the car of Nazi chief of security, SS Obergruppenführer Reinhard Heydrich. He dies six days days later. In a revenge masterminded by SS chief Heinrich Himmler, 1,331 Czechs die and the village of Lidice is levelled. Its men are killed while women and children are interned.

Actor John Barrymore, a matinée idol and accomplished Shakespearean actor, dies aged 60 after a life hallmarked by outrageous drinking and womanising.

Sunday 31: Cologne is devastated by a thousand-bomber raid by the Royal Air Force. More than 2,000 tons of explosives were dropped on the city.

Sydney is raided by three Japanese midget submarines.

◆ EYE WITNESS ◆

Eric Williams joined the Royal Corps of Signals as a boy soldier in 1935 and was serving in India when the war broke out. He was captured by the Italians in North Africa in 1942.

❝ I was captured just outside Benghazi. As the driver for the General's reconnaissance, we were always sent in advance. Our lines of communications were so long we got cut off.

We were taken by cattle boat back to Italy, battened down in the hold. Then we were moved to Ancona on the east coast. In Italy there was a funeral a day. People just gave up. If they felt ill, they never fought it.

One morning we could hear the gunfire which sounded as though it was getting closer. The Colonel in command of the prisoners told us: "The British are coming." The next morning soldiers did turn up but they were in the wrong uniforms – it was the Germans. They put us in cattle trucks and took us to Freiburg in eastern Germany where we worked in a flax factory from 6am to 6pm. There was lots of forced labour there, including many girls from Poland.

If it hadn't been for Red Cross parcels containing tinned cheese, bacon and milk we would have starved. The food, particularly in Germany, was nothing but a slop. We did a sit-down strike on one occasion. The soldiers simply moved us along using their rifle butts. We stole food when we could and the Polish girls brought stuff in for us.

Eventually we were liberated by the Russians. Their treatment of the locals was appalling – but then the Russians had suffered a lot at the hands of the Germans. A friend and I commandeered a horse and cart and managed to get to American lines. I was finally flown to Aylesbury. But before I was allowed back in the country I was sprayed with DDT.

My mother lost three children and a son-in-law during the war. I was a prisoner of war missing for five months while my younger brother served in the Middle East. ❞

Above: Cologne cathedral stands defiantly among the debris following a thousand-bomber raid.

Right: Screen star John Barrymore died after a lifetime of dramatic achievement and living.

■ JUNE ■

Monday 1: Mexico declares war on Germany and Italy.

Thursday 4: Battle of Midway, between US and Japanese naval forces, commences in the Pacific. It is a turning point in the Pacific war.

Saturday 6: Mail from US servicemen serving overseas arrives in the US photographed on microfilm. It is then photostated and sent on to relatives.

Monday 8: Japanese forces bombard Sydney and Newcastle.

Thursday 11: A pit company deducts half a day's wages from the widow of a man killed in a midday mining accident to account for the time he wasn't at work, an outraged MP reports to Britain's House of Commons.

Tuesday 16: In the Mediterranean, one Italian cruiser and two destroyers are lost to the British in the battle of the convoys.

Thursday 18: Musician and future Beatle Paul McCartney is born.

Sunday 21: Tobruk falls after South African General Klopper surrenders to Rommel. British forces in North Africa fall back into Egypt.

Monday 22: In a national broadcast, Pierre Laval, deputy leader of Vichy, France, announces: 'I wish victory for Germany.'

Thursday 25: Cairo is in danger of falling into German hands after recent breakthroughs by Rommel.

Sunday 28: All Jews aged six and over in Vichy France are compelled to wear the Star of David.

■ JULY ■

Wednesday 1: Vichy France's Pierre Laval allows German soldiers to seek out Resistance hideaways in unoccupied France.

Friday 3: Sevastopol, the Black Sea port held under seige by 100,000 Soviet soldiers, falls to the Germans after almost a month of fierce fighting.

Saturday 4: First US Army Air Forces plane sees action in Europe, a Douglas A-20G Havoc.

Monday 6: The British 8th Army, under Auchinleck sends Rommel into retreat at El Alamein.

Wednesday 8: Hollywood movie actor Cary Grant marries Woolworth heiress Barbara Hutton.

Friday 10: The remnants of Convoy PQ17 from Britain to the USSR reach the safety of a Russian port. After instructions from the British Admiralty that the convoy was to scatter, U-boats and German aircraft picked off 29 merchant ships abandoned by their Royal Navy escorts.

Saturday 11: RAF Lancasters attack the Danzig docks, aiming to put U-boats out of commission.

Monday 13: Hitler orders General Paulus to capture Stalingrad.

Tuesday 14: In Yugoslavia the occupying Germans murder 700 people in retaliation for the killing of a Gestapo officer.

Above: **Born Archibald Leach, he was better known as Cary Grant. His marriage to Barbara Hutton lasted just three years.**

◆ EYE WITNESS ◆

An anonymous American in training wrote these words in 1943.

❛ We are scared easily. A blast on a whistle sends us running; the word "ten-Shun!" stops us from breathing; the sight of the Sergeant makes us tremble. The boys who were scared of dying, and those who weren't, see now that it will be a long time before they have an opportunity to do any dying; they are now scared of sergeants, commissioned officers, KP, and humiliation before their fellow men. ❜

Wednesday 15: The RAF carries out its first daylight raid on the Ruhr.

Monday 27: Sweet rationing begins in Britain.

Thursday 30: Conscription is introduced in Canada.

Friday 31: Leisure-motoring is banned in a British government move to conserve fuel.

Air Marshal Sir Arthur Harris, Bomber Command chief, announces in a radio broadcast to Germany that the RAF and USAAF will carry out daily and nightly air raids 'come rain, blow or snow'.

A group of concerned observers including a university professor aiming to aid refugees in Europe christen themselves the Oxford Committee for Famine Relief – or Oxfam for short.

■ AUGUST ■

Monday 3: Prime Minister Churchill arrives in Cairo to personally investigate the fall of Tobruk.

Friday 7: US Marines land on Guadalcanal, in the Solomons.

Sunday 9: Civil unrest spreads in India after the arrest of Mahatma Gandhi and other eminent leaders of the Indian Congress after they voted

to press colonial England to leave their country once and for all.

Wednesday 12: Monty arrives in North Africa to take command of the desert army.

Wednesday 19: The ill-fated commando raid by Canadian and British forces against German-held Dieppe, France, ends in disarray with large numbers of casualties and about 1,500 prisoners taken.

The ill-fated commando raid against German-held Dieppe ends in disarray

---

Thursday 20: First US aircraft fly into Henderson's Field, Guadalcanal.

Saturday 22: Following the loss of elements of its merchant fleet to U-boats, Brazil declares war against Germany and Italy.

Monday 24: Sea battle off the Solomons commences.

The Duke of Kent, youngest brother of Britain's King George VI, is killed in a flying-boat crash on a trip to Iceland.

JOIN THE MODERN ARMY

The Modern Army gives young men interesting work with mechanized training

Wednesday 26: Japanese land at Milne Bay, Papua New Guinea.

Jewish residents of occupied France fall victim to the notorious Nazi round-ups for concentration or extermination camps.

Monday 31: Beginning of the Battle of Alam Halfa in North Africa.

Australians attack the Japanese along Papua New Guinea's treacherous Kokoda trail

■ **SEPTEMBER** ■

Friday 4: The execution of a 19-year-old IRA member causes fury among Republicans in Northern Ireland, sparking clashes between police and protesters in Belfast.

Saturday 5: Australians drive Japanese from Milne Bay.

Sunday 6: Two police officers are shot dead by the IRA in Belfast.

Thursday 10: The RAF carries out a massive bombing raid against Düsseldorf, dropping 100,000 bombs in an hour.

Friday 11: Japanese forces halted on the Kokoda trail, Papua New Guinea.

Saturday 12: British transport ship Laconia is torpedoed and sunk by a U-boat, killing about 800 of the 1,800 Italian

prisoners of war aboard.

Sunday 13: 'Operation Daffodil' begins in North Africa, comprising commando raids on Benghazi, Barce and Tobruk.

RAF raids disrupt oil production in Ploesti, Romania, the site of a vital oil installation.

Wednesday 16: German 6th Army penetrates the suburbs of Stalingrad.

Friday 18: British troops seize a major port in Madagascar, threatening the capital, held by forces loyal to Vichy France.

Sunday 20: In Paris, 116 people are killed by German occupying forces in reprisal for a spate of attacks directed at German army officers.

Wednesday 23: Australians attack the Japanese along Papua New Guinea's treacherous Kokoda trail.

■ **OCTOBER** ■

Saturday 3: President Roosevelt freezes wages, rents and farm prices.

Sunday 11: Battle of Cape Esperance off Guadalacanal.

Above: Street urchins like this Greek girl were the target of compassionate observers who founded Oxfam.

Right: Following sea battles off Guadalcanal, Solomon Islands, involving Japanese and US warships and warplanes, the US Marines were able to reinforce and re-stock the key island.

Right: Boxer Joe Louis quits the ring and throws his weight behind the war effort.

US boxer Joe Louis retires from the ring.

Wednesday 14: Australian forces embroiled in fierce fighting with the Japanese high in the Owen Stanley mountains on Papua New Guinea.

Henderson Field, Guadalcanal, comes under fierce land, air and sea attack from the Japanese.

Saturday 17: Convoys assemble for 'Operation Torch', the Allied landings in Morocco.

Friday 23: Montgomery's 'Operation Lightfoot' begins in North Africa along the coast at El Alamein.

Sunday 25: The RAF causes havoc in northern Italy, carrying out 24-hour raids on the key centres of Milan, Genoa and Turin.

'Operation Torch' begins with Allied landings at Algiers, Oran and Casablanca

Wedding cakes made of cardboard decorated with chalk icing are the fashion in Britain after sugar-coated confectionery is banned.

Monday 26: Aircraft carrier USS Hornet is sunk by Japanese aircraft in the Battle of Santa Cruz.

Brutal street fighting continues in Stalingrad.

Tuesday 27: Monty regroups his troops of the 8th Army for a second offensive at El Alamein.

Friday 30: Afrika Korps trapped by advancing Australians near Alamein.

Right : Many Americans got their first taste of action in the 'Torch' landings in North Africa which finally settled the desert war.

Pvt. Joe Louis says—

"We're going to do our part ...and we'll win because we're on God's side"

■ NOVEMBER ■

Monday 2: 'Operation Supercharge', the second El Alamein offensive, gets underway in the desert, forcing Rommel to retreat.

Friday 6: Heavy rain hampers the whirlwind advance made by Montgomery at Mersa Matruh.

Women are finally permitted to enter church in England without wearing hats.

Sunday 8: 'Operation Torch' begins with Allied landings at Algiers, Oran and Casablanca.

Pierre Laval cuts diplomatic relations with the US.

Monday 9: Field-Marshal Rommel recieves long-awaited reinforcements in Tunisia.

Tuesday 10: Resistance to the Allies in Algeria comes to an end following an order to lay down arms from Admiral Jean François Darlan, the military commander representing Vichy France.

Wednesday 11: German troops move into Vichy France in 'Operation Anton'. The last vestiges of French independence are removed.

Thursday 12: First naval battle at Guadalcanal.

Friday 13: Libyan port of Tobruk back in Allied hands.

Saturday 14: The US triumphs in the second sea battle of Guadalcanal.

Australian troops find fresh success in Papua New Guinea.

Sunday 15: Monty triumphs in the second Battle of El Alamein.

Japanese convoy destroyed by US off Guadalcanal.

Thusday 19: Red Army opens its winter offensive with counter-attack on the German flanks at Stalingrad.

Friday 20: Turin suffers the worst bombing raid inflicted on Italy during the war.

Monty reaches Benghazi.

◆ EYE WITNESS ◆

John Hughes, 76, from Portsmouth, was a seaman serving on long-range destroyer escorts. Most of this service was with HMS *Vesper* guarding Atlantic convoys.

❝ We had a lot of contact with American servicemen. On many crossings we'd tie up alongside USS *Prairie*, which was permanently stationed in Newfoundland as a repair ship. Anyone who has regularly sailed the North Atlantic would understand just how regularly we needed repairs.

That was when I realised how close the war had brought the British and the Americans. Of course, there was a bit of barracking – there always is – but it was mostly good humoured.

The Yanks were very generous. We didn't have a lot of money in those days but whenever we went aboard the *Prairie* we'd end up with chocolates, cigarettes, stockings and other bits and pieces for our girlfriends. Some sweethearts did very well out of the *Prairie*, I can tell you.

I've never forgotten the way we were treated. It reminded us that when the chips were down, the Americans were in there with us. The only way we could repay them was to do our utmost to get their ships safely across the ocean. ❞

Monday 23: German 6th Army and four Panzer divisions, under General Paulus, encircled and trapped at Stalingrad, as Russians launch 'Operation Uranus'.

French West Africa switches sides and joins the Allies.

Friday 27: French fleet scuttled as Germans enter Toulon, Vichy France.

Sunday 29: Coffee rationing gets underway in the US.

German 16th Army and four Panzer divisions encircled and trapped at Stalingrad

---

■ DECEMBER ■

Tuesday 1: Australians capture Gona, New Guinea.

Petrol rationing starts in US.

Britain's blueprint for the welfare state is unveiled. The plan, drawn up by Sir William Beveridge, is backed by the unions but opposed in some sectors of commerce.

Tuesday 8: Rommel's hard-pressed forces withdraw to Tunis.

Sunday 13: Britain's Jewish population marks the suffering and killings among their counterparts in Europe with a day of mourning.

Monday 21: British and Indian troops embark on the first Arakan offensive in Burma.

Tuesday 22: Four children aged between two and 15 are killed in an explosion at their home in Margate, Kent. It is thought to have been caused by an unexploded mortar bomb found and brought home by the eldest of the children.

Wednesday 23: Britain has ordered from Canada powdered eggs equivalent to 63,000,000 shell eggs, it is announced in Ottawa.

A mother of two from Bedford,

England, is killed when a plane crashes in flames on to her house following a mid-air collision. The woman's children were rescued from the wreckage.

Thursday 24: Admiral Darlan, military chief in Algeria, pays the ultimate price for switching his allegiances from Vichy France to the Allies. He is shot by an assailant and dies before he reaching hospital. His assassin was a Frenchman loyal to Marshal Pétain, presently held captive by the Germans.

Friday 25: British 8th Army reaches Libyan coastal town of Sirte but finds toughening resistance from Afrika Korps units ensconced in hilltop defensive positions.

Thursday 31: Battle of Barents Sea.

Above: **French warships lie crippled at their moorings after being scuttled following Nazi moves on the port of Toulon, southern France.**

1943

The first seeds of an Allied victory are sown with Rommel being ousted from North Africa, a strike at Italy and the rout of Germany in Russia at the key battle of Kursk. In the Pacific, US forces and Australians begin clawing back Japanese-occupied territory.

JANUARY

Monday 4: Japan begins evacuation of Guadalcanal.

Tuesday 5: Lieutenant-General Mark Clark appointed commander of the US 5th Army.

Thursday 14: Churchill and Roosevelt attend Casablanca Conference with de Gaulle.

Monday 18: Tiger tanks used for the first time by the Germans in Tunisia.

Saturday 23: Britain's 8th Army moves into Tripoli.

End of Casablanca Conference – Roosevelt demands 'unconditional surrender' of the Axis powers.

Tuesday 26: Russians capture Voronezh on the River Do, taking 52,000 German prisoners.

Wednesday 27: US 8th Air Force undertakes first bombing raid on Germany, targeting Wilhelmshaven and Emden.

Sunday 31: Paulus surrenders at Stalingrad. It is the first field defeat experienced by Germany.

The RAF makes two daylight raids on Berlin, disrupting speeches by Nazi bigwigs to mark ten years of fascism in Germany.

FEBRUARY

Thursday 4: 8th Army units enter Tunisia, to meet a volley of German counter-attacks in the coming weeks.

Friday 5: Mussolini sacks his son-in-law Count Ciano and assumes the post of foreign minister himself.

Saturday 6: Matinée idol Errol Flynn is acquitted on three rape charges.

Above: **Lieutenant-General Mark Clark, soon to command the invasion of Sicily.**

Two women claimed the star had molested them. Flynn, 33, denied the allegations. It took a jury 13 hours to come to its decision.

Monday 8: Russians liberate the city of Kursk in central USSR.

Wednesday 10: Gandhi begins a 21-day fast in protest at his incarceration in Poona jail.

Sunday 14: Chindits cross the River Chindwin in Burma.

Above: **The Casablanca Conference.**
Left: **Major-General George Patton.**

Right: **Heart-throb Hollywood star Errol Flynn is cleared of rape.**

Surrender at Stalingrad. It is the first field defeat experienced by Germany

Above: **Stuttgart is a city in ruins after giant new bombs rain down on its industrial heart. The weapons used were the 8,000lb 'Blockbuster' and the 4,000lb 'Factory-smasher'.**

Tuesday 16: SS chief Himmler launches plans to eliminate the Jewish ghetto in Warsaw.

Thursday 18: Labour MPs cause uproar in the House of Commons when the coalition government refuses to name the day for the introduction of the welfare state.

■ MARCH ■

Monday 1: Weak from lack of food, Mahatma Gandhi brings his protest fast to an end.

Tuesday 2: Battle of the Bismarck Sea commences.

Berlin is the target for an explosive 900-ton air raid by the RAF.

Saturday 6: Rommel leaves Africa.

Sunday 14: Strategic foothold of Kharkov in Russia is recoccupied by the Germans.

Wednesday 24: Cabinet Secretary Lord Maurice Hankey brands the measures taken to combat the U-boat menace 'our greatest failure'.

Friday 26: All Britons in Vichy France are put under arrest by a jittery German army. They fear an Allied invasion is imminent.

First Arakan offensive ends in retreat for the British and Indian forces

---

Saturday 27: German resistance workers explode bridges on the River Oder in Frankfurt.

Sunday 28: Russian-born composer Sergei Rachmaninov dies at his home in Beverly Hills, aged 69.

Tuesday 30: First Arakan offensive ends in retreat for the British and Indian forces.

■ APRIL ■

Monday 5: The Vichy regime hands Daladier, Blum, Reynaud and Mandel, all prominent politicians before the war who have resisted Nazism, to the Germans.

Monday 12: Another stringent budget puts a 100 per cent tax on luxury goods.

Wednesday 14: Rommel evacuates his troops from Tunis.

Thursday 15: A mighty 8,000lb bomb called a 'Blockbuster' is dropped on Stuttgart along with 4,000lb 'Factory-smasher' bombs.

Sunday 18: Admiral Yamamoto killed over Bougainville when his plane is shot down by American fighter aircraft.

Tuesday 20: In Britain, church bells, banned except to indicate the launch of a German invasion, are being permitted to ring again by a government convinced that the risk of German occupation is past.

Monday 26: A row between Stalin

RAF Lancasters from 617 Squadron carry out the famous 'Dambusters' raid on the Ruhr

and the Allies blows up over German claims that Russian secret police officers murdered 4,000 Polish army officers. The Germans uncovered a mass grave at Katyn near the Russian city of Smolensk. They claim the

officers were taken prisoner by Russia after the fall of Poland in 1939. The Polish government-in-exile is anxiously seeking clarification while Stalin is allegedly furious over the issue.

Thursday 29: The RAF embarks on its biggest mine-laying exercise of the war in the busy Baltic Sea.

■ MAY ■

Saturday 1: American miners announce a strike in protest at a pay freeze.

Sunday 2: As Roosevelt is poised to seize the mines to prevent the stoppages, miners, unions in America call off the dispute.

Monday 3: The British government makes part-time war work compulsory for women between the ages of 18 and 45.

Above: **Actor Leslie Howard perished in a plane crash en route from Spain.**

Tuesday 4: The rift between Poland and Russia is patched up with General Sikorski, the Polish leader, instructing Poles to ally with Russia. Soon afterwards, Stalin announces his plans for a strong and free Poland at the end of the war.

Friday 7: Tunis falls to Allies. The North African campaign is over.

Second Washington Conference of Allied leaders gets underway.

Sunday 9: Martial law is declared in Holland by Germans convinced that an Allied invasion is coming.

Friday 14: A hospital ship is torpedoed off Australia by a Japanese submarine, killing up to 300 people.

Monday 17: RAF Lancasters from 617 Squadron carry out the famous 'Dambusters' raid on the Mohne and Eder dams, bringing flooding and severe disruption to the Ruhr.

Thursday 20: More than 100 aircraft are destroyed when Allied planes attack Italian airfields.

Sunday 30: Churchill and de Gaulle arrive in triumph at Algiers.

Monday 31: A French 'provisional government' is established by General de Gaulle and General Giraud in Algiers.

◆ EYE WITNESS ◆

Olive Boddill was working in a factory before she joined the Land Army in 1943.

❝ I was 18 when I volunteered for the Land Army. I left my home in Leeds, Yorkshire, to work on farms in Grantham, Lincs.

There I lived in a hostel with 39 other Land Army girls. We were posted out to different farms, potato-picking or other work, including driving. I had never driven before and I didn't do it very well, either.

We wanted to get away from parental control and enjoy ourselves. I didn't think too deeply about the reasons behind volunteering.

We worked alongside Italian prisoners of war. They were glad to be in England. They admitted they didn't like fighting which is why they surrendered very quickly. We used to trade our cigarettes for their cake.

One day when I forgot my packed lunch a farmer invited me in for something to eat. All my friends were jealous, thinking I was going to have a slap-up meal. Instead, he showed me the orchard out the back and told me to eat all the rotten apples on the ground.

We had to make our own entertainment at first until troops including the US air force were stationed near us. Then there was plenty to do.

The village "pub" was run by Stan Laurel's sister Olga, a former music hall artiste, in her living room.

The Americans had lots of money and they were very generous when our boys couldn't afford to be. We got a lot of cigarettes, sweets and goodies. Every birthday they threw a party and sent down a truck for us. Many were there one minute and gone the next. We were very hard about these things. We just accepted it.

We saw a lot of planes crash – damaged planes trying to make their way home. People were immune to death during the war.

One day I saw two planes collide in mid-air. That weekend I was hitch-hiking home to Leeds. A bloke jumped on the same lorry. He was going to Leeds too, to inform the parents of one of the men in those planes that their son was dead. It was upsetting but you got very blasé about these things in wartime. ❞

■ JUNE ■

Thursday 1: British actor Leslie Howard dies when the airliner he is travelling on is shot down in the Bay of Biscay. Howard, best remembered as Ashley Wilkes in Gone with the Wind had been visiting Spain, in an effort to persuade cinemas there to screen British-made movies.

Monday 7: Italian troops begin to pull out of Albania.

Friday 11: The Mediterranean island of Pantelleria surrenders to the Allies

Epic tank and air battle for Kursk begins between Germans and Russians

after 13 days of continuous air bombardment. The island – a halfway point between Tunis, now in Allied hands, and Sicily – was battered into submission by waves of attack aircraft and fell before a seaborne invasion was necessary.

Friday 16: Japanese lose 100 aircraft over Guadalcanal.

Sunday 18: Field-Marshal Wavell, once sacked from North Africa, is appointed Viceroy of India.

Monday 19: In Berlin, Goebbels triumphantly reports the city is 'free of Jews'.

Wednesday 21: French Resistance leader Jean Moulin is arrested after a meeting of undercover agents was betrayed to the Gestapo.

Sunday 25: Sicily comes under fire from Allies.

Friday 30: Amphibious offensive against Japanese in the Solomon Islands begins.

Right: **The invasion of Sicily was a vital blow at Hitler's Europe. Despite its success, many Germans escaped.**

■ JULY ■

Sunday 4: General Wladyslaw Sikorski, leader of the Free Polish government and army, is killed in an air crash. The Liberator plane ran into trouble soon after leaving Gibraltar and crashed into the sea.

Monday 5: Epic tank and air battle for Kursk begins between Germans and Russians.

Thursday 8: President of the National Resistance Council Jean Moulin is dead after lengthy torture by the Gestapo. The 44-year-old was also known as 'Max'.

Saturday 10: The invasion of Sicily by Allied Forces, 'Operation Husky', gets underway.

Tuesday 13: The tank battle at Kursk ends in defeat for Germany.

Sunday 18: A German U-boat shoots down a US airship off Florida Keys, the only airship lost by America during the war.

Monday 19: A bombing raid by US planes over Rome causes hundreds of casualties. Yet despite the immense tonnage of explosives dropped by the aircraft, the architectural treasures of the city remain intact.

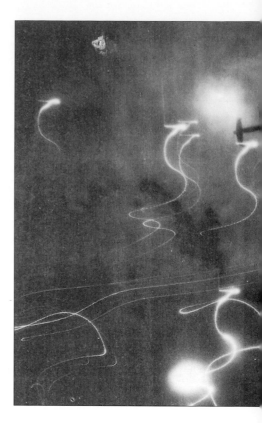

Thursday 22: US 7th Army, led by General Patton, seizes Palermo, Sicily, and heads for Messina. Meanwhile Monty's 8th Army is held up by retreating Kesselring.

Sunday 25: Mussolini resigns and is arrested. In his place as Prime Minister comes Marshal Badoglio.

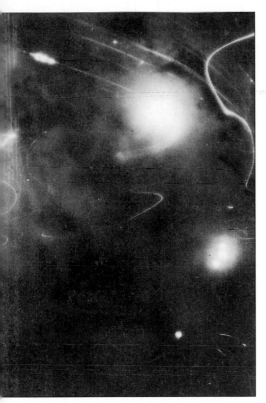

Above: Flares light up the path of a Lancaster bomber over Hamburg.

Tuesday 27: A firestorm rages in the German city of Hanover after an incendiary raid by the Royal Air Force. It followed three days of continuous raids on the city.

■ **AUGUST** ■

Monday 2: A further raid by the RAF on Hamburg brings the death toll there to 40,000, with 37,000 seriously injured.

Friday 6: Naval battle of Vella Gulf in the Solomon Islands.

Saturday 14: Rome declared an 'open city'.

Sunday 15: Marshal Badoglio, now heading a new Italian government, sends a peace emissary to Spain.

Tuesday 17: German soldiers in Sicily are finally either captured or escape to the mainland.

Tuesday 24: Quadrant Conference in Quebec between Churchill, Roosevelt and Canadian prime minister Mackenzie King ends after eight

◆ THE BATTLE OF KURSK

The high point of the German push east was reached in November 1942. The Soviets then launched a winter offensive that formed a bulge, or salient, in the invaders' line around the city of Kursk. In summer 1943, the Germans attacked Kursk, with the 9th Army, under General Kluge, striking from the north and the 4th Panzer Army, under Field-Marshal Manstein, attacking from the south in a pincer movement. Unfortunately for the Germans, the Russians had forewarning of the operation, cancelling the element of surprise and enabling them to assemble a formidable defence. In the ensuing battle 6,000 tanks were involved, along with two million men and 4,000 aircraft. The battle was an epic, but when it was over, it was the Germans who were in retreat.

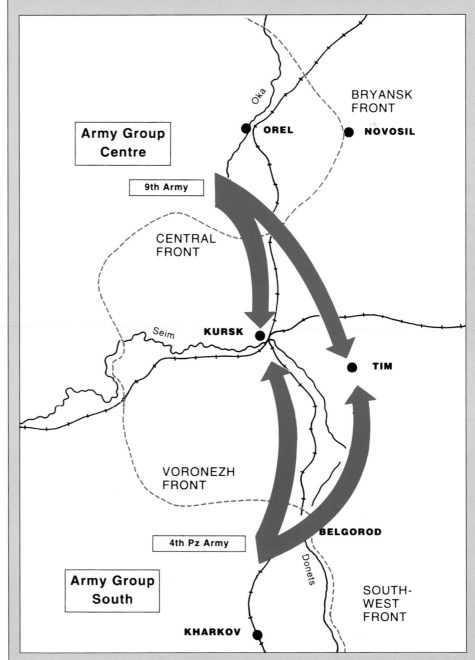

Above: **Popular pianist Fats Waller was just 39 when he died in 1943.**

days, with all leaders confident that victory is within their grasp.

Wednesday 25: Admiral Mountbatten is appointed Supreme Allied Commander in South East Asia.

Thursday 26: Russian forces begin a five-pronged assault on the German-held Ukraine.

Saturday 28: Bulgaria's King Boris dies after being shot by an assassin.

■ SEPTEMBER ■

Friday 3: Invasion of Italy begins. A ceasefire between Italy and the Allies is agreed but kept under wraps for five days.

Thursday 9: Allies land at Salerno in 'Operation Avalanche' in the face of fierce defensive fire from defending German forces.

Friday 10: German troops under von Vietinghoff seize Rome.

Sunday 12: Mussolini is sprung from prison in a plan approved by Hitler.

Monday 13: Germans stage a counter-attack at Salerno.

Friday 17: British and American forces join up in Italy to push back the Germans.

Monday 20: British Chancellor, Sir Kingsley Wood, dies suddenly, and is replaced by Sir John Anderson.

Wednesday 22: The introduction of Pay As You Earn (PAYE) is announced to British tax-payers. For the first time everyone will get a tax code number and their revenue dues will be deducted at source instead of demanded subsequently.

Wednesday 29: Polish trades union leader turned president Lech Walesa is born.

■ OCTOBER ■

Friday 1: US 5th Army reaches Naples, a key Italian port.

Monday 4: The island of Corsica is taken by the French Resistance, their first victory in their struggle to oust the Germans from their homeland.

Tuesday 5: US starts shelling Wake Island in the Pacific.

Monday 11: British midget submarines attempt to sink *Tirpitz*,

◆ EYE WITNESS ◆

Derek Brooks, from Porchester, England, served on board HMS *Ramillies* and saw action at D-Day as the battleship gave supporting fire to paratroops storming Pegasus Bridge.

❝ During a lull in the gunfire I managed to snatch a few moments' fitful sleep while sitting at the anti-aircraft artillery. Something woke me up and I peered my head over the side of the placement to see what it was. At that very moment both the 15-inch gun turrets engaged simultaneously. The shock waves blew me straight out of my seat.

They don't make alarm clocks like that any more. ❞

the mighty German battleship.

Wednesday 13: Italy declares war on Germany.

Tuesday 19: In the first exchange of its kind, 4,200 British prisoners of war are swapped for a similar number of Germans on neutral Swedish territory.

Italian partisans join forces with Tito's Yugoslav resistance movement to fight the Germans.

Thursday 21: A daring exploit by the French Resistance in Lyon springs 14 of their colleagues from jail.

Allied troops encounter stiff resistance from Germans holed up around Monte Cassino

Friday 29: Troops stand in for striking dockers in London.

Sunday 31: Allied troops encounter stiff resistance from Germans holed up around Monte Cassino.

■ NOVEMBER ■

Monday 1: US Marines land at Bougainville in the Solomons.

Saturday 6: Red Army enters Kiev, in German hands since the first thrust of 'Barbarossa'.

Thursday 11: The Lebanese government is arrested and held for ten days by irate French troops after making a declaration of independence.

Tuesday 16: German forces defeat the defending British and Italian garrison of Leros in the Dodecanese.

Thursday 18: Massive bombing raid by RAF on Berlin with 350 4,000lb bombs falling on the Reich's capital.

Saturday 20: Sir Oswald Mosley, leader of the British Union of Fascists, is released from jail on the grounds of ill-health. He will remain under house arrest.

Monday 22: Churchill and Roosevelt meet with China's Chiang Kai-shek in North Africa in an historic conference on the war against Japan.

Tuesday 23: Tarawa, in the Gilbert Islands, is captured by the US Marines with just 17 of the defending Japanese force of more than 4,500 left alive. More than 1,000 Marines died in 'Operation Galvanic', one of the most arduous amphibious landings experienced by the Americans during the war.

Sunday 28: Teheran Conference begins, with the big three, Churchill, Roosevelt and Stalin, meeting to discuss the war efforts.

■ DECEMBER ■

Thursday 2: Ernest Bevin, the Minister of Labour, announces that one in ten men called up between the ages of 18 and 25 will be sent to work at the coal face. The government is concerned about the shortage of miners after an exodus of young men to join the forces. The 'Bevin Boys', as they have been tagged, will be selected by ballot.

Saturday 4: Churchill and Roosevelt meet Turkish president Ismet Inonu in a bid to forge closer links between the three countries.

Eisenhower is named as supreme commander for the Allied invasion of western Europe

Sunday 5: Tito forms a provisional government of Yugoslavia.

Friday 10: Roosevelt visits Malta to witness for himself the effects of months of siege laid by the Germans and Italians.

Sunday 12: Rommel appointed commander in chief of German defences along the Atlantic Wall.

Wednesday 15: US jazz pianist and composer Thomas 'Fats' Waller dies, aged 39.

Sunday 19: A war crimes trial held in Kharkov, Russia, finds three Germans guilty. All are hanged.

Wednesday 22: British children's author and illustrator Beatrix Potter dies, aged 77.

According to government figures, there will be enough turkeys for only one in ten families this Christmas.

Friday 24: US General Dwight D. Eisenhower is named as supreme commander for the Allied invasion of western Europe.

Saturday 25: US Marines land on New Britain.

Sunday 26: Battle of the North Cape. German surface raider, the battle-cruiser *Scharnhorst,* is sunk by the Home Fleet, spearheaded by HMS *Duke of York.*

Below: General Dwight D. Eisenhower launched plans for D-Day months before it took place.

Halfway through the year, the Allies played a trump card. The invasion of Normandy was a sparkling success, even though there were still months of grinding battle to endure before an overall triumph was secured.

■ JANUARY ■

Sunday 2: Russian armies are within 20 miles of Poland.

Tuesday 4: Hitler presses all children over the age of ten into the war effort.

Thursday 6: Russian forces move into Poland.

Tuesday 11: Mussolini has his son-in-law Count Ciano executed on a charge of treason.

Saturday 15: Germans dig in around Monte Cassino.

The abbey atop Monte Cassino is destroyed by air and artillery attacks, but resistance continues

---

Sunday 16: Eisenhower appointed Supreme Commander of the Allied Expeditionary Force.

Saturday 22: Allies land at Anzio. However, a plan to cut through the German flank is doomed.

Above: A German shell smashes into one of the landing vehicles at Anzio, Italy.
Right: Inspired by Gauguin and van Gogh, Edvard Munch was best known for his painting *The Scream*.
Far left: The US 7th Army at Saarbrucken.

Sunday 23: Norwegian artist Edvard Munch dies, aged 81. His work became a major influence on 20th century impressionism.

Thursday 27: Leningrad is relieved after a siege lasting 900 days.

Monday 31: After first pounding it from the air and the sea, US forces land on Kwajalein in the Marshall Islands. A week-long battle leaves 16,300 Japanese dead with just 264 taken prisoner.

■ FEBRUARY ■

Wednesday 2: All French men aged between 16 and 60 are forced to work in Germany.

Sunday 6: Second Arakan offensive ends in failure for Britain.

Tuesday 8: 'Operation Overlord', the

invasion of Europe, is given the green light in Whitehall. Now begins months of detailed planning in time for the massive amphibious landing to take place in Normandy in June.

Sunday 13: Weapons for the French Resistance are dropped by the Allies in Haute-Savoie, south east France.

Tuesday 15: The abbey atop Monte Cassino is destroyed by air and artillery attacks but resistance by the Germans continues. Governments on both sides of the Atlantic are forced to defend the decision to bomb the Christian cultural treasure.

Wednesday 16: Allies at Anzio under pressure from German counter-attack.

Thursday 17: Plans for a national health service at the end of the war are announced in Britain.

Friday 18: Truk, in the Central Pacific, comes under US fire with its airfield and harbour being destroyed.

Luftwaffe commences another blitz of London.

Eisenhower receives Russia's highest military honour, the Order of Suvorov First Class.

Tuesday 29: US troops landed on the Admiralty Islands, in the South West Pacific, in 'Operation Brewer'.

■ MARCH ■

Wednesday 1: Chindits enter Burma once again, this time by glider.

Saturday 4: It is announced that tests in Bath, Britain, prove that children conceived in the winter are more intelligent.

Wednesday 8: Japanese launch 'Operation U-Go' against British troops in Burma.

The engine of Britain's Spitfire aircraft is is to be enlarged.

Japanese forces drive a wedge between British forces at Kohima and Imphal in Burma

---

Thursday 9: Japanese take action against Bougainville.

Sunday 12: Travel between England and all parts of Ireland is banned to prevent word of the invasion plan reaching Germany.

Wednesday 15: Further attacks

Above: **A plane crash claimed the life of Major-General Charles Orde Wingate.**

against the German-held strongpoint of Monte Cassino carried out by Allied forces.

Thursday 16: Japanese forces drive a wedge between British forces at Kohima and Imphal in Burma.

Friday 17: New Zealand forces reach the railway station at Monte Cassino.

Saturday 18: Imphal is reinforced by an Indian division from Arakan.

Germans begin an occupation of Hungary.

Friday 24: Major-General Orde Wingate, creator and commander of the Chindits, dies in a plane crash.

Tuesday 28: MPs vote to give women and men teachers equal pay.

Wednesday 29: Allied forces under siege at Imphal by Japanese troops under Lieutenant-General Mutaguchi.

■ APRIL ■

Saturday 1: Fifty people die when US bombs neutral Switzerland in error.

Sunday 2: Russians enter Romania.

Wednesday 5: Kohima is under seige.

Germany begins rounding up and deporting Jews from Hungary.

Sunday 9: General Charles de Gaulle is created commander in chief of the Free French forces.

Monday 10: Odessa is freed by the advancing Red Army.

Sunday 16: Stalin orders his troops not to allow any retreating Germans to escape as Russian forces surge through the Crimea.

Tuesday 18: Kohima is reinforced.

Thursday 20: Troops drive London's buses following a strike.

The Royal Air Force drops 4,500 tons of bombs on occupied Europe.

Saturday 22: US troops land in Hollandia, New Guinea.

Thursday 27: The British government bans foreign travel in a bid to keep the invasion plans quiet. Visitors are already barred from approaching within ten miles of the British coast.

Sunday 30: Britain's first pre-fabricated homes go on show in London. After the war, the steel-framed single-

---

Above: **Londoners were riding high while the troops operated the bus services, offering free transport on selected routes.**

storey homes will alleviate the housing shortage after the war brought about by enemy bombing.

■ MAY ■

Wednesday 3: British and Indian troops notch up a triumph at Arakan by taking a vital link road.
Tuesday 9: Sevastopol is liberated by the Red Army.
Friday 12: Final German forces are evacuated from the Crimea.
Monday 15: Rommel clamps down in Vichy France, cancelling all passenger train services and raiding the diplomatic bags for foreign powers held at the Vichy war ministry. His aim is to stop the Resistance sending and receiving messages.

Tuesday 16: Gustav line in Italy finally penetrated by Allied forces.
Wednesday 17: German forces withdraw from Cassino.
Thursday 18: Monte Cassino falls to Polish troops. The Gustav line of defences is ruptured.

The 'Great Escape' from Stalag Luft III ends in disaster when 47 recaptured airmen are shot

Tuesday 23: Allied troops held down in Anzio finally break out.
Thursday 25: Chindits forced to

withdraw under heavy counter-attack from Japanese.

Tito flees to a hilltop hideaway as Germans seize Bosnia.
Sunday 28: The 'Great Escape' by officers from Stalag Luft III in Silesia. It ended in disaster when 47 recaptured airmen were shot by Gestapo.
Wednesday 31: For the first time in months, Britain suffers no civilian casualties during May.

■ JUNE ■

Saturday 3: Battle of Kohima ends in Allied victory.

◆ EYE WITNESS ◆

Melvin Marr Middleton was with the Third Brigade of the 7th Canadian Infantry Division. He joined up at the end of 1940 when he was 26.

'After six months training in Canada I arrived over here with nothing but my grey coat and some spare socks in my pocket. I was issued with a Bren gun which I carried through the war. But I never had a single round of ammunition. They just didn't give me any. It did seem ridiculous to me but at the same time I just had to get on with it. If we ever ran into action, I hoped they would give me some ammunition.

I was in a mobile workshop repairing optical equipment like binoculars, dial sights and range-finders. I landed in France on D-Day-plus-four and was based five miles outside Caen. Still nobody in the workshop had ammunition. Perhaps they were afraid we would shoot ourselves.

We followed the infantry up to service their instruments. Because we were in a truck we became a target. The soldiers used to bring up their instruments in the middle of the night, put them outside the door and disappear. They would come the next night to collect them.

While I was in Europe I travelled in a Jeep when the Germans started shelling. The driver hit a shell crater and I bounced up in the air, landing with my back across the seat. At the time the medics told me it was bad bruising. Only when I left the forces in 1963 was I told that I had caused permanent damage to my back which puts me in a wheelchair today.'

This man is your **FRIEND**

Canadian

He fights for **FREEDOM**
★ ★ ★

Sunday 4: Rome falls to Allies.
Monday 5 June: Twelve British minesweepers clear the waters in preparation for the Normandy landings. Airborne forces are dropped behind enemy lines.

King Victor Emmanuel III of Italy abdicates in favour of Crown Prince Umberto.
Tuesday 6: D-Day begins.
Wednesday 7: British take Bayeux.
Thursday 8: American forces capture Ste Mère Eglise.
Friday 9: Invading allied armies meet up in Normandy.
Saturday 10: An England XI beats the West Indies by 166 runs at Lords in a benefit match for the Colonial Comforts Fund.

Right: **A triumphant British newspaper announces the arrival of troops in Rome.**

Sunday 11: London newspaper The Observer reports that relations between the British and Americans on one side and Free French leader General Charles de Gaulle on the other remain 'the outstanding problem of Allied diplomacy'. Disagreements between the two sides arose after America refused to acknowledge de Gaulle's left-of-centre French Committee as the provisional government of France.
Tuesday 13: First V1 flying bomb lands in England.

In the Battle of Villers-Bocage, British tanks take a hammering and are forced to withdraw.

D-Day begins.
British take Bayeux.
American forces capture
Ste Mère Eglise

Thursday 15: US Marines land on Saipan in the Marianas.
Friday 16: Sustained attacks by V1 bombs over southern England.

King George VI visits Normandy invasion forces behind the front line.
Sunday 18: Assisi in Italy is taken by the 8th Army.
Monday 19: Battle of the Philippine Sea in which 250 Japanese aircraft are brought down in the 'Great Marianas Turkey Shoot'.

BLACKOUT TIMES

Daily Herald STOP PRESS No. 8625 MONDAY, JUNE 5, 1944 ONE PENNY TANKS IN ROME

Tanks, Guns Race Up Highway Six, Storm Into First Axis Capital

ALLIES IN ROME
Yard-By-Yard Battle Through Streets

HORDES OF PRISONERS MARCH OUT

Another Explosion In Arms Train

"Shall Fight On," Said Rome Radio

All-Day Blows At Invasion Coast

Gales wreck the giant Mulberry harbours ferried to Normandy to provide unloading facilities for the invading Allies.

Wednesday 21: A thousand-bomber raid on Berlin is staged by the US Army Air Forces.

Thursday 22: Imphal is relieved.

Allies seize V1 rocket site at Cherbourg, northern France.

Monday 26: 'Operation Epsom' to take Caen in Normandy is mounted by British and Canadian troops.

Thursday 29: Cherbourg is liberated by US forces.

Friday 30: Civilian casualties in Britain during June amounted to 1,935 dead and more than 5,900 injured, due to the V1 bombs.

'Epsom' ends with five-mile gain, but Caen is still in German hands.

■ JULY ■

Monday 3: Russians recapture town of Minsk.

London children face evacuation again due to the danger of V1 'doodlebug' flying bombs.

Thursday 6: Appalled at the progress of the Allies in France, Hitler sacks von Runstedt as supreme commander of his western forces.

Friday 7: Caen is comprehensively bombed by the Royal Air Force.

Sunday 9: Caen is finally taken by British forces.

Wednesday 12: US 5th Army, under Lieutenant-General Mark Clark, pushes through Tuscany, northern Italy.

Thursday 13: Red Army seizes Vilna, the capital of Lithuania.

Monday 17: 8th Army under General Leese crosses the River Arno and is poised to take Florence.

US forces capture the town of St Lô in Normandy.

Rommel is badly injured in an aircraft attack.

Tuesday 18: 'Operation Goodwood' on the outskirts of Caen, designed to wipe out lingering German resistance, gets underway.

Wednesday 19: Russian troops enter Latvia on the Baltic.

Thursday 20: Roosevelt wins the

Above: **An LST is crammed full on its way to the beaches of Normandy and the liberation of France.**

nomination to run for a fourth term of office. Harry S. Truman is his running-mate.

High-ranking German officers Colonel Count von Stauffenberg and Lieutenant-General Olbricht make an unsuccessful attempt on the life of

Like the D-Day forces, US troops in the Pacific faced tough and dangerous landings, such as this one on Saipan.

the Führer. Three German officers are killed when a bomb concealed in a suitcase went off under a conference table in an East Prussian headquarters. Hitler, who was shaken but unharmed, broadcast to Germany afterwards. 'A very small clique of ambitious, unscrupulous and, at the same time, criminally stupid officers laid a plot to remove me.'

Friday 21: US Marines land on Guam in the Marianas.
Monday 24: 'Operation Cobra'

Below: **British infantrymen march out of the shadow of the Duomo, the grand cathedral of Florence.**

pulled off by the US forces shatters the stalemate in Normandy.
Tuesday 25: Canadians force their way south of Caen.
Wednesday 26: Japanese counter-attack on Guam.
Thursday 27: Guam is captured by the Americans.
Friday 28: Red Army captures Brest-Litovsk on the River Bug.

High-ranking German officers make an unsuccessful attempt on the life of the Führer

■ AUGUST ■

Tuesday 1: Warsaw up rising begins as the Polish Home Army takes on the German occupying forces.
Thursday 3: German occupying forces leave the Channel Islands.
Saturday 5: Japanese prisoners of war held at Cowra Camp, New South Wales, Australia, stage a mass break-out. In the early hours, 1,100 storm the barbed wire, overcome a machine-gun post and kill its crew. A fire begun in the camp huts kills 12 of them; 31 committed suicide, 200 were killed by guards and 108 were wounded. The rest were recaptured.

Tuesday 8: Canadians head towards Falaise in Normandy, soon to be joined by the US 3rd Army after it completes its clearance of St Malo and Le Mans.

One field-marshal, four generals and three other officers are sentenced to death for their part in the July bomb plot to assassinate Hitler. They are to be hanged by piano wire from meat hooks.
Thursday 10: Japanese resistance on Guam virtually eliminated – although the last Japanese soldier to surrender fails to emerge from the jungle there until 1972.
Saturday 12: The 'Pluto' pipeline from the Isle of Wight to Cherbourg begins operations to supply the Allies with adequate fuel for their operations in France.
Tuesday 15: 'Operation Anvil', the

invasion through southern France, gets underway.

Wednesday 16: Canadian forces take Falaise in Normandy.

Saturday 19: Field-Marshal von Kluge, a senior German officer aligned to the July bomb plot to assassinate Hitler, commits suicide.

Marshal Pétain is arrested by the Germans and taken to Belfort.

Sunday 20: French troops liberate Toulon on the south coast of France.

Russians follow the Danube south.

Monday 21: Falaise gap is finally closed to fleeing German troops.

Tuesday 22: German battleship Tirpitz, sister ship to Bismarck, comes under attack from Allied aircraft.

Wednesday 23: Romania concedes

defeat to the Soviet Red Army.

Friday 25: Paris is liberated by Free French troops led by General Leclerc. German commander von Choltitz defies Hitler's orders by refusing to burn the city.

Romania declares war on Germany.

Saturday 26: US and British forces head east of the River Seine.

Bulgaria withdraws from war.

Sunday 27: Chindits evacuated to India from Burma.

Monday 28: Marseilles is freed by invading forces.

Thursday 31: Monty is promoted to the rank of field-marshal.

■ SEPTEMBER ■

Friday 1: Canadian troops take Dieppe and Rouen. The US 5th Army takes Pisa.

Sunday 3: The British Guards Armoured Division liberates Brussels.

The Allies wreck 900 German motorised vehicles and 750 horse-drawn vehicles on the Mons to Brussels road.

Wednesday 6: The Red Army reaches Yugoslavia.

Friday 8: First V2 attack on London.

The Belgian government returns to its homeland from exile in London.

The Red Army takes Bulgaria.

Paris is liberated by the Free French troops, led by General Leclerc

Sunday 10: Prague falls to Russian The Red Army takes Bulgaria, while Finland signs a peace accord with Stalin.

US troops enter Luxembourg.

Tuesday 12: US 1st Army in Germany near Aachen.

Remaining German pocket at Le Havre surrenders.

Below: **A bomber lies upturned on the beaches at Guam in the Marianas, where US Marines are landing.**

Above: **Allied troops parade at the Arc de Triomphe following the recapture of Paris. The city was liberated by the Free French.**

Friday 15: Siegfried line is broken by the US 1st Army.

US forces land in the Palau Islands.

Sunday 17: 'Operation Market Garden', in which Allied troops

British 2nd Army, under General Dempsey, reaches the Rhine

---

parachute into Nijmegen and Arnhem, begins.

Tuesday 19: British paratroopers of 1st Airborne Division isolated at Arnhem when bad weather prevents the arrival of reinforcements.

Finland signs a ceasefire with the Soviet Union.

Sunday 24: British 2nd Army, under

Right: **Paratroopers salvage what they can from a crashed glider after descending into Arnhem.**

Lieutenant-General Dempsey, reaches the Rhine.

Monday 25: Chinese commander Chiang Kai-shek requests that US General 'Vinegar' Joe Stilwell, mastermind of Chinese defences against Japan, be sacked.

Tuesday 26: Remnants of the British airborne force that dropped at Arnhem are withdrawn.

Wednesday 27: German forces counter-attack at Nijmegen.

■ OCTOBER ■

Monday 2: The Greek capital, Athens, is evacuated by Germans.

British troops land on Crete.

Monday 9: Churchill visits Moscow for talks with Stalin.

Wednesday 11: US aircraft attack Luzon in the Philippines.

Saturday 14: Rommel, another senior German incriminated in the July bomb plot to kill Hitler, commits suicide rather than risk public

condemnation as a traitor. The world is told he died after his car crashed during an aircraft attack in July.

British forces enter Athens.
Monday 16: Hungary withdraws its request for peace with the Allies when its head of state's son is kidnapped by crack German commando officer Otto Skorzeny.
Wednesday 18: A people's guard, or Volksturm, is created by Hitler for the defence of the Fatherland.

Left: The 'dragon's teeth' defences of Germany's Siegfried line, also known as the West Wall, hold no fears for these conquering US soldiers.

Thursday 19: Germans pull out of Belgrade, the Yugoslav capital.
Friday 20: US forces land on Leyte in the Philippines.

Aachen, the first German town to fall into the hands of the Allies, capitulates to the US 1st Army.
Monday 23: The three-day naval Battle of Leyte Gulf begins.
Friday 27: Kamikaze attacks launched on American ships operating in the Philippines.
Saturday 28: De Gaulle orders French Resistance fighters to lay down their arms.
Monday 30: Organised mass exterminations come to an end at Auschwitz concentration camp.

■ NOVEMBER ■

Thursday 2: Germans pull out of Greece altogether.
Friday 3: Flushing in Holland is taken by the British and Canadians.
Friday 10: The Allies acknowledge the government of Albania headed by

Left: US Marines plunge through the surf, determined to chase the Japanese out of the Philippines.

◆ THE ALLIES BOMB GERMANY

By 1944, systematic bombing of Germany by RAF and USAAF aircraft was well underway. In general terms the RAF's Bomber Command, under Air Marshal Sir Arthur Harris, concentrated on high-volume area bombing by night, whereas the UK-based US 8th Air Force favoured precision attacks against specific targets by day. In the early days of the offensive, the latter course was very costly in terms of men and machines, since Allied fighter escorts were limited in range and once they had turned for home the bombers were at the mercy of Luftwaffe interceptors. In time however, fighter-escort range increased, until by 1944 bombers could be protected right across Germany.

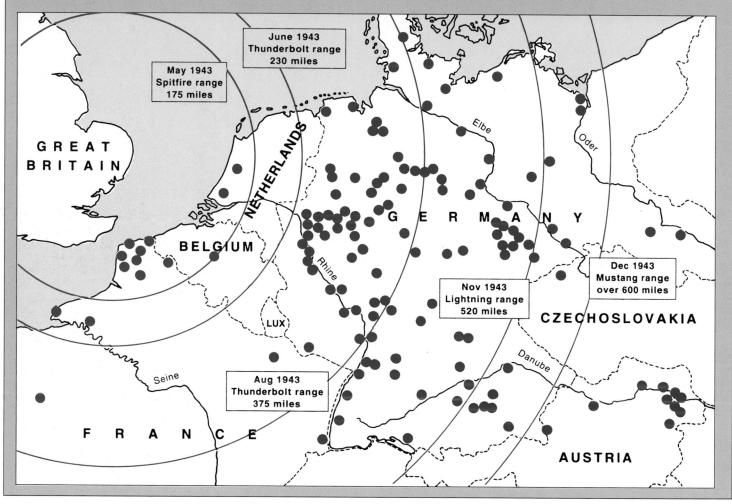

partisan Enver Hoxha.

Saturday 11: Britain's Home Guard dissolved today after four and a half years domestic defence.

Sunday 12: Tirpitz, the giant German battleship, comes under attack once more in Norway by the RAF. The units involved include 617 Squadron (Dambusters). This time the vessel sinks under the onslaught of 12,000lb 'Tallboy' bombs.

Saturday 18: US 3rd Army enters Germany in force.

Friday 24: Allies breach the Saar, putting the industrial arm of Germany under threat.

Sunday 26: Antwerp is open for merchant ships to supply the Allies, at last providing a fresh supply source for the front-line British and American forces.

Monday 27: American B-29 planes bomb Tokyo.

In Britain, 70 people are killed by a massive explosion at an RAF bomb dump near Burton on Trent.

Thursday 30: Churchill celebrates his 70th birthday.

■ **DECEMBER** ■

Friday 1: Germans pull out of the hotly contended Suda Bay, Crete.

Sunday 10: De Gaulle signs a treaty of alliance with Stalin.

Wednesay 13: The development of 'new towns', to be created for Londoners miles away from the capital, is unveiled today in a blueprint for the future drawn up by

Top: **Incendiaries shower down on Tokyo, causing mammoth damage.**

Above: **Bandleader Glenn Miller disappeared on a flight to France.**

Professor Patrick Abercrombie. Other suggestions include ring-roads around London and the development of Heathrow airport, at this time little more than an airstrip with huts.

Saturday 16: Battle of the Bulge, also known as the Battle of the Ardennes, the surprise German counter-attack, gets underway in the Ardennes. A total of 24 German divisions, including ten armoured divisions, combine for the push, which aims to capture the Belgian port of Antwerp. In fact, only one is up to full strength. Still, the Germans force a wedge between the two Allied prongs of attack and race towards their target.

Bandleader Glenn Miller goes missing on a flight to France. The man who was turned down for active service so he could entertain the troops with his distinctive sound was 40 years old.

Monday 18: British troops in Greece act to quell a left-wing rebellion aiming to seize control of the country.

Friday 22: German Panzers are driven back from the Meuse.

Japanese resistance on the Philippine island of Leyte is ended.

◆ **EYE WITNESS** ◆

Major Chester 'Chet' Hansen was aide to Lieutenant-General Omar Bradley, commander of the American ground forces in Europe.

❝ One of the sticking points came in the matter of Antwerp in the British sector. Had Monty cleared the resistance there quickly we would have been able to bring supplies in through Antwerp. We didn't get supplies through the port until November. We lost the whole month of October and that was critical. Bradley thought it was the most outrageous mistake of the war.

Had we been able to use Antwerp and bring in supplies we might have been able to avoid the dreadful winter. We all got bogged down and took terrible casualties. The advance was pretty well stopped.

The Battle of the Bulge made relations worse between the US and the British. It came as a terrible surprise. No one ever expected the Germans to mount a counter-offensive in that force. Many people thought the war was coming to a close. Back in the Pentagon they were already planning the movement of troops to the Pacific.

We felt Monty delayed too long in attacking the German flank. The British still had memories of Dunkirk when Hitler had cut off the BEF in the same way. But we thought the British panicked.

When the Bulge was reduced Monty had a little press conference. He made it appear he had come like St George to save to US forces from disaster. It infuriated us. He admitted afterwards it was a dumb thing to do. ❞

1945

At last the evil regime of Hitler was ended and peace returned to Europe. It took a further four months to halt the fighting in the east. Japan refused to bow to the inevitable Allied victory until two atomic bombs killed thousands of its people.

Left: **Brave Polish fighters took on German troops in the Warsaw uprising, only to be cruelly defeated.**

The Battle of the Bulge ends, with 120,000 Germans dead, injured or taken captive

■ FEBRUARY ■

Thursday 1: US 6th Army pushes towards Manila in the Philippines.

Saturday 3: Berlin is raided by 1,000 B-17 bombers, flying with a 900-strong fighter plane escort.

Sunday 4: The Allied conference gets underway at Yalta in the Crimea.

Tuesday 6: SS commander Himmler reports that German commanders in Poland have been shot for 'cowardice and dereliction'.

Wednesday 7: German engineers sabotage the Schwammanuel Dam in the face of advancing US troops.

Sunday 11: German resistance in Budapest is eliminated.

Monday 12: Yalta Conference ends with major players Churchill, Roosevelt and Stalin working out a

■ JANUARY ■

Monday 1: The final attempt by the Luftwaffe to halt the Allied invasion, code-named 'Operation Bodenplatte', gets underway with widespread bombing of French, Belgian and Dutch airfields.

Wednesday 10: US 6th Army lands on Luzon, Philippines, running into fierce Japanese opposition.

Wednesday 17: Warsaw liberated by Polish troops.

Thursday 18: Germans mount a push to break through Russian lines and reach the Danube.

Monday 22: Vital supplies route, the Burma Road, is reopened, providing a crucial boost to China's war effort.

Tuesday 23: St Vith, the last remaining German stronghold in the Bulge, is overwhelmed by American troops.

Thursday 25: Germans begin evacuating troops from Prussia and Pomerania across the Baltic to sidestep a Russian pincer action.

Left: **Eisenhower and Tedder after the German surrender at Rheims.**

Right: **Allied troops were taken by surprise by the German winter counter-attack that led to the Battle of the Bulge.**

Saturday 27: Auschwitz concentration camp, in southern Poland, is liberated by the Red Army.

Sunday 28: The Battle of the Bulge ends with 120,000 Germans dead, injured or captive. Americans lose 8,600 troops with a further 47,100 wounded and more than 21,000 posted missing.

Tuesday: Hungry Berliners riot as they try to seize extra food. Several women are killed when they upturn a potato truck.

◆ EYE WITNESS ◆

John Strachan joined the US army in 1941 when he was 17 and was in the first wave of soldiers to hit Utah beach. Subsequently, he fought through Normandy and in the Battle of the Bulge.

❝ I was cautious and scared. I guess that is why I lasted as long as I did. Morale was very high. Here was a group of men ready to fight. We were so geared up, young boys who became men overnight. We did some street fighting in Cherbourg. Then we went all the way to Paris. The reception from the French people was unreal. It meant freedom for them. The wine flowed and there was dancing in the streets. They really celebrated – and we joined in, too.

Getting injured during the Battle of the Bulge was the worst part of the war. I was hurt by a German 88 in both legs and my right arm. It felt like someone had driven a freight train into me. My nerves were severed. I never realised something could hurt as much as that did. They shot me with morphine before I was flown home. Afterwards, I was in hospital for two years. ❞

final plan to defeat Hitler and Japan. Also, the zones of influence around Europe and the world for each country have been drawn up.

Tuesday 13: RAF sparks firestorm in Dresden in a night raid involving 800 Lancaster bombers, causing as many as 250,000 deaths. American B-17s

The US Marines capture Mount Suribachi, the highest point on Iwo Jima

continued the attack in daylight. Condemnation of the destruction is immediately voiced in London.

Wednesday 14: Russian troops make important gains in Silesia, one of the manufacturing centres of the Reich.

Friday 16: US Navy pounds the island of Iwo Jima.

Monday 19: US Marines land on Iwo Jima for a bloody battle.

Thursday 22: 'Operation Clarion', in

Right: **US Marines nose down in the sands of Iwo Jima.**

which the Allies hope to paralyse German communications by destroying road and rail networks, gets underway.

Friday 23: After four days of bitter conflict, the US Marines capture Mount Suribachi, the highest point on Iwo Jima, and raise the US flag.

Saturday 24: Premier Ahmed Maher Pasha is shot dead after declaring Egypt to be at war with the Axis powers. His killer, 28-year-old lawyer

Mahmoud Essawy, who was pro-Hitler and anti-British colonialists, was later hanged.

Tuesday 27: The Allies enter the German town of Mönchengladbach.

Wednesday 28: A lend-lease agreement is signed between the US and France.

■ MARCH ■

Friday 2: Japanese resistance on Corregidor is ended.

Sunday 4: Meiktila in Burma is seized for the Allies.

Monday 5: The city of Cologne falls to the Allies.

A bridgehead is established east of the Rhine

Wednesday 7: A bridgehead is established east of the Rhine when the US 1st Army crosses the broad river at Remagen Bridge. When a sergeant spotted the bridge intact, he raced to it with his men, forcing the Germans nearby to flee. Booby traps placed on the bridge exploded but were too small to cause any serious damage.

Above: **Ambulances wait for the injured after the collapse of the Remagen Bridge.**

Thursday 8: American troops move into Bonn.

Saturday 10: A fire raid by Boeing B-29 Superfortresses devastates Tokyo, leaving thousands dead.

Tran Kim declares that Vietnam is now independent.

Sunday 11: Cambodia, following the example of neighbouring Vietnam, declares itself independent.

Monday 12: Dutch Jewish girl Anne Frank dies in Belsen. The 15-year-old kept a diary about her harrowing months in hiding in her native Amsterdam before being rounded up by the Nazis and taken to the concentration camp with her family.

Thursday 15: The Duke of Windsor resigns as governor of the Bahamas.

Sunday 18: In Japan, anyone over the age of six is ordered to assist in the war effort.

Left: **Anne Frank recorded the moving and mundane in her daily diary.**

◆ EYE WITNESS ◆

Peter Strachan was in the 147th Brigade of the Royal Army Signals Corps and joined the invasion of Normandy.

❝ Unknown to me, the Germans had pushed us back. I was driving along according to a map reference I had been given. It was pitch dark amongst some trees. I saw some trenches about 50 yards long. They looked nice and safe so I stopped the truck and hopped in one to get some kip. I saw shadows further up, about 30 yards away. They didn't talk and I didn't talk. I dozed off. As day broke these shadows moved off. Some men in the British infantry later came up and asked what I was doing. "You shouldn't be here," they told me and went on to explain the area – and the trench itself – had been in the hands of the Germans overnight. I slept with the enemy without even realising it. ❞

■ APRIL ■

Sunday 1: US 10th Army, under General Buckner, lands on Okinawa.
Friday 6: Numerous kamikaze attacks on the US fleet off Okinawa.
Saturday 7: Russian troops reach the gates of Vienna.
Giant Japanese battleship Yamato is sunk by US naval air action.

President Franklin Delano Roosevelt, four times elected to office, dies, aged 63

Monday 9: Fifty-nine-day seige at Königsberg, East Prussia, ends when Russians storm the fortress there.
Thursday 12: US president Franklin Delano Roosevelt, four times elected to office, dies, aged 63. Harry S. Truman takes over as president.
Friday 13: Allies liberate Belsen and Buchenwald concentration camps.

Monday 19: The Burmese city of Mandalay is cleared of Japanese forces and subsequently falls to Slim's 14th Army.
Sunday 25: Mayor of Aachen Karl Oppenhoff is assassinated by fanatical German youths called the 'Werewolves' who objected to his co-operation with American forces.

Below: Harry S. Truman is sworn in as president, following Roosevelt's death.

Monday 26: Final Japanese counter-attack on Iwo Jima, where just 216 Japanese prisoners are taken out of a force numbering 21,000. American casualties are high, almost 20,000 dead or wounded.
David Lloyd George, Britain's leader in World War I, dies, aged 82.
Tuesday 27: Battles rage for control of Danzig and Gdynia, on Polish territory, between German and Russian forces.

Friday 20: US 7th Army, under General Patch, reaches Nuremberg.

Hitler celebrates his 56th birthday.

Monday 23: US 8th Army captures Cebu in the Philippines.

Blackout restrictions are lifted in London.

Hitler orders the arrest of Göring after the Luftwaffe supremo attempts to take command of Germany.

Wednesday 25: US troops meet their Red Army counterparts on the banks of the Elbe at Torgau.

Delegates meet at the San Fransisco Opera House to structure the United Nations.

Thursday 26: Brutal fighting continues on Okinawa.

Marshal Pétain, leader of Vichy France, is arrested as he tries to flee across the Swiss border.

Saturday 28: Mussolini is captured and killed by Italian communist partisans. His body is hung by the ankles alongside that of his mistress Clara Petacci outside a petrol station in the Piazza Loretta, Milan. Mussolini, wearing a German cap, had been hiding under a pile of coats in a convoy of cars stopped and searched by the partisans. Commu-

◆ EYE WITNESS ◆

George Greenaway, of New Westminster Bridge, British Colombia, served with 85 Canadian Bridge Company of the Royal Canadian Army Service Corps. He was attached to the British 21st Army Group following the D-Day invasion.

'There was a great deal of work for us, especially once the advance reached Belgium and Holland. There was just so much water about.

We were equipped with bridges like the Kapok, for foot soldiers, or the Bailey, for vehicles. These would be prepared downstream, away from enemy action, and then towed or steered up on their own motors to the spot where they were needed. Very often, we had to move fast to a location at extremely short notice.

This sometimes backfired on us. I remember when we arrived in Brussels it was decided the men wouldn't be confined to barracks. After the hard battles of Normandy it was felt they could relax a little.

Of course it didn't take the guys long to disappear into the backstreets of Brussels. Almost as soon as they had gone, however, we got an order to move out immediately. It got our CO rather overexcited. He ended up firing his pistol into the air at random in an attempt to recall all his men!

One thing struck me during our advance through Normandy and that was the way the French had stored away a few little luxuries, even though they had lived through some horrendous hardships. In the towns and villages there would always be people lining the streets and holding out bottles of liquor for us. Some of it was Calvados and it laid out some of our people stiff like boards.'

nist partisan leader Cino Moscatelli held a short trial before he was condemned to death and shot with a machine gun.

Sunday 29: Hitler weds Eva Braun and appoints navy chief Grand Admiral Karl Dönitz to succeed him as Führer.

Monday 30: Hitler shoots himself in his Berlin bunker. His new wife dies by his side having taken poison.

Kamikaze attacks sink 20 ships off Okinawa.

US troops liberate the concentration camp at Dachau, near Munich.

Left: Another Japanese-held island, this time Cebu, is taken by US forces.

■ MAY ■

Tuesday 1: British airborne troops drop south of Rangoon.

Wednesday 2: Berlin is occupied by the Red Army.

German forces in Italy surrender to Field-Marshal Harold Alexander, Supreme Allied Commander in the Mediterranean.

Germany's General Alfred Jodl signs the instrument of surrender of all German forces

---

Thursday 3: British take Rangoon.

Friday 4: Surrender of German troops in Holland, Denmark and north west Germany is made to Field-Marshal Montgomery.

Saturday 5: Kamikaze attackers claim another 17 ships off Okinawa.

Germans in Norway surrender.

Monday 7: Germany's General Alfred Jodl, army chief of staff, signs the instrument of surrender of all German forces in the Allied HQ at Rheims. Afterwards, he said: 'With this signature the German people and the German armed forces are, for better or worse, delivered into the victors' hands.' For the Allies, General Bedell Smith, Eisenhower's chief of staff, signed the document.

Tuesday 8: VE Day.

Wednesday 9: Germany's surrender is ratified in Berlin.

Prague is occupied by the Red Army to the cheers of its residents.

Thursday 10: Japanese forces west of the Irrawaddy river are isolated.

Saturday 12: German forces on the island of Crete surrender.

Monday 14: An incendiary bombing raid on the city of Nagoya aims to knock out vital Japanese industrial bases, the first in a series of annihilating aerial attacks.

Saturday 19: Japanese resistance on Luzon is mopped up.

Monday: Belsen concentration camp is razed.

Wednesday 23: SS commander Heinrich Himmler commits suicide while in British custody.

Friday 25: Invasion of the Japanese home islands is planned.

Monday 28: More than 100 Japanese aircraft shot down over Okinawa.

Tuesday 29: William Joyce, the traitor 'Lord Haw-Haw', is arrested after being shot in the thigh by two British officers on the Danish border.

■ JUNE ■

Friday 1: Japanese forces in retreat on Okinawa.

Tuesday 5: Division of Germany into four zones of occupation drafted.

Wednesday 6: Hitler's remains are discovered under the Chancellery.

Thursday 7: Papua New Guinea's Wawek Harbour welcomes its first Allied cargo ship for three years.

Saturday 9: The Royal Air Force introduces its latest plane, the Vampire jet fighter.

Sunday 10: Australian forces invade Borneo.

Left: President Truman is just one of the dignitaries signing the UN Charter.

◆ EYE WITNESS ◆

Isaac Banks, from Edinburgh, was called up on his 28th birthday and became a machine-gunner in the Middlesex Regiment. Of Russian-Jewish descent, he spent months driving trainees for the Special Operations Executive before requesting to go back to his battalion. He landed in Normandy two weeks after D-Day.

In Holland I was driving a lorry which was used as an ambulance. I saw my mate Tommy White standing in the doorway of a house. As I looked at him he was killed by an explosion, just like that. It was so quick. I had known him since 1940 as we joined up together. I had to take his body to the burial ground in the truck.

I saw plenty of anti-Jewish signs. In the Dutch parks I tore down signs reading "Juden Verboten" (Jews Forbidden). I met a young lady in Holland and asked her if there were any Jewish people about. She directed me to a friend who had spent the war in hiding. I used to bring bread and other bits of food to the family.

Tuesday 12: General Dwight D. Eisenhower is awarded the freedom of the City of London and the Order of Merit.

Friday 15: German foreign minister Ribbentrop is captured by the British in Hamburg.

Monday 18: Lieutenant-General Simon Bolivar Buckner, commander of the US 10th Army, is killed by shrapnel on Okinawa.

Britain begins demobilisation.

Wednesday 20: Japanese forces begin surrender on Okinawa.

Monday 25: World Charter of Security is presented at the San Francisco Conference, signed by delegates of 50 countries, laying the foundations of the United Nations.

■ JULY ■

Friday 6: Allied troops hold a victory parade in Berlin.

Saturday 14: The ban on Allied troops fraternising with German

Above: The war is over in Europe but not in the east, as phosphorous shells explode over Japanese lines on Okinawa.

women is lifted.

Sunday 15: London's West End lit up once more, along with the nation's street lamps, after years of blackout.

Monday 16: First atomic explosion takes place at Los Alamos in the New Mexico desert.

Japan is told by Allied heads to surrender or face 'prompt and utter destruction'

Tuesday 17: Potsdam Conference opens. Subjects to be covered include postwar division of Germany.

A massive air raid involving 1,500 American and British bombers

attacks Tokyo. Meanwhile, Honshu is bombarded from the sea.

Monday 23: Marshal Pétain goes on trial for treason in Paris.

Thursday 26: Labour Party achieves sweeping triumph in the British general election, winning 393 seats to the Tories 213. Clement Attlee become prime minister.

Japan is told to surrender by the Allied heads at Potsdam or face 'prompt and utter destruction'.

Saturday 28: Carrier aircraft numbering 2,000 attack targets on the Japanese home islands.

An American B-25 bomber hits the Empire State Building when it is shrouded in fog, killing 13 people and injuring 26.

Tuesday 31: The Potsdam Conference ends in discord as the Allied leaders fall out over the face of postwar Europe. The sticking points are the new German and Polish boundaries and the insistence by Britain and America on free elections in Eastern Europe.

First atomic bomb is dropped on Hiroshima, killing about 80,000

■ AUGUST ■

Wednesday 1: Pierre Laval, the pro-Nazi former deputy leader of Vichy France, is put on trial for treason after being handed over to the French by the Americans.

Thursday 2: Boeing Superfortresses drop 6,600 tons of incendiaries on five Japanese cities.

Monday 6: First atomic bomb is dropped on Hiroshima, killing about 80,000 people and injuring 80,000.

Tuesday 7: Marshal Tito bars King Peter II from returning to Yugoslavia.

Wednesday 8: Russia declares war on Japan and invades Manchukuo.

Thursday 9: A second A-bomb is dropped, this time on Nagasaki. The death toll is about 40,000 with 60,000 injured.

Friday 10: Japan indicates its willingness to surrender.

Monday 13: In the absence of an

Above: **Attlee sweeps into power after the British general election.**

unconditional surrender from Japan, carrier aircraft launch a propaganda attack on Tokyo.

Tuesday 14: Japan agrees to an unconditional surrender.

Wednesday 15: VJ Day.

Pétain, 89, is sentenced to death for treason but reprieved by de Gaulle on account of his age.

Thursday 16: Japan's Emperor Hirohito appeals to all Japanese troops to lay down their arms.

Friday 17: The government plans to demobilise servicemen at a rate of 171,000 a month.

Sunday 19: Japanese surrender in Manila and Java.

Monday 20: Vidkun Quisling, the Norwegian traitor who supported the Nazis, goes on trial.

Tuesday 28: Japanese forces surrender in Rangoon.

Wednesday 29: Allied occupation of Japan begins.

Thursday 30: The world's largest submarines, built by Japan, surrender to the Allies after just one voyage.

Left: **The destructive power of the atomic bomb is illustrated at Hiroshima.**

■ SEPTEMBER ■

Sunday 2: Formal surrender document signed by Japan aboard the USS Missouri in Tokyo Bay.

Wednesday 5: The British return to Singapore.

Friday 7: Shanghai is surrendered by the Japanese, two days before hostilities cease throughout China.

Saturday 8: General Hideki Tojo attempts suicide by shooting himself in the heart. However, American medics arrived in time to save his life.

'Tokyo Rose', the US-born Iva Togori, who broadcast Japanese propaganda messages to US troops is arrested. She was later sentenced to ten years' imprisonment and fined $10,000. In 1977, she received a pardon from President Gerald Ford.

Monday 10: Quisling is found guilty of treason and sentenced to death.

Wednesday 12: Admiral Mountbatten receives surrender of all Japanese forces in South East Asia.

Below: **Thousands flocked to the White House to mark Japan's surrender.**

◆ EYE WITNESS ◆

Peggy Morris Riley was a WAAF based at Portreath in Cornwall. She worked in the operations room, plotting aircraft positions. She met and married an American sailor and left Britain in 1946 to live in the US.

❛In the ops room, we had four different watches. I was in D watch. We worked for six days then we had 56 hours' leave. The two girls I worked with – who were later my bridesmaids – and I would hitch-hike down to Falmouth which was where the action was. There were probably eight men to one woman. I danced with everyone, from the Free French to Poles and even Russians. That is where I met my husband in July 1944, after he had been involved in the D-Day landings. We were engaged in December 1944 and got married in May 1945.

I arrived in New York on 3 March 1946. I was 21 years old. It was an adventure for me. I loved my husband. And although I missed my parents and two brothers at first, they came out to join us in 1948.

At first I couldn't understand a word my mother-in-law said. I could understand anything the men said but the women seemed to be talking a different language.

I didn't know anything about domesticity – I didn't even know how to cook an egg. One day we went out to lunch in a restaurant. I had never seen a hamburger before in my life. This one was about four inches thick. After rationing at home, it looked enormous to me. The others tucked in but there was no way could I get my mouth around it. I came to the conclusion then and there that you had to have a big mouth to be in the USA.❜

Thursday 13: Japanese forces surrender in Burma.

Sunday 16: Japanese forces surrender in Hong Kong.

Monday 17: The commandant of Belsen and guards from Belsen and Auschwitz go on trial at Lüneberg.

William Joyce is tried for treason in London.

Wednesday 19: Prime Minister Clement Attlee announces that it is the British government's intention to allow India its independence 'at the earliest possible date'.

■ OCTOBER ■

Tuesday 2: Peace is negotiated between warring Vietnamese fighters and French troops.

Thursday 4: In Britain 17,000 dockers go on strike for more pay.

Friday 5: Japan's new premier is to be Baron Kijuro Shidehara.

Sunday 7: The first prisoners of war to return home from the Far East arrive in Southampton. Their emaciated figures and tales of appalling treatment shock the waiting relatives.

Tuesday 9: Laval is sentenced to death for treason.

Wednesday 10: Joseph Darnand, head of the pro-Nazi French Militia, which helped round up Jews in France, is executed.

Above: **General de Gaulle, war hero, wins the presidency of France.**

Above: **Peace returns to the world with the official international ceremony.**
Right: **The Japanese surrender papers.**

Monday 15: Pierre Laval is executed by firing squad.

Wednesday 17: A military coup fails when Colonel Juan Peron is returned to power in Argentina by popular demand.

Tuesday 23: Communists emerge as the biggest party in the French elections after clinching 142 seats to the Socialists' 140.

Wednesday 24: Quisling is executed in Norway by firing squad.

Nazis, including Hess, Göring, Ribbentrop and Dönitz, go on trial at Nuremberg

---

Wednesday 31: Allied troops on alert after a British brigadier is killed trying to negotiate a peace between the Dutch government and rebels on the islands of the Dutch East Indies.

■ NOVEMBER ■

Saturday 3: Britain's dockers end a seven-week unofficial strike over pay.

Monday 12: Tito wins a landslide victory in the Yugoslav elections.

Tuesday 13: General Charles de Gaulle is elected president of France.

Friday 16: The United Nations Educational, Scientific and Cultural Organisation (UNESCO) is founded.

Saturday 17: Josef Kramer, otherwise known as 'the butcher of Belsen', is sentenced to death.

Tuesday 20: Nazis, including Hess, Göring, Ribbentrop and Dönitz, go on trial at Nuremberg.

■ DECEMBER ■

Thursday 6: An Anglo-US loan agreement is signed, amounting to £1,100 million for British coffers.

Monday 10: The minimum daily wage for British workers is fixed at ten shillings. In America the figure is 75 cents.

Friday 21: US general George Smith Patton dies in a German hospital from injuries he received in a car crash. The 60-year-old general won plenty of enemies among the Allies thanks to his blunt speaking and apparent lust for action.

Saturday 22: Britain and the US recognise Marshal Tito's government in Yugoslavia.

Thursday 27: An International Monetary Fund (IMF) and a world-wide bank to boost world economy are launched.